ILAN PAPPE is Professor of History at the College of Social Sciences and International Studies and Director of the European Centre for Palestine Studies at the University of Exeter. He is the author of over a dozen books including the bestselling *The Ethnic Cleansing of Palestine*. In 2017, Pappe was awarded the Middle East Monitor's Lifetime Achievement Award at the Palestine Book Awards.

Praise for *The Biggest Prison on Earth*

'Israeli expat historian Pappe (*The Idea of Israel*)...boldly and persuasively argues for understanding the occupied territories as the world's "largest ever mega-prison." ... Pappe's conclusions won't be welcomed in all quarters but this detailed history is rigorously supported by primary sources.'
Publishers Weekly

'A diagnostic survey of Israel's long-planned occupation of the Palestinian's land... A grim, hard-hitting look at the nuts and bolts of Israeli occupation.'
Kirkus Reviews

'Pappe's book is critical for understanding the present situation and looking forward to possible solutions.' *CHOICE reviews*

'What is new in *The Biggest Prison on Earth* is Pappe's detailed accounting of exactly what the Israeli planners were contemplating in 1963; namely, "the largest ever mega-prison for a million and a half people."'
Electronic Intifada

T0321484

THE BIGGEST
PRISON ON EARTH

A History of the Occupied Territories

ILAN PAPPE

A Oneworld Book

First published in North America, Great Britain and
Australia by Oneworld Publications Ltd, 2017

This paperback edition published 2019
Reprinted, 2020, 2023 (twice), 2024 (three times)

ISBN 978-1-78607-341-9
eISBN 978-1-78074-433-9

Typeset by Hewer Text UK Ltd, Edinburgh
Printed and bound in Great Britain by Clays Ltd, Elcograf S.p.A.

Oneworld Publications Ltd
10 Bloomsbury Street
London WC1B 3SR
England

Stay up to date with the latest books,
special offers, and exclusive content from
Oneworld with our newsletter

Sign up on our website
oneworld-publications.com

MIX
Paper | Supporting
responsible forestry
FSC® C018072

To the Palestinian children, killed, wounded and traumatized
by living in the biggest prison on earth.

Contents

List of Maps

List of Maps

Preface: One Hill,
Two Prisons and
Three Agencies

THE UNIVERSITY ON THE HILL

Givat Ram, the Hill of Ram, is a sprawling, hilly neighbourhood on the very western edge of present-day Jerusalem. Various government ministries, the Knesset, part of the Hebrew University and the Bank of Israel are located there. Israelis of a certain age, ethnic origin and socio-economic background have developed a great nostalgia for the place. The hill makes a very brief and pastoral appearance in Amos Oz's first and most famous novel, *My Michael*, published in 1968. It is the place 'where a small herd of sheep graze alongside the Prime Minister's Office'.[1] There are no sheep to be seen these days and the grazing fields of yesteryear are long gone. They have been replaced by an elaborate system of highways, metal gates, suspension bridges and a rather beautiful rose garden.

It is highly unlikely that sheep were to be found anywhere near the Prime Minister's Office when Oz's book was first published. However, sheep did graze this hillside when the rural Palestinian village of Sheikh al-Badr was situated there. A few of its houses still remain, next to the American hotels frequented by Israeli members of the Knesset who do not live in Jerusalem. The village was gradually swallowed by the city, becoming part of the urban sprawl until it was ethnically cleansed by Israeli forces in 1948. It was a famous part of the city, as it overlooked one of Jerusalem's best-known landmarks: the Valley of the Cross. Tradition has it that the tree that provided the wood for Christ's cross stood there and this is why it is said that on that spot Greek Orthodox monks built an impressive monastery, still there today, albeit surrounded by new Jewish neighbourhoods and ring roads.

West of the monastery lies one of the two main campuses of the Hebrew University in Jerusalem. It was built on land confiscated from Sheikh al-Badr and sold to the university by the Israeli Custodian of Absentee Property[2] (allegedly held pending a decision about its future, but in reality sold to any Jewish individual or enterprise prepared to pay the ridiculously low price for it). Until 1948 the university was situated on Mount Scopus, which became a 'no man's land', an island within the Jordanian party of the city, and therefore inaccessible. After the June 1967 war, many of the Givat Ram campus's departments were transferred back to the old campus on Mount Scopus, which was then expanded significantly over confiscated Palestinian land.

North of the newly built campus, and at roughly the same time, a new home for the Israeli government was erected. Whereas the buildings of the campus were modest in appearance and laid out with pleasant lawns and accompanying greenery, the serene charm of this hilltop did not apparently inspire the architects who designed the government site of the Jewish State. Paying little attention to the pastoral scenery or its biblical heritage, they opted for what look like huge lumps of concrete spreading all over the hill, scarring the natural beauty of this crest of the Jerusalem mountains.

In summer 1963 a group of unusual students were enrolled on this campus for a month-long course. Almost all of them had a legal background of one sort or another. Some were members of the military administration that was controlling the areas in which the 1948 Palestinians (the Israeli Arabs as they were called then) lived under a strict rule that robbed them of most of their basic rights. Others were officers in the legal section of the Israeli army or officials of the Ministry of the Interior, and one or two were private lawyers.

They had been invited by the Department of Political Science in the Hebrew University. The course included lectures on military rule in general and on the political situation in the West Bank and the Gaza Strip, as well as a discussion on the lessons to be learned from Israel's military rule in the Sinai and Gaza in 1956 and inside Israel since 1948. A short introduction to Islam was also part of the curriculum and it closed with a lecture on the 1948 ethnic cleansing of Jerusalem (though of course not described in this manner by the lecturer, who probably referred to it as Operation *Yevusi* of April 1948), in which scores of Palestinian villages were wiped out and their inhabitants expelled. This, reported one of the participants, was followed by 'a celebratory meal and everyone was in an excellent mood'.[3]

Their presence on Givat Ram in 1963 was part of a new overarching military strategy initiated by the Israeli Chief of the General Staff. The strategy was presented by the CoGS to the army on 1 May 1963 and was meant to prepare the army for controlling the West Bank as an occupied military area.

The West Bank, of course, was not yet occupied, but the fact that four years before the actual occupation the Israeli military was ready with a judicial and administrative infrastructure for ruling the lives of one million Palestinians is highly significant.

Discussion in Israel of how to run occupied Arab areas began during the Sinai operation, when, in collusion with Britain and France, the Jewish State tried to topple the Egyptian president, Gamal Abdel Nasser, in October 1956. As part of the campaign the Gaza Strip was occupied for a few months, and the sense among the strategists and army commanders was that the IDF (Israel Defense Forces) was ill-prepared for the mission. The lesson learned was that a more systematic approach was needed. The opportunity to devise a more structured strategy arose in 1963. That year, growing instability in Jordan led the chiefs of staff to prepare seriously for the eventuality of the fall of the Hashemite Kingdom, which would lead to a possible war with Israel. They began contemplating more seriously the occupation of the West Bank.[4] For this they needed a plan.

In the first chapter of this book, this plan will be seen to have been located within a wider historical context that shows that since 1948, and even more since 1956, Israel's military and political elite was looking for the right historical moment to occupy the West Bank.

The plan was code-named the 'Shacham Plan' and it divided the West Bank into eight districts so as to facilitate the imposition of an organized military rule. Mishael Shacham was the general military governor of the Palestinian territories inside Israel (and one of the founders, together with Ariel Sharon, of unit 101, a notorious commando unit that carried out daring, and brutal, retaliatory operations against Palestinian guerrillas and farmers attempting to smuggle their way into Palestine). The official name of the programme was 'the Organization of Military Rule in the Occupied Territories'.[5]

There were three groups behind the plan: members of the legal section of the army, academics of the Hebrew University and officials of the Ministry of the Interior. The latter were mainly people already serving in one capacity or another in the military administration imposed on the Palestinians in 1948, which was still intact in 1963.

The plan included the appointment of a legal advisor to the future Governor General of the Occupied Territories and four military courts. The appendices to the plan consisted of a translation into Arabic of the Jordanian law as well as the 1945 Mandatory regulations. Although the latter were already used inside Israel, for some reason the Israelis did not have the Arabic translation. This may have been because theoretically, according to Israeli law, these draconian measures, of which more later, were imposed on Jews and non-Jews alike. In the case of the West Bank it was meant to apply to Palestinians only (and indeed when the Jewish settlers arrived they would be exempt from this legal regime).

Zvi Inbar was a senior member of the military Attorney General's team – he was the Attorney General for Southern Command. In his memoirs he revealed for the first time the details of the plan, explaining that every term had to be transferred from the reality of the Mandatory period, when these regulations were issued by the British government in 1945, to the prospective occupation of the West Bank and the Gaza Strip in 1963. Thus, the 'High Commissioner' and 'His Majesty's government' were irrelevant terms and were replaced by 'a general military governor' and the IDF, respectively.[6]

Other parts of the plan suggest that the compatibility of international law and the Geneva Convention with just such an occupation was also a matter of concern during these deliberations. Ominously for the Palestinians, the main concern was that the Geneva Convention did not permit executions. As this book will show, a year into the occupation Israel decided that the Convention did not apply to the occupation and, as for executions, the Israelis would not adopt the death penalty but instead resorted to other equally lethal means of execution.

Jordanian law was also studied to ascertain which of the Hashemite laws would need to be abolished immediately so as not to interfere with the Israeli strategy and objectives. 'It is impossible for us to leave a law which would contradict, or render illegitimate, Israeli laws,' recollected Inbar. But in other respects the mode of rule in the Jordanian period fitted the Israeli conceptions of control well. It was as comprehensive as the Israelis hoped it would be; it even included a list of the books censored in the West Bank, especially for children. The Jordanian list included *The Diary of Anne Frank*, while the Israeli list named Thomas Kuhn's *The Structure of Scientific Revolutions* (presumably because it contained in the title the word 'revolution').[7]

The Shacham Plan also suggested the names of people who should be appointed to senior posts in the future occupation. Some of them would indeed be there in 1967, men such as Chaim Herzog and the plan's mastermind, Colonel Mishael Shacham himself. In 1963 Herzog was released from active military service with the rank of a general.

He was immediately appointed the future Governor General of the West Bank. The appointment of such a senior officer indicated the significance of the military and judicial preparations in 1963 Israel.

Herzog appointed a bank director by the name of David Shoham as the 'finance minister' in waiting of the Occupied Territories, and Memi De-Shalit to be the 'minister of tourism'. The official titles were Staff Officer for finance and tourism, respectively.[8]

One major result of these preparations was a dossier on economic conditions in the West Bank. The report was put together by the head of the national military college near Tel Aviv and later the Chief of the Central Command during the 1967 war, Uzi Narkiss. At the time he rejected requests from Shacham and his colleagues to prepare an even more detailed plan of how to rule the West Bank (in 1963 he did not foresee such a scenario as imminent). Shacham received a more encouraging response from the military intelligence, which began to prepare files on personalities, installations and institutions in the West Bank (and of course the Gaza Strip). The preparations in 1963 culminated in an exercise in which the early days of takeover were practised.[9]

A year later Shacham invited another group of potential recruits to the Hebrew University. For this new course, the university produced with the army a special guidebook for the 'students' titled 'Military Rule in Occupied Territories'.[10] The detailed guidebook provided precise instructions on how to deal with local municipalities and councils in the West Bank and the Gaza Strip, and how to manage the educational system. In summarizing the guidebook, Shlomo Gazit, who became the military officer coordinating government policy in the Occupied Territories, said it explained how 'to cleanse it from hostile elements' and 'encourage collaborators and punish those who would resist the occupation'. All in all, 'The aim was to encourage the emergence of new local collaborative leadership with the occupation (unless of course the local leadership on the ground would behave well; then it can remain intact.')[11]

Within three years the team was ready for the eventuality of a military occupation, which indeed occurred in June 1967. The various courses moved to Beit Hayahl, 'the soldiers' dormitory' of Jerusalem. The structure of the courses and their main purpose were the same: to prepare for the day when the military rule in the West Bank and the Gaza Strip would commence on the ground.

The military Attorney General's team had its own code name for the plan, *Granit* ('granite'), which was combined with the overall Shacham Plan and became far more workable by May 1967. At this point, military governors and military judges had already been appointed to the West Bank and Gaza Strip, and the Shacham Plan became fully operational (it even included preparations for installing a regime in what the army referred to as 'Syria'). The *Granit* Plan was the most detailed and structured of all of Israel's pre-1967 preparations for how to manage the occupation of the West Bank and the Gaza Strip.

In May 1967 each potential military governor as well as legal and political advisors received a box (*argaz*). Each box included the following: instructions on how to govern an occupied Arab area; the Geneva and the Hague conventions; the Arabic translation of the emergency regulations; *The Occupation of Enemy Territory: a Commentary on the Law and Practice of Belligerent Occupation* by Gerhard von Glahn; and lastly a set of international law reports on administrative rule published in 1929 by Elihu Lauterpacht, C. J. Greenwood and A. G. Oppenheimer.

The major source was von Glahn's book. Had it indeed been the book on which future policies in the Occupied Territories were to have been based, the history of these areas would have been quite different from the way it unfolded. This book determined that occupation cannot change the *de jure* status of an area, that occupation is only temporary and the occupier can only use assets of any kind (such as land, houses, etc.) but cannot own, sell or buy them.

I mention these materials in the box in detail because they were either prepared before the occupation of Germany in 1945 or based on lessons learned from that occupation. In hindsight, however, one can say that despite the elaborate preparations, in practice an easier way was chosen: a simple extension of the military rule imposed on one Palestinian group (the minority inside Israel) to another Palestinian group (the people of the West Bank and the Gaza Strip). The Palestinian minority in Israel was put under military rule between 1948 and 1966 (in fact, Mishael Shacham was the last Governor General of that rule); thus there was a ready-made rule that could be reimposed in the Occupied Territories. The basis for the old and the new imposition was the same: the British Mandatory emergency regulations. The Israeli interpretation of these regulations – in 1948 as well as in 1967 – gave a military governor unlimited control over every aspect of the life of the people in his area. The rulers became what the first head of the military rule regime in 1948, Colonel Elimelech Avner, described as 'absolute monarchs' in their own small domains.[12]

When these regulations were first imposed in 1948 and again in 1967, no one mentioned the fact that when they were originally introduced by the British Mandate they were condemned by all Zionist leaders as Nazi legislation. These leaders described them as regulations with 'no parallel in any enlightened country', and continued that 'even in Nazi Germany there were no such rules, and the actions of Maydanek and its like had been done out of violation of the written law'.[13]

The two most notorious regulations were and still are No. 109, allowing the governor to expel the population, and No. 110, which gave him the right to summon any citizen to a police station whenever he saw fit. Another infamous regulation was No. 111, which sanctioned administrative arrest – an arrest for an unlimited period with neither explanation nor trial. This would become a more familiar feature of the 1967 occupation than the oppression of the Palestinians in Israel. One practice that stemmed from an interpretation of several regulations was the right of governors to resort to pre-emptive measures, the most common of which was to declare entire villages 'closed military areas' whenever the Shin Beit or the Shabak (the General Security Services – GSS) had prior knowledge of a forthcoming meeting or demonstration. This was first used in Israel in

1949 when the Palestinians demonstrated against land expropriation and would be constantly used to silence protests in the West Bank up to the present day and in the Gaza Strip until 2005.

The Mandatory emergency regulations became the legal infrastructure for the military courts, those institutions through which hundreds of thousands of Palestinians would pass, arrested without trial, sent to be tortured and abused. Only rarely did they emerge from them unscathed. The judges were all army officers, and were not required to have a legal background. Courts had either one, two or three judges. Those courts with three judges had the right to order executions or sentence people to life imprisonment. Among the theoretical institutions envisaged in 1963 was a special military court of appeal that would become operational in 1967, sanctioning the decisions of the lower courts in order to show to the world a system that apparently had the right to appeal built into it.

The boxes were quickly distributed in May 1967 and were given to a new body duly named 'the Special Unit', which was attached to the occupying forces a month later. The graduates of the course on Givat Ram were among them and they took over the military judicial administration of the West Bank and the Gaza Strip. Zvi Inbar, for instance, was attached to the forces that occupied the Gaza Strip, and within two days he and others had set up the military rule and judiciary system in the Strip. The four years of preparation facilitated a swift takeover and the creation of a regime that would in all but name remain in place for the next fifty years.

What they contemplated and executed, and what successive generations of Israeli bureaucrats would maintain, was the largest ever mega-prison for a million and a half people – a number that would rise to four million – who are still today, in one way or another, incarcerated within the real or imaginary walls of this prison. This book tells the story of the origins of this prison and tries to capture what life was, and still is, like within its confines.

THE GOVERNMENT ON THE HILL

The government complex erected in the early 1950s and completed just before the 1967 war consisted of three buildings. These huge cubic edifices tower above the summit of Givat Ram, and now comprise the Knesset, the Supreme Court of Israel and the Bank of Israel.

The actual Prime Minister's Office was, and still is, on the third floor of the building closest to the university campus. On the same floor is the government boardroom, with an enormous rectangular wooden table in the middle; this table can sometimes be seen on television when a news item relating to the Israeli government appears in a bulletin. Since the 1960s and up to the present day, the government has used another boardroom built for it on the second floor of the Israeli Parliament, the Knesset; here they sit around an oval table, another familiar image in the televised history of the Jewish State.

The thirteenth government of Israel convened almost daily around both tables in the immediate aftermath of the 1967 war, debating intensively the fate of the West Bank and the Gaza Strip and the future of the people living in them. After almost three months of deliberation, they concluded their discussions with a series of decisions, all of which in one way or another condemned those living in the West Bank and the Gaza Strip to life imprisonment in the biggest ever mega-prison of the modern age. The Palestinians living there were incarcerated for crimes they never committed and for offences that were never committed, confessed or defined. As this book is being written, a third generation of such 'inmates' have begun their lives in that mega-prison.

This particular government, the one that took that most callous and inhumane of decisions, represented the widest possible Zionist consensus: every ideological stream and viewpoint was presented around those oval and rectangular tables. Socialists from the Mapam party sat alongside the revisionist Menachem Begin and shared the glory and the power with the various factions that made up the

Zionist Labour movement. They were joined by members of the most secular liberal and the most religious and ultra-religious political parties. Never before, or since, this government's term in office would such a consensual partnership lead the State of Israel in its future and critical decisions.

Contrary to conventional wisdom about the history of the West Bank and the Gaza Strip, no one apart from the government of Israel has played a crucial role, then or now, in deciding the fate of these territories or the people living in them. What these ministers decided in the second half of June 1967, and in the following months of July and August, has remained the cornerstone of Israeli policy towards the Occupied Territories to this day. None of the successive Israeli governments have deviated from this path, and nor have they ever wanted to, in any shape or form.

The resolutions adopted in that short period, between June and August 1967, clearly charted the principles to which future Israeli governments would religiously adhere and from which they would not diverge, even during the most dramatic events that followed, be it the first or second Intifada or the Oslo peace process and the Camp David Summit of 2000.

One explanation for the resilience of this set of decisions is the extraordinary composition of the 1967 government. As mentioned, this government represented, as never before or since, the widest possible Zionist consensus. This can also be attributed to the euphoric mood in the wake of the total devastation of three Arab armies by the IDF and the successful blitzkrieg that ended with the military occupation of vast areas of Arab lands and countries. An almost messianic aura surrounded the decision-makers in those days, encouraging them to take bold decisions of historical consequence that their successors would find hard to refute or change.

All these plausible explanations tend to see the policies as the direct product of the particular and extraordinary circumstances of June 1967. But as the first chapter of this book will try to show, these decisions were mainly the inevitable outcome of Zionist ideology and history (however one chooses to define this ideology or insist on its shades and innuendoes). The particular circumstances made it easier to remind the politicians of their ideological heritage and reconnected them once more, as in 1948, to the Zionist drive to Judaize as much of historical Palestine as possible. The principles of how to adapt the dramatic events of June 1967 to the ideological vision were laid down in those frequent meetings at Givat Ram and in the Knesset. Because the decisions taken reflected the consensual Zionist interpretation of the past and present reality of Palestine as an exclusive Jewish State, none of the developments occurring thereafter appeared to undermine their validity for future Israeli policymakers. The only way of challenging the decision taken then was by questioning the very validity of Zionism itself.

Two fundamentals of Zionist ideology were still unfailingly adhered to by the politicians of 1967, just as they had been by their predecessors. The struggle for the survival of the Jewish State depended, on the one hand, on its ability to control most of historical Palestine, and, on the other, on its capacity to reduce considerably the number of Palestinians living in it. Realpolitik in Zionist terms meant reconciling oneself to the possibility of not being able to achieve these two goals fully. There were times when leaders such as David Ben-Gurion attempted to quantify these two objectives (namely, how much of Palestine was needed and how many Palestinians could be tolerated in a Jewish State), but more often than not the conclusion reached was that the best options were more land in the first instance and fewer Palestinians in the second. When Palestine was clearly defined as a geopolitical entity by the British Mandate after the First World War, having most of the country meant possession of most of Mandatory Palestine (Israel today with the Occupied Territories).

In terms of population, the consensus dictated a wish for a purely ethnic Jewish State. Again, there were sometimes attempts to ascertain what would constitute a tolerable non-Jewish minority within a Jewish State, but the unspoken (and at times spoken) desire was to have only Jews in what was considered to be the ancient Land of Israel.

1948 provided the historical opportunity to realize both goals: taking over much of the land and getting rid of most of the local population. Several discrete processes came together to allow the Zionist movement to ethnically cleanse Palestine that year: the British decision to withdraw from Palestine after thirty years of rule; the impact of the Holocaust on Western public opinion; the disarray in the Arab and Palestinian worlds; and, finally, the crystallization of a particularly determined Zionist leadership. As a result, half of the country's native population was expelled, half of its villages and towns destroyed and 80 per cent of Mandatory Palestine became the Jewish State of Israel.

The dispossession was witnessed at close hand by representatives of the international community: delegates of the International Red Cross, correspondents of the Western press and UN personnel. The Western world, however, was not interested in listening to their incriminating reports; the political elites chose to ignore them. The message from Europe and the US was clear: whatever happens in Palestine is the inevitable final act of the Second World War. Something had to be done so that Europe could atone for the crimes committed on its soil against the Jewish people – and therefore a last, massive dispossession of Palestinians was needed so that the West could move on to post-war peace and reconciliation. The situation in Palestine, of course, had nothing to do with the movement of populations in Europe in the wake of the Second World War or with the genocide of Europe's Jews; it was the culmination not of the war in Europe but of Zionist colonization of the land that had begun at the end of the nineteenth century. It was the final act in the making of a modern-day settler Jewish State at a time when the international community seemed to view colonization as unacceptable and an example of the deplorable ideology of the past.

But not in the case of Palestine. The message from the enlightened world was unambiguous: the Israeli dispossession of the Palestinians as well as the takeover of most of Palestine were both legitimate and acceptable. Almost half of the ministers attending the 1967 meetings were themselves veterans of the 1948 ethnic cleansing of Palestine.

Some were members of the small cabal that took the decision to expel almost a million Palestinians, destroy their villages and towns and prevent them from ever returning to their homeland. Others were generals or officers in the machinery that perpetrated the crime. All of them were fully aware of the international indifference in 1948 when the Zionist movement took over 78 per cent of Palestine. And this is why they, and their colleagues, were convinced that the international community would allow them once more to act unilaterally now that the Israeli army occupied the remaining 22 per cent of the land. Having acted with impunity in 1948, there was no reason to expect any serious rebuke for, or obstacles to, a similar policy of ethnic cleansing in June 1967.

There was, though, one huge difference between 1948 and 1967. In 1948 the decisions about the fate of the Palestinians were taken before the war, whereas in 1967 they were formulated after the war. Therefore, in 1967, there was more time to ponder the ramifications of any massive expulsion that might be carried out without any war going on. The government was determined, almost en masse, to decide unilaterally about the territories' future, but was more divided about the possibility or the wisdom of another huge ethnic cleansing[14] after the official end of hostilities. The counter-arguments were clear: a post-war ethnic cleansing could have awakened an otherwise dormant Western conscience. Furthermore, it was also doubtful if the army had the will and mentality to carry it out, as it was unclear whether it had sufficient means to accomplish it. The 1967 government was also a larger forum than the one that devised the 1948 ethnic cleansing. The thirteenth government included quite a few conscientious ministers who would have objected to such a master plan on moral grounds.

Notwithstanding the decision to refrain from mass expulsion, very few members of that government and those that succeeded it objected to the incremental expulsions and dispossession that have reduced significantly the number of Palestinians in the Occupied Territories (nor did they object to the harassment that triggered emigration from Palestine). The fewer the Palestinians, the easier it would be to police them in the new mega-prison that was constructed.

So, ethnic cleansing on a grand scale was ruled out. However, the prevailing sense in those boardroom meetings was that the international community would not act against Israel's land expansion – not as an endorsement of expansionism per se but more as a reflection of an unwillingness to confront it. But there was one crucial caveat: there could not be a *de jure* annexation of the territories, only a *de facto* one. There were two reasons for this: first, the West Bank and the Gaza Strip were regarded by international law as occupied territories, whereas the areas Israel occupied during the operations in 1948 were all recognized by the United Nations as part of the State of Israel. Second, if the population could not be expelled, it could also not be fully integrated as equal citizens of the Jewish State, given their number and potential natural growth that would have endangered the decisive Jewish majority in Israel.

There was then, and there is now, an Israeli consensus and an overwhelming desire to keep the West Bank and the Gaza Strip for ever, while at the same time there was and still is the two-fold recognition of the undesirability of officially annexing these territories and the inability to expel the population en masse. And yet keeping these territories, with the population in them, seemed as vital as the need to maintain a decisive Jewish majority in whatever constituted a Jewish State.

The minutes of the meetings are now in the public domain. They expose both the impossibility and incompatibility of these two driving forces: the appetite for possessing new lands and the reluctance either to drive out or to fully incorporate the people living on them. The documents also reveal a congratulatory self-satisfaction about the early discovery of a way out of the ostensibly logical deadlock and theoretical impasse. Ministers were convinced, as all the ministers after them would be, that they had found the formula that would enable Israel to keep the territories it coveted, without annexing the people it negated, while safeguarding immunity against international condemnation and rebuke.

In fact, they had not discovered anything new. Since 1948 they had faced a similar predicament when they and their predecessors had had to decide how to treat the Palestinian minority inside Israel. They imposed on them a military rule that was only lifted after eighteen years and replaced by a new kind of regime of inspection, control and coercion. With time, this eased somewhat but became more hidden and complex. But by now there were more people in the West Bank and the Gaza Strip; therefore, while the limited citizenship granted to the Palestinian minority in Israel seemed to tally with the aim of maintaining a decisive Jewish majority in the state, the same would not have been the case had similar citizenship been extended to the people of the West Bank and the Gaza Strip. Thus, there was a need to keep the territories, not to expel the people in them, but at the same time not to grant them citizenship. These three parameters or presumptions have remained unchanged to this day. They remain the unholy trinity of the consensual Zionist catechism.

When three such goals are translated into actual policies they can only produce an inhumane and merciless reality on the ground. There can be no benign or enlightened version of a policy intended to keep people in limbo, without citizenship, for long periods. Only one thing created by man operates in such a way as to rob, temporarily or long term, the basic human and civil rights of the citizen: the modern-day prison. The prison, the penitentiary and the correctional facility are contemporary institutions that impose exactly this, either as part of a ruthless dictatorship or as a consequence of a long legal process in democracies.

Officially, some of the West Bankers had Jordanian citizenship; however, under the occupation this 'citizenship' had no value whatsoever within the occupied West Bank and hence for all intents and purposes from June 1967 these were citizen-less inhabitants. Moreover, in the wake of events in September 1970 (the internal war between the Palestine Liberation Organization and the Hashemite Kingdom) and the official Jordanian disengagement in 1988 from the West Bank, the number of citizenship holders decreased.

Today's prison resembles the Panopticon, originally conceived by Jeremy Bentham, the first modern philosopher to justify the rationale of imprisonment within a new coercive penal system. The Panopticon prison, which was notorious in the early nineteenth century, was designed to allow guards to see their prisoners but not vice versa. The building was circular, with prisoners' cells lining the outer perimeter, and in the centre of the circle was a large, round observational tower. At any given time guards could be looking down into each prisoner's cell – and thereby monitor potentially unruly behaviour – but carefully situated blinds prevented prisoners from seeing the guards, so that they did not know if or when they were being monitored. Bentham believed that the 'gaze' of the Panopticon would force prisoners to behave morally. As if under the all-seeing eye of God, they would feel shame at their wicked ways.

If we substitute moral conduct for collaborating with the occupation, and we change the circular structure of the Panopticon to a variety of geometrical parameters of imprisonment, the 1967 Israeli decision was to isolate the Palestinians in the West Bank and the Gaza Strip in a modern Panopticon. And for those readers familiar with the further Foucauldian elaboration of the Panopticon model, this could also be a useful tool for partly understanding the edifice built by Israel in 1967 and thereafter. But Foucault, like Bentham, stressed the nature of the Panopticon prison as a system of control that had no need of physical barriers and where the guards are unseen. As we shall see, and as most readers probably know, this applies to only one element in the matrix of power that caged the Palestinian population in Israel's mega-prison in the twentieth century. Others were intentionally forcing the 'prisoners' to look at the guards and to sense in the most physical way possible the barriers, the wall and barbed wire surrounding them.

In 1967 the official Israeli navigation between impossible nationalist and colonialist ambitions turned a million and a half people into inmates of just such a mega-prison. But it was not a prison for a few inmates wrongly or rightly incarcerated: it was imposed on a society as a whole. It was, and still is, a malicious system that was constructed for the vilest of motives, but more than that. Some of its architects genuinely looked for the most humane model possible for this prison, probably because they were aware that this was a collective punishment for a crime never committed. Others did not even bother to look for a softer version or a more humane one. But the two camps existed and therefore the government offered both versions of the mega-prison to the people of the West Bank and the Gaza Strip. One was an open-air Panopticon prison, the other a maximum security one. If they did not accept the former, they would get the latter.

The 'open-air prison' allowed a measure of autonomous life under indirect and direct Israeli control; the 'maximum security prison' robbed the Palestinians of all autonomy and subjected them to a harsh policy of punishments, restriction and, in the worst-case scenario, execution. The reality was that the open-air prison was harsh enough and sufficiently inhuman to trigger resistance from the enclaved population, and the maximum security model was imposed in retaliation to this resistance. The softer model was tried out twice between 1967 and 1987, and from 1993 to 2000, and resistance took place in 1987 until 1993 and in 2000 until 2009 (and in the Gaza Strip to this day). The open-air prison also became Israel's peace plan, endorsed by the USA and European countries. This plan formed the basis of diplomatic efforts and the 'peace process'. In Israel and in the West, a vast laundering of words and a very cooperative media and academic community were essential for maintaining the moral and political validity of the open-air prison option as the best solution for the 'conflict' and as an idealized vision of normal and healthy life in the occupied West Bank and the Gaza Strip.

'Autonomy', 'self-determination' and, finally, 'independence' were words used, and mainly abused, to describe the best version of an open-air prison model the Israelis could offer the Palestinians in the West Bank and the Gaza Strip.

But this laundering did not cleanse the reality of the situation, and the hyperbole of peace and independence did not deafen the conscientious members of all the societies involved: in the Occupied Territories, in Israel and the outside world. In the age of the internet, an independent press, active civil society and energetic NGOs, it was hard to play the charade of peace and reconciliation on the ground where people were incarcerated in the biggest ever human prison witnessed in modern history. This book is dedicated to those who relentlessly tried to alert decent human beings to the importance of not standing by and watching while millions of people were being treated in such an inhumane and dehumanizing way – just because they were not Jews. These virtuous people provided descriptions and analyses that confronted the Western mainstream media's indifferent, and often quite distorted, coverage of life in the West Bank and the Gaza Strip since 1967. Along with Palestinian resistance, they continue, so far with little success, to question the sweeping immunity the West has granted the State of Israel for its criminal policies towards the Palestinians.

THE BUREAUCRACY ON THE HILL

The open-air prison and the maximum security prison required a huge staff to run them. These thousands of soldiers, officers, officials, judges, physicians, architects, police officers, tax collectors, academic advisors and politicians are the principal human face of this monument to inhumanity.

At the top of the bureaucratic pyramid stood a committee of the ministerial Directors General. This committee was established on 15 June 1967 and in the subsequent months devised the economic, legal and administrative infrastructure for controlling and maintaining the Occupied Territories. Its meetings are contained in two volumes of thousands of pages minuting their every deliberation. This group of government officials enlisted the leading academics of the time and veteran members of the previous system of control employed in the Palestinian areas inside Israel. This book is as much about these officials, academics and bureaucrats as it is about the system they built in June 1967 and that is still maintained today. A second generation is already in place and a third is imminent. Once you cross that generational gap any discourse about temporality or even finality is useless. It becomes a living organism that is very hard to combat or dismantle, hence the understandable desperation in recent years that takes the form of suicide bombs or rocket attacks, neither of which have any hope of persuading Israelis to dismantle this monstrosity.

The focus on the bureaucracy is essential in order to avoid falling into the trap of demonization; thus this book does not seek to demonize Israeli society as a whole, although many of its members support the mega-prison and many others choose to turn a blind eye. This book distinguishes as much as it can between the system and the people working within it. It singles out the politicians and academics who in 1967 established the mechanism of the creation of an enclave and imprisonment, as well as the thousands of officials, officers, soldiers and police who ran it. Some who appear in this book are as guilty as those individuals all over the world, and throughout history, who stood by and did nothing about the crimes committed on their behalf, in their name and before their very eyes. These Israelis, who either support or do not object to the oppression, are still hailed in the Western world as champions of peace and humanity, endowed with an endless stream of undeserved prizes and awards. But that said, there are very few really evil people in modern human history but there are quite a few evil systems. The mega-prison of Palestine is one of them.

The villains of the piece, of this book, are therefore the Israelis who worked out the fine detail of the system to begin with, those who upheld it for all those years and those who 'perfected' its operation: namely, its power to abuse, humiliate and destroy. They were and are servants of the bureaucracy of evil. They come quite innocent into the system but only very few among them fail to succumb to its raison d'être, to its modus operandi. As wardens of this largest prison on earth, they are constant abusers, dehumanizers and destroyers of Palestinian rights and lives. Only when the last of them has been discharged from this service will we know that the mega-prison of Palestine has been abolished for ever.

Introduction: Re-reading the Narrative of Occupation

When the sixth day of the June 1967 war came to an end, the State of Israel extended over an area three times larger than its original size and added one million Palestinians to the 300,000 already resident in the state since 1948. That figure was more or less the same number of Palestinians expelled by Israel in 1948. The million doubled, tripled and continued to grow as the years passed, and reached, together with the Palestinians in Israel, almost five million by the beginning of the twenty-first century. Along with them, in more than fifty years of colonization, half a million Jewish settlers have also inhabited vast areas within the Occupied Territories, and as I write they continue to flow in and encroach upon the limited space allotted to the Palestinians.

The fate of these Palestinians and of the land on which they were living was debated by the Israeli government in June 1967. The final decision, reached before the end of the month, was to exclude to all intents and purposes the West Bank and the Gaza Strip from any future peace negotiations. The wish was to make a unilateral decision on the territories and to seek international endorsement of the new policy, whatever that might be. This decision is the fulcrum around which this book's narrative revolves.

Even the weakest critics of that decision refer to the strategy and the reality that followed as an 'occupation'. The legal and military measures described in the Preface indicate that official Israel was preparing to rule the lives of the Palestinians in the West Bank and the Gaza Strip in the same manner in which it controlled those of the Palestinians inside Israel proper. These Palestinians lived mainly in areas allocated to a Palestinian state by the United Nations in 1947 but which had now been annexed by Israel without international discussion or rebuke. The individuals involved in the early 1960s preparations, and the nature of these preliminary steps, are indicative of the problems associated with applying the word 'occupation' to the history of the West Bank and the Gaza Strip under Israeli rule since 1967 and up to the present day.

This book sits uneasily with the term 'occupation'. There are two specific reasons for this reservation, although I accept that it is widely and commonly used in reference to the reality of life in the West Bank and Gaza Strip (both by those who oppose the Israeli presence there and by some mainstream Israeli and Western politicians who did not, or have no wish to, end it).

One reservation is that adherence to this term creates the idea of a false separation between Israel and the occupied areas. It indirectly legitimizes the Israeli presence everywhere else in what used to be Mandatory Palestine and produces the unacceptable dichotomy between 'democratic' Israel and the 'non-democratic' Occupied Territories.

The second reservation concerns the political and legal implications usually associated with the term 'occupation'. It is generally regarded as a temporary means of securing a territory following armed conflict or a war. This has a beginning and an end and there are very clear international regulations and imperatives that stem from the temporality of any given occupation.

The reality in the West Bank and the Gaza Strip is different in two very significant aspects. One that emerges from this book is that temporality is not part of the story of this 'occupation'. The powers that be that hold to the territories and those who support the 'occupier' accept the reality of 'occupation' as a given for years to come. By 1987 it had already entered history as the longest existing military occupation and that record is unlikely to be broken in the foreseeable future.

The second aspect that distinguishes it from known cases of military occupation is the totality of control exercised by the occupier. Such instances of absolute control are to be seen in the early days of any military occupation, but, unless you were part of a group designated for elimination or genocide, they never lasted too long. The extent of these practices of total control in what became known as the Occupied Territories leads one to search for better terminology.

In fact, analysis provided here prompts the suspicion that the legal international meanings and associations with the term 'occupation' are not only inapplicable to the reality on the ground, but also, in hindsight, allowed the State of Israel to evade any serious global rebuke or condemnation.

In recent years the academic world has applied the paradigm of settler colonialism to the case study of Israel and Palestine. Settler colonialism is the movement of Europeans into other parts of the world with the purpose of building a new and permanent life. Such a move was quite often triggered by persecution, as indeed was the case with the Jewish settlers in Palestine. Immigration into a new homeland almost always entailed a clash with the indigenous population. In many cases such an encounter ended in the genocide of the local population, or, in rare cases such as Algeria, South Africa and Zimbabwe, with the demise of the settler colonialism project itself.

Palestine is an exceptional case. We do not yet know how it will end. Will the logic of settler colonialism, so brilliantly defined by the late Patrick Wolfe as 'the logic of the elimination of the native', continue to be implemented in Palestine through ethnic cleansing and colonization, or will it make way for the logic of human and civil rights? Time will tell. What we can say, again with reference to Patrick Wolfe, is that settler colonialism is a structure not an event. A structure of displacement and replacement, or, to paraphrase Edward Said's words, substituting presence with absence. It began in 1882, reached a certain peak in 1948, continued with vehemence in 1967 and is still alive and kicking today.[1] The mega-prison is one of the many methods the settler colonial State of Israel employed to keep the project alive. The mega-prison was created in a matter of a few days and became a reality of a kind not seen anywhere else in modern history. Prisons are permanent structures, immune from international scrutiny, and function as a world of their own.

The mega-prison was created in June 1967 not in order to maintain an occupation but, rather, as a practical response to the ideological prerequisites of Zionism: the need to control as much as possible of historical Palestine and create an absolute – if possible, exclusive – Jewish majority in it. These impetuses led to the ethnic cleansing of Palestine in 1948 and informed the policy formulated in June 1967, just as it feeds Israeli actions today.

The mega-prison was the logical and inevitable consequence of Zionist history and ideology. Thus, the first chapter of this book presents the background to the 1967 policy as a sequel to strategies adopted by Zionism since 1882 and in particular in 1948. It is in essence a survey of the period between 1948 and 1967 as an integral prelude to both the 1967 war and the policy pursued thereafter. It is a story of a consistent drive to occupy the West Bank, and to a lesser extent the Gaza Strip, a drive unfulfilled because of lack of opportunities rather than strategic temporizing.

The first four chapters describe the way the 1967 decisions were implemented. An early geographical and demographic demarcation of the mega-prison is followed by an articulation of the legal infrastructure for the bureaucratic management of the territories. The Israeli government first decided where to settle Jews in a number of wedges it drove into the West Bank and the Gaza Strip; then made a clear decision about the judicial system that would run the affairs of the occupied population but left open the question of their legal status (which is still unresolved today).

After examining the progress of demarcating the territorial and demographical boundaries of the mega-prison, the book then takes a closer look, in chronological order, at the two models 'offered' to the Palestinians. The first, the open-air prison, was in place between 1967 and the outbreak of the first Intifada in 1987. It was oppressive enough to engender significant resistance from the local population, later enhanced and supported by the Palestine Liberation Organization (PLO) in Tunisia.

The Israeli response was ruthless and between 1987 and 1993 the harsher model of a maximum security prison was imposed. International pressure led to yet another attempt to introduce an open-air prison. This lasted from 1993 to 2000 and was unveiled to the wider world as a 'peace process' initiated and led by the USA.

The basis for this process was a charade of an internal debate within the occupying power between two camps, 'peace' and 'national', one wishing to end the occupation, the other to maintain it. So, in theory, you could push forward a peace process because of the presence of a large number of Israelis wishing to end the occupation. It was a charade not because there were no Israelis wishing to end the occupation, but because they were insignificant and marginal, and, as in 1967, so in the 1990s, the political and military elite continued to adhere to the same principles that led them to occupy the territories in the first place.

In fact, the result of such a gap between a dialogue about peace and the absence of any change in the reality of occupation was far worse. On the ground diplomatic endeavour has allowed Israel to solidify and strengthen its grip over the territories and the people living in them, while enjoying immunity from international pressure or rebuke.

The paradigm this book offers requires a new dictionary and a new vocabulary. This is illustrated in particular by the way I approach the diplomatic efforts, which I have chosen to illustrate as part of the Israeli endeavour to solidify the open-prison model and how, in this, I reject the accepted notion that this was and is a genuine effort to reach reconciliation and understanding with the Palestinian people.

Through the prism of the mega-prison, internal Israeli debates about the territories are a narrative of sham and illusion. The primary Israeli strategic decisions on the occupied areas' fate were taken immediately after the 1967 war, which rendered most of the political discussions that allegedly ensued between a 'peace camp' and a 'war camp' in Israel insignificant at best and dishonest at worst. If this is a fair assessment, then the peace process that evolved entirely around this 'debate' was doomed to fail the moment it was launched.

The book ends, as a historical narrative, with the re-imposition of the second maximum security prison on the West Bank and Gaza Strip in the present century. Some observers believe that a new open-prison version was once again on offer in 2006, but only for the West Bank, while the Gaza Strip, that same year, became an even more extreme version of a maximum security prison. These two assumptions are examined at the very end of the book.

This is not a comprehensive or a full history of the West Bank and the Gaza Strip since 1967 (as much as such a book needs to be written). It dwells on some crucial, and by now quite familiar, moments in this history but, contrary to the usual narrative of these events, they are examined here as an adaptation of the mega-prison model by the bureaucrats to the changing circumstances. It seems that nothing that has occurred since June 1967 up to the present day has diminished the determination of the Israeli authorities to keep the West Bank and the Gaza Strip under strict Israeli control, to cage the people living in it in a huge prison and to disregard any international pressure to end its criminal policy. The model is a faulty one since at the same time as caging the Palestinians the controlling authorities do not mind if they leave and do not return to the prison. But if you are determined or you do not want to join the millions of homeless refugees in the Middle East in the twenty-first century, your only option is the mega-prison.

It is also more a history of the occupiers than the occupied in the sense that it attempts to explain the mechanism created for ruling the millions of Palestinians and less to reconstruct their lives. The

Palestinians do appear in the book but it is more of a narrative of their oppression than a narrative of their aspirations, social fabric, cultural production and other aspects of life so worthy of the history that I hope will one day be written. Their resistance and steadfastness deserve to be chronicled and highlighted for the generations to come.

The particular prism through which this book should be viewed, that of the mega-prison, means that familiar subjects and themes are treated here in a different context from the way they have been analysed in some of the best books so far written on the occupation. Thus, for instance, the Jewish settlers and settlements are considered here as a means for confining the space of Palestinian life and for reducing their numbers in the territories – rather than as a response to an ideological Zionist desire to expand into the rest of Palestine.

I only briefly consider the economic aspect, despite the crucial role it plays in this history. Economics appears here as a set of considerations affecting the policymakers both when the model of the open-air prison was tried out and when the maximum security model was imposed. In this context I also include the Israeli use of the American, and generally Western, financial aid without which Israel could not have sustained its control. More sinisterly, senior bureaucrats perceived the international funds that flowed to the territories from concerned governments and civil societies as a vital means of keeping down the Israeli costs of looking after the 'residents' (as the people of the West Bank and the Gaza Strip are referred to in, and by, the Jewish State).

There is no separate chapter on the Palestine Authority (PA) either, a subject dealt with exhaustively by some recent books. It is presented here as it has been perceived by the Israeli policymakers and bureaucrats down the years. For them the PA was an integral and crucial component in the open-air prison model suggested in the 1990s, and one which the pragmatic elite of Israel still hopes to instate in the West Bank, at least in the near future.

From the first page to the last this book describes a historical move that in many ways began in the late nineteenth century, continued in 1948 and is now in its third stage, one that began in 1967. Time will tell if this is a final stage. Palestinian resistance and steadfastness and wide support in the world's civil societies have so far prevented it from being so. This is a record of Zionist and Israeli enterprise to the present day, with a particular focus on the phase that began with those governmental meetings of 1967.

Chapter One

The War of Choice

One afternoon, on 10 March 1948, the leaders of the Jewish community in Palestine, together with their military commanders, took the decision to occupy 78 per cent of the country. Since 1917 Palestine had been under British Mandatory rule. At the time one million Palestinians were living in that 78 per cent of the country (which equates to Israel today without the Occupied Territories). The leadership decided to expel most of the population. That evening, orders were despatched to the forces on the ground to prepare for a systematic eviction of the Palestinians from large areas of the country. The orders specified how the expulsion would take place: large-scale intimidation, laying siege to villages, bombing neighbourhoods, setting fire to houses and fields, forced expulsion and, finally, the planting of TNT in the rubble to prevent any of the expelled inhabitants from returning. Each military unit received a list of villages and neighbourhoods to be demolished and its inhabitants to be expelled. The plan and the means by which it was to be carried out were included in a clutch of documents called Plan *Dalet*, or Plan D, which followed Plans A, B and C, all prepared by the Zionist leadership from 1937 onwards, and which first broached the idea of ethnically cleansing Palestine.[1]

This historical decision by the leaders of the Jewish community was the inevitable result of the ideological Zionist impetus to achieve an exclusive Jewish presence in Palestine. Zionism emerged as a movement seeking a safe haven from European anti-Semitism and looking for a territory where it could redefine Judaism as a nationality. Since the choice was an inhabited country it became a settler colonialist project, and since the movement's founding fathers wished to create a democratic state they were preoccupied with the question of the demographic balance, a preoccupation that led to the decision taken in March 1948. In other settler colonial projects, such as in the Americas and Australia, such a demographic concern led to genocides of the indigenous population; in Palestine it triggered a never-ending process of ethnic cleansing.

The month of March 1948, or so it seems in hindsight, was deemed by the Zionist leadership as the best time to implement their strategy of Judaizing Palestine. Several developments led to this 'ideal' historical junction. The first was the British decision to leave Palestine and entrust its future to the United Nations. The second was the pro-Zionist constellation in the UN, which reflected the international balance of power. The Western political elites were hostile towards the Palestinian community and in particular shunned its leader, Haj Amin al-Husseini, whom they regarded as an ally of the Nazis during the Second World War. More importantly, they wished to bury the genocidal chapter of the Nazi extermination of the Jews by allowing the Zionist movement to dispossess Palestine. As a result, the UN rejected out of hand the Palestinian leadership's demand for a democratic process for determining the future of the country (the Palestinians constituted 66 per cent of the overall population) and instead endorsed a Zionist solution for partitioning Palestine into two states, one Arab, one Jewish. Partition was rejected by the Palestinians and the neighbouring Arab states. The Arab states threatened to foil the plan by force, while the Palestinians went on strike, wrote petitions and for a week or so randomly attacked Jewish settlements and convoys.[2]

Six months later, the coveted 78 per cent of Palestine became Israel, built on the ruins of hundreds of destroyed villages, demolished towns and expropriated cultivated land. The land and real estate were expropriated after hostilities ended as part of a special legislation initiated by the state in order to take over the property, first, of those expelled and, second, of those Palestinians who were allowed to stay (although the latter in some cases were offered compensation or alternative land and in other cases were allowed to purchase their original land for a much higher price). The remaining 22 per cent was made up of the West Bank and Gaza Strip. The West Bank was not occupied thanks to a tacit understanding with the Hashemite Kingdom in Jordan, which annexed the region in return for a limited Jordanian intervention in the 1948 war.[3]

The exclusion of the West Bank from the future State of Israel was thus not the result of a military defeat but, rather, the fruit of a strategic political decision. The decision was never officially adopted as policy by the Zionist leadership because the West Bank, or Judea and Samaria in Zionist jargon, was part of 'Eretz Israel' (Land of Israel) as much as were the Galilee or the Negev. When the deal with the Jordanians was exposed, many officers and politicians in Israel regarded the decision as a grave national mistake. In response, very early on they introduced into the Israeli public scene the discourse of 'the missed opportunity', later adopted by the mainstream parties and media, and which was to play a crucial role in the subsequent support for the 1967 occupation of the West Bank. What was missed, according to those who put the idea forward, was a historical opportunity to occupy the West Bank during the 1948 war.

Motivated by a sense of urgency, a significant group of generals began searching for a pretext that would force their government to renege on its commitment to the Jordanians. They beat the war drums frequently, accusing the Hashemite Kingdom of violating the armistice agreement of 1949 that had finalized the borders between the two states. This was not an easy undertaking as the Jordanians adhered faithfully to the armistice's principal points. It would be another eighteen years before a new golden opportunity, similar to that available in 1948, would enable the creation of the coveted Greater Israel.

The Gaza Strip was, at least until 1967, a different story. In many ways it was Egyptian steadfastness that deterred an Israeli occupation between 1948 and 1956, and the Strip, nearly 2 per cent of historical Palestine, was put under military rule after the 1948 war, which the Egyptian government assured the Arab League and the Palestinians would be terminated once Palestine was fully liberated.

But the Gaza Strip, very much like the West Bank, was traditionally deemed by mainstream Israeli leaders to be part of ancient Israel, and in the romantic vision of the protagonists of Greater Israel the Jewish State needed to possess both areas in order to thrive and prosper. Some politicians coveted these regions on strategic grounds; they regarded the 1949 armistice lines as the 'Auschwitz borders', as it was crudely put by Abba Eban, Israel's Foreign Minister for most of its early years.[4] This was a paranoid and alarming expression from someone who represented the liberal and moderate camp in Zionist Israel (and one, as we shall see, which in the moment of truth tried to pre-empt the Israeli aggressiveness in 1967). But most Israelis indeed felt that Israel's cartographical shape – with a narrow corridor between the north and the south, around the greater Tel Aviv area – posed a constant threat to Israel's existence. Any Arab army coming from the West Bank could, warned Israeli strategists, easily bisect the state.

So the focus of expansionism was on the West Bank. The expansionist group within the Israeli military and political elite consisted of some of the state's highest profile politicians and generals. Foremost among them was David Ben-Gurion, the very man who engineered the first collusion with Jordan, but who then had second thoughts about its wisdom. He was Israel's Prime Minister for two terms until 1963, with the exception of two years when the position was held by Moshe Sharett. Ben-Gurion began seriously to consider a forceful annexation of the West Bank in the early 1950s. On three different occasions his government considered the incorporation of the West Bank into Israel, but was thrice deterred by the fear of a strong British reaction that could have led to an open military confrontation with Jordan's main ally and protector.[5]

The pretext in the early 1950s was Jordan's alleged violations of the armistice agreement. Later, at the end of that decade, other reasons were put forward.[6] The main argument in favour of a military invasion of the West Bank was the weakness of the Hashemite dynasty after the assassination of its founding father, King Abdullah, in July 1951. A new threat was concocted: the Arab radical threat. Its centre was Cairo where the Free Officers took power in 1952 and pursued an energetic pan-Arabist policy, encouraging the replacement of pro-Western traditional Arab monarchies and republics by their model of ruling. In hindsight this seemed a far more important pretext than that of the armistice violations. The Israeli lobby in favour of annexing the West Bank relentlessly used this new regional development as justification for a possible occupation of the West Bank. Every time it seemed that the downfall of the dynasty in Amman was imminent, this group, led quite often by the Prime Minister, would explore plans either for dividing Jordan with the sister Hashemite Kingdom of Iraq or for ceding the West Bank from a future 'radical' Jordan.

Indeed, the government and army in Israel as a whole took a deep interest in the political affairs of Jordan after the rise to power in Egypt of Gamal Abdel Nasser in 1954 and of similar 'radical' leaders in other parts of the Arab world. The emergence of this new brand of Arab nationalism, with branches in Jordan, generated a more active, and at times aggressive, Israeli involvement in the politics of the neighbouring states. The policy and orientation of those who were regarded as spokesmen for Arab nationalism, however, never warranted such a combative Israeli attitude. In the early 1950s, the acknowledged leader of this movement of change, Nasser, was willing to investigate the possibility of peace with Israel. Whether the chances for peace were real or not depended in part on Israeli domestic politics, more specifically on the outcome of the rivalry between David Ben-Gurion and Moshe Sharett, the two leaders of the ruling Mapai party, which represented the Zionist Labour movement.[7]

During Sharett's term in office as Prime Minister (1953–1955), these opportunities for an alternative history seemed more genuine.

Sharett, unlike Ben-Gurion, was keen to establish a substantial dialogue with Nasser. Unfortunately, the Egyptian side's most signifi-cant peace gambit came before Sharett was appointed Prime Minister and while he was still Foreign Minister. In mid-May 1953 Nasser wrote to Abdel-Rahman Sadiq, the Press Attaché at the Egyptian embassy in Paris, indicating that he was willing to reach an agreement with the Jewish State. Sadiq had conducted secret talks with his coun-terpart in the Israeli embassy over the previous two years. Nasser addressed his letter to Sadiq but directed it to the Israeli government. In it he asked for Israeli understanding of his position in the area as a whole but particularly in Egypt. He stressed his commitment to peace negotiations between the two states, but asked for time. As a first step he was willing to refrain from making any aggressive declarations, and he asked the Israeli government to exercise its influence in Washington in Egypt's favour, particularly to persuade Washington to support the Egyptian demand for a total British withdrawal from his country. Whereas Sharett, as Foreign Minister, was willing to use the new channel, Prime Minister Ben-Gurion, as before at such historical junctures, showed no enthusiasm, and nothing came out of this initiative.[8]

It seems that during those same months Ben-Gurion formulated his uncompromising attitude towards Arab 'radicalism', which he now saw as Communism in disguise, or more accurately as an anti-Israeli and anti-Western version of Communism. He feared its ideo-logical orientation, but, more importantly, he was alarmed by the military capability that the USSR could offer the 'radical' regimes. In early 1953 he was in favour of a pre-emptive Israeli action against these regimes.[9] He regarded them as more committed to the armed struggle against Israel than the 'inefficient' traditional regimes, and believed the former would perform better on the battlefield, unless defeated by a pre-emptive Israeli attack.

Unexpectedly, Sharett became Prime Minister in December 1953, and soon resumed negotiations with Nasser. Talks progressed from vague promises to concrete details. Egypt wanted part of the Negev in return for peace and asked Israel to acknowledge its principal role in creating the Palestinian refugee problem. But at this stage the peace process came to a halt. In February 1955 the Israeli army struck an Egyptian base in Gaza. Sharett was led by the army generals to believe that this would be a limited retaliatory action against continued Palestinian guerrilla infiltration from the Egyptian-controlled Gaza Strip. In the event, it proved to have been devised in such a manner that it could only harm Nasser's prestige rather than reduce the Palestinian guerrilla effort. Not surprisingly, Nasser abandoned his peaceful intentions and moved to a more aggressive policy towards the Jewish State.[10]

While Sharett was Prime Minister, Ben-Gurion conducted an 'alternative' government from a place he named 'my voluntary exile', a kibbutz in the south of the country called Sdeh Boker. From this desert location he preached an active Israeli policy, singling out as a crucial goal the need to contain the improvement of Egyptian–American relations, which he saw as a most harmful development. He was confident that such a relationship would impair Israel's ability to influence American politics.[11]

Sharett had very little control over the military policies in Israel even before Ben-Gurion deposed him in 1955. It was Moshe Dayan who took most of the important decisions in this area and he would remain a crucial figure in Israeli policymaking in the 1960s, pushing the state into the 1967 war. In Moshe Sharett's personal diaries there is an entry from May 1955 in which he quotes Moshe Dayan:

We do not need a security pact with the U.S.A; such a pact will only constitute an obstacle for us. We face no danger at all of an Arab advantage of force for the next 8–10 years. Even if they receive massive military aid from the West, we shall maintain our military superiority thanks to our infinitely greater capacity to assimilate new armaments. The security pact will only handcuff us and deny us the freedom of action we need in the coming years. Reprisal actions which we couldn't carry out if we were tied to a security pace are our vital lymph . . . They make it possible for us to maintain a high level of tension among our population and in the army. Without these actions we would have ceased to be a combative people and without the discipline of a combative people we are lost. We have to cry out that the Negev is in danger, so that young men will go there[12]

Livia Rokach, whose father was a pillar of the Zionist movement in its early stages in Palestine, but who herself gradually became anti-Zionist, commented on what that message conveyed (based in part on her intimate knowledge of the personalities involved):

This State has no international obligations, no economic problems, the question of peace is non-existent . . . it must calculate its steps narrow-mindedly and live on its sword. It must see the sword as the main, if not the only instrument with which to keep its morale high and retain its moral tension. Towards this end it may, no – it must – invent dangers, and to do this it must adopt the method of provocation-and-revenge . . . And above all – let us hope for a new war with the Arab countries, so that we may finally get rid of our troubles and acquire our space.[13]

In any case, in the 1950s it was still Ben-Gurion who was the principal policymaker. When he returned to power he translated these aggressive thoughts into action. In collusion with Britain and France, he led Israel into a war against Egypt in October 1956, the Suez campaign, and, despite being forced to withdraw from the Sinai by both the US and USSR, he did not abandon this belligerent policy.

For a moment during the Suez campaign the possibility of invading the West Bank emerged once more. During the tripartite negotiations between Israel, France and Britain in preparation for the joint venture, the Israeli Prime Minister seriously discussed with Guy Mollet, his French counterpart, the possibility of annexing the West Bank within the overall framework of the 1956 attack against Egypt and Arab 'radicalism'. The Americans somehow got wind of this exchange and explicitly warned Ben-Gurion against such action.[14]

But Ben-Gurion did not give up the idea. After the end of the Suez operation, the political situation in Jordan deteriorated and young King Hussein's position seemed so untenable that in April 1957 the Iraqi government, still Hashemite in those days, despatched troops to help him. Ben-Gurion believed this might have provided the opportunity he was looking for and ordered the army to prepare for a takeover of the West Bank. He was confident the Iraqis would be unable to sustain Hussein, in which case his army would step into the West Bank. Hussein, however, survived.[15]

At that time the Israeli public was well aware of the high alert in the army and the possibility of a military operation. The press was subsequently told that any such operation had been averted because the United States had sent the Sixth Fleet to the eastern Mediterranean to deter Israel from taking aggressive action. Commentators in the local press (and also in the United States) called the US efforts to curb Israel the 'boldest American move since Korea'. The culprit, according to the Israeli press, was the Secretary of State, John Foster Dulles, who, it was reported, had personally despatched the fleet. But in fact, according to US documents, the fleet was sent to counter anti-American developments in Syria, not to check Israeli expansionist policies. Washington nonetheless elected to deter Israel by other less dramatic means, and it succeeded. In the circumstances, acquiring more territory and retaining American sympathy were contradictory aims. As we shall see, the reconciliation of these two initiatives enabled the 1967 occupation and annexation.[16] It is important to note that, although the USA did not recognize the Jordanian annexation of the West Bank, it was committed with France and Britain, through a tripartite declaration in 1950, to maintain the territorial status quo in historical Palestine.

Despite basic American unease with Israel's aggressive policy, Ben-Gurion did not hold back and, in the immediate aftermath of the Suez campaign, led his government into one of Israel's most intransigent and harsh positions towards the Arab world in general and its neighbours in particular. This uncompromising attitude was also translated at home into the further imposition of oppressive military rule on the Palestinian minority living inside Israel. By 1958, a decade of systematic military rule over these Palestinians had passed, long enough to build a method of control that nine years later would be transferred to the West Bank and the Gaza Strip.

At the same time Ben-Gurion strove to align Israel fully with the United States, with a particular emphasis on empowering the embryo American Israel Public Affairs Committee (AIPAC), the pro-Zionist lobby in Washington, to help in this goal. He also sent his army shopping around the world to equip the IDF with the latest and most up-to-date weaponry on earth.[17]

Ben-Gurion's attention was focused on both the southern and northern borders of Israel. The emergence of the Ba'ath party as the ruling power in Syria was regarded in the same way as the rise of Nasserism in Egypt. The political upheavals in Syria that ended with the formation of the United Arab Republic in early 1958 were constantly cited as a possible cause for military action against Syria.

The pretext for attacking Syria was the persistent friction and skirmishing between the Israeli and Syrian armies in the so-called no man's land, territory that, according to the armistice signed between them in the summer of 1949, belonged to neither of them. Since then clashes in this zone were sparked by provocative Israeli policy. Israel encouraged its farmers to cultivate the land there, and the inevitable Syrian fire directed at those farmers escalated quickly into an artillery duel and at times into air raids from both sides.[18]

In 1957 this border was still extremely unstable with the Israelis and Syrians alternately violating the shaky armistice between them. The Israeli press was particularly anti-Syrian, and portrayed Damascus as an anti-Israeli stronghold from which only the worst could be expected. Few voices, however, pointed out that many of the border clashes were actually triggered by Israeli provocation. Martin Buber and Ernest Simon were among the few critics within Ben-Gurion's own party who took the Prime Minister to task in no uncertain terms, accusing him of acting against the interests of peace in the Middle East.

David Ben-Gurion hoped that France would be Israel's principal ally for military action against Syria. In a conversation with General Maurice Challe, the French Deputy to the Chief of Staff of the Air Force, he portrayed Syria as 'the problem of the world, not just of Israel'. The danger was so acute, he said, that France should urgently work to include Israel in NATO officially, or at least encourage the organization to accept it as a privileged ally. France, of course, could not do this, but it delivered arms in large quantities. Moreover, in 1957 France supplied Israel with its nuclear infrastructure. One result of the French aid was that it provided Israel with a military capacity to expand and strengthen the political elite's self-confidence and uncompromising mood.[19]

Worried about Syria's anti-French role in the Algerian war of liberation, most French politicians accepted the necessity of this alliance, and France granted Israel $30 million credit, most of which was used to buy arms and weapons. The strong alliance with France never distracted Ben-Gurion from the search for an even stronger alliance with the United States. Appearing in front of his party's members at the Knesset, Ben-Gurion declared:

> The most popular people in Israel are now the French. But this is not good enough. We need the Americans. We cannot rely on Britain, since unlike the United States, the Jews have no political influence over there. Thus for instance, the British Labour party 'are purely "Goyim" [Gentiles]'.[20]

In many ways, the success of solidifying the military alliance with the United States, which only came about in 1966 and 1967, seemed to be a pre-condition for the successful implementation of the dream of a greater, expanded Israel. You needed American might behind you not for occupying more of Palestine, but for maintaining that occupation.

This was particularly true in relation to the West Bank, which was regarded by the US as Jordanian territory (even if its annexation was never formally acknowledged). None of even the most belligerent American administrations would have backed an Israeli occupation of the West Bank, but all of them supported it after it took place.

REHEARSING THE GREATER ISRAEL OPTION

The unification of Syria with Egypt in February, the civil war that erupted in Lebanon in May and, finally, the revolution in Baghdad in July 1958 were events that drew Israel's attention to its eastern border. But as volatile and precarious as the situation in those countries might have seemed to Israeli policymakers, a military operation against them was not on the cards, particularly where Syria, Lebanon and Iraq were concerned.

But Jordan was a different case altogether. In the eyes of this important group of Israeli politicians and generals it possessed an integral part of the Jewish homeland. If radicalization in the other Arab countries spilled over to Jordan and toppled the Hashemites, it might provide the pretext and justification for the occupation of the West Bank.

Consequently, while there was no will to invade a 'radical' Syria or a potentially 'radical' Lebanon in 1958, there was a strong initiative to occupy the West Bank, should Jordan become radicalized or – and this is extremely important in understanding the Israeli decision in June 1967 – should it seem about to be radicalized. The problem in 1958 was that of timing and capabilities, not intention or will. As readers may recall, Jordan was not radicalized and the Hashemite dynasty remained in power, so when Israeli politicians and generals discussed the option of occupation they did so before a 'radical' take-over had occurred. In 1958 no one wanted to go to a war with a Hashemite Jordan, an embattled ally that was still valued as being able to play a positive role, despite the urge and desire to cede from it the West Bank.[21]

Nonetheless it was some time before Israeli policymakers were convinced that the opportunity to take over the West Bank had slipped. The 'radicalization' of the political scene in the Hashemite Kingdom was a process that was closely watched by Israeli intelligence and the Research Department of the Foreign Ministry. Monthly reports were delivered to the policymakers, in all of which Israeli experts strongly recommended keeping intact the *de facto* alliance with the Jordanians. The problem for Israeli policymakers was that, while determined to occupy the West Bank, on the brink of the Hashemites' fall, they realized that in such an eventuality the West would itself prefer to act to save the Hashemites and would not allow Israel to take independent action; which is precisely what happened in 1958.[22]

While it would seem unthinkable today, it was actually the Americans who in 1958 worked closely with the United Nations' Secretary General, Dag Hammarskjöld, to curb Israel's expansionist ambitions. Hammarskjöld had no doubt that the Israeli Prime Minister had only one aim in mind in those tense days in 1958 – when the West dreaded what its leaders termed 'the radicalization of the Arab World' – and that was the annexation of the West Bank. No wonder, then, that Israel's relationship with the United Nations in 1958 sank to an unprecedented low.[23]

It is unclear whether Hammarskjöld understood Ben-Gurion's bizarre state of mind in those anxious moments of crisis. In the midst of it all, this man who regarded the decision not to occupy the West Bank in 1948 as a fatal mistake, and indeed prepared his army for its takeover in April 1957, began to doubt the wisdom of such a policy in 1958. His diary reveals a growing concern about the demographic implications of annexing the West Bank without chasing the Palestinians out of there. 'Regrettably this time the Palestinians would not flee,' he wrote in one entry, meaning that he feared this time Israel would not be able to force them to flee. His fears were echoed by the heads of the military intelligence who voiced opposition to an occupation of the West Bank on precisely these grounds.[24]

Ten years later, in 1968, Ben-Gurion would recommend immediate and unilateral Israeli withdrawal from the West Bank (apart from Jerusalem) in order to maintain the demographic achievements of 1948, namely the ethnic cleansing of Palestine. But, of course, from 1963 onwards he was no longer part of the decision-making process. Back in 1958, when such hesitation was translated into military orders delivered to an Israeli army ready and willing for action, they revealed a blueprint for a very limited military operation in the West Bank. Ben-Gurion authorized only the occupation of the Arab neighbourhoods connecting Mount Scopus with West Jerusalem. The army chiefs and some of the government ministers were deeply disappointed with the plan and recommended an overall takeover. It was all in vain.[25]

These generals and politicians were supported by an ultra-nationalist and aggressive press. Or, to put it another way, given the very centralized nature of the media, the press was precisely in tune with the jingoistic attitude these politicians were so keen to encourage. Both the press and leading members of the government discussed openly and enthusiastically the possibility of a Greater Israel in 1958. The main reason for pushing the option then, according to the press, was that world opinion would tolerate such an expansion, quite apart from any other justification for redeeming the 'heart of the Jewish homeland'. Such redemption was deeply integrated in the curricula and subtexts of the Israeli educational system and, as Tom Segev points out, could also be found in children's toy boxes, in games that included maps of an Israel stretching over the West Bank and consisted of its imaginary occupation.[26]

But the Israelis failed in their attempts to exploit the 1958 crisis. They were frustrated, as they would be again many years later during the 1991 Gulf War, by the subordinate role the West had allocated to them. The Western powers were willing to employ every possible means available to them, including the most lethal and ruthless ones, to contain Gamal Abdel Nasser, the Iraqi officers in Iraq, the Ba'ath party in Syria and the pro-Nasserite forces in Lebanon. They were all deemed, wrongly one has to say, to be proxies of the Soviet Union and a grave danger to the chances of building a strong American imperial hold over the Middle East and its rich natural resources. However, the leaders of this camp, the US administration, did not trust the Israelis and did not want them to play a significant role in this effort.

Israel was thus a 'junior partner' on the scene, unable to pursue its own policy. Hence it was a Western solution to the threat of radicalism that was eventually implemented – keeping a Hashemite Kingdom intact at any cost. Israel's solutions were not welcomed by the West and thus it had to bide its time.

REHEARSING THE 1967 WAR

After the end of the 1958 crisis, the desire to take military action against any of the 'radical' countries seemed to abate for a while in Israel. In fact, it would be fair to say that for most of the time Israeli politicians were content to maintain the status quo, as most politicians would in such circumstances. But the generals and some other important figures never stopped looking for opportunities and searching for new pretexts to take action. One of those most active in a calculated and subversive effort was Yigal Alon.

In 1960 he quite clearly charted the way forward in his autobiography, *Masach Hol* ('A Curtain of Sand').[27] In this book, Alon, a hero of the 1948 war and one of the prime ethnic cleansers of the Palestinians, listed a set of contingencies, each of which constituted for Israel a cause for war. One of them was the downfall of the Hashemite monarchy of Jordan. In such an event, according to Alon, Israel should occupy the West Bank and possibly parts of the East Bank of the River Jordan. Other scenarios related to aggressive Arab actions such as the closure of the Straits of Tiran or the diversion of the estuaries of the Jordan in Arab countries in such a way as to threaten Israel's precious water supply.

Alon was quite specific about what was required for the collapse of the Hashemite Kingdom. Israel's need to act owed nothing to past alliances with King Abdullah or his grandson, King Hussein. Alon, and other Israeli leaders, claimed that a radical takeover in Jordan constituted a grave danger to Israel's security, indeed to the state's very existence. Alon did not explain why. He took it for granted that his Israeli followers would understand that radical regimes would naturally be obsessed with the wish to eliminate the State of Israel.

But there was more to it. Alon had other reasons for describing domestic changes in Jordan as a *casus belli* scenario. He was one of the leaders of Ahdut Ha'avoda, a political party that represented a mixture of socialism and romantic nationalism. For its members Israel's 1948 borders were unacceptable. In their hearts they found it hard to forgive the political leaders of the 1948 ethnic cleansing for allowing Jordan to annex the West Bank and for failing to exploit the result of the 1948 war to occupy what they regarded as the heart of the Jewish homeland – the towns of Hebron, Nablus and, of course, the whole of Jerusalem. As a young general in 1948, Alon had demanded that Israel occupy the Gaza Strip and part of Sinai, but at the time Ben-Gurion had not allowed him to proceed with these plans.

Despite their failure to do so in 1958, Alon and other members of the political and military elite did not give up their intention to occupy the West Bank. Two years later they were joined by others in yet another attempt to grab land by military force, which was once more presented as part of an Israeli plan to defeat Arab radicalism and Palestinian nationalism. It began with a provocative Israeli intrusion into no man's land on the Israeli–Syrian border, which led to a serious escalation on that front. A chain of events that included Egyptian forces entering the Sinai Peninsula and Israeli preparation for a pre-emptive strike, code-named Operation *Rotem*, ended when Egyptian leaders decided to withdraw their forces from the Sinai. Had the military operation got under way it would have included a military takeover of the West Bank and the Gaza Strip. As such, it turned out to be a grand rehearsal for 1967.[28]

It is interesting to note that this was the same plan of action that would eventually lead to the 1967 war: escalation on the Syrian border, triggered by Israeli provocation, leading to rumours of an imminent attack on Damascus and public hysteria in Syria. All the following scenarios are familiar: Nasser rushing forces to the Sinai Peninsula and ordering the UN to concentrate its units in several locations instead of being spread along the armistice lines. Then Israel in turn reacting by calling up reserves in preparation for an attack on Egypt. The last pieces of the jigsaw had to wait until 1967. An Israeli attack and a symbolic Jordanian retaliation were missing in 1958. There was no need at that point, as there would be in 1967, for the insecure King of Jordan to show that he was not entirely in the pocket of the Western powers and thus Jordan was not involved at all in the 1960 crisis.

The difference between 1960 and 1967 was the presence of a wise UN Secretary General who allowed Nasser to play his patriotic pan-Arabist role by showing commitment to defend Egypt and Syria, and who therefore did not object to Egyptian forces replacing the UN units. Instead, he waited patiently for the Egyptian forces to leave two months later. In 1967 a much less sophisticated UN Secretary General would order the complete withdrawal of UN forces and, in so doing, helped to create a golden opportunity for Israel to implement its expansionist dreams.

The chain of events that followed Operation *Rotem*, which eventually culminated in the June 1967 war, continued with yet another round of serious military clashes between Israel and Syria in 1964 and 1965. The bone of contention this time was control over the River Jordan's estuaries. Syria, backed by the veteran Arab League and a new outfit, the Arab Summit, confronted Israel's attempt to expropriate the water for its sole consumption. In 1964 the Israelis initiated a diversion of these water sources to a new mega-reservoir inside Israel. Every now and then further small incidents would escalate into full-scale confrontation. Another source of friction was the launch of Palestinian guerrilla operations from Syrian soil. This was expanded to the Israeli–Jordanian border in 1965 and resulted in a series of Israeli 'retaliations', which took the form of monthly raids into the West Bank attacking villages and police stations.[29]

In August 1965 the Israeli air force was poised for the first time to implement Operation *Moked* ('Focus') – the pre-emptive destruction of the Arab air forces in preparation for war. It involved both a limited option, whereby only the Syrian air force would be targeted, and an extended one, which would be aimed at the destruction of several Arab air forces, including the Jordanian one. The crisis ended two days later, but the extended plan was eventually implemented on 5 June 1967. The Jordanian air force was designated as a target since the West Bank was a key objective in the event of war breaking out.[30]

For a brief moment in 1966, the drive towards strong military reactions subsided. This was mainly due to the weakening of Israel's links with France on the one hand, and, on the other, implicit Soviet threats to Israel should it take on the Ba'ath regime in Damascus. But such worries soon evaporated. A new American administration, that of Lyndon B. Johnson, proved to be the most loyal ally the Israelis could have hoped for. In his first year in office LBJ provided civilian aid worth \$52 million, along with Skyhawk aircraft and Patton tanks – the most up-to-date and lethal weapons in the American arsenal – and more was about to follow.[31] The Israeli military achievements of the 1967 war were due in part to superior US weaponry, including advanced fighter technology, which proved pivotal when Israel launched its surprise attack on the Arab armies during the morning of the first day of fighting.[32]

Armed with new weapons and a mighty ally, the Israeli army stepped up its operations against the Palestinian organizations that occasionally infiltrated the Jewish State from the West Bank. In November 1966 the Israeli army raided several Palestinian towns and villages, killing dozens of citizens and wounding hundreds of others, leaving behind them scores of demolished houses and blocks of flats. As in 1936 and again in 1948, the main weapon against the Palestinian people was collective punishment, whether during a war or a period of relative calm. The official reason for the punitive action was retaliation against intrusions and guerrilla actions by Fatah (the major Palestinian faction that founded and ran the PLO), but one cannot help recognizing the intentional brutality of the same leaders and generals who carried out the ethnic cleansing in 1948. Their targets were innocent West Bankers who had very little to do with Fatah, a worrying forerunner of the operations that were to become institutionalized, routine, collective punishment after 1967.[33]

These punitive missions culminated on 13 November 1966 with the attack on the village of Samu with its five thousand inhabitants. Almost all of Samu's houses were demolished. Despite a relatively bold Jordanian attempt to defend the place, which cost the lives of more than a dozen Arab Legion soldiers, the population felt totally exposed to Israel's will and power. They would soon find out how right they were.

So the plans, ambitions and motive for occupying at least the West Bank were firmly in place long before the June 1967 war. But these expansionist drives did not yet have a definite timetable. That was determined by circumstances unforeseen and unpredicted by Israel's political and military elite. When the opportunity emerged – as a result of escalation on Israel's northern border caused mainly by the army's aggressive actions on that front – the ambitions were swiftly translated into actual policy on the ground.

As stated in the Preface, by 1966 professional teams were already preparing for – and had been since 1963 – administrative, legal and military rule of the West Bank and the Gaza Strip, using as a model the one already implemented in the Arab areas of Israel. The army was prepared, as was the framework for occupation.

It was the Syrian border once more that saw the immediate prelude to the 1967 war. While the Jordanian army was relatively restrained in its response to Israeli operations in the West Bank, the Syrian army continued to answer every Israeli provocation with ever-growing fire and air power. The Israeli air force in particular proved to be far superior in the quality of its aircraft and the capacity of its pilots. As each incident seemed more severe than the previous one, it seems plausible that the Syrian leadership, and in particular its Soviet advisors, began to realize that around the corner a huge military operation, even a war, awaited them. The Syrian leaders joined forces first with Egypt, then with Iraq and Jordan, in the hope of deterring an Israeli attack. Defence pacts between the Arab countries and a series of rather bold, and some would say in retrospect irresponsible, acts by Nasser followed. The by now familiar sequence of events concludes this chapter.

THE FINAL ESCALATION: THE MYTH
OF THE PRE-EMPTIVE STRIKE

The eastern borders of the State of Israel were anything but quiet at the end of 1966 and the beginning of 1967. The reasons for the tension were the same as before: the unresolved question of control in the no man's land between Israel and Syria and the Israeli attempt to divert the River Jordan and its estuaries into its own water system. Similarly, continued guerrilla activity by Fatah and other Palestinian groups prompted yet more Israeli reprisals and attacks.

It was in the very first days of 1967 that new winds of war began to blow, first gently and then ferociously, from Israel's political and military headquarters. The language of the leaders, as later revealed in internal governmental debates, showed an inclination to describe this situation as being dramatically different from anything that had occurred before, even though the reality on the ground reflected a more cyclical wave of escalation and de-escalation since 1948. But those in favour of war and annexation suggested a new interpretation of reality and, more importantly, demanded an unprecedented response to problems that had clearly existed since the creation of the State of Israel.

The first hints of this new mood came in one of the government's first meetings in 1967. It convened in the Prime Minister's Office in Givat Ram on 17 January. The Prime Minister, Levy Eshkol, told his cabinet that the escalation of tension on the Israeli–Jordanian border was unacceptable. Over the next few weeks, similar language was used to describe the situation on the Syrian border, followed by tougher action on the ground. Years later, in an interview with *The New York Times*, Moshe Dayan admitted that Israel's policy in that period was provocative and was pursued specifically to appease the Jewish settlers near the Syrian border. These settlers, explained Dayan, had since 1949 been demanding that Israel occupy the Golan Heights: 'Many of the fire fights with the Syrians were deliberately provoked by Israel, pressed by the Kibbutzim residents'. In hindsight Dayan did not put down the settlers' main concerns to a desire for greater protection from Syrian bombardment, but, rather, to their appetite for more farmland. 'They did not even try to hide their greed for the land', he stated.[34]

The result was a far more aggressive policy on the part of the Israeli air force. Israeli pilots were brought into the picture by extending their routine manoeuvres and exercises beyond Israel's border and into Syrian airspace. This, some of the pilots recalled years later, was a policy intended to escalate the tension. The inevitable dog fights that erupted between the two air forces culminated in the shooting down of six Syrian aeroplanes on 7 April 1967 – the anniversary of the founding of the Ba'ath party in Syria – and thus the actions were meant 'to humiliate the Syrian regime'.[35]

In Egypt, Gamal Abdel Nasser was convinced that Israel was intent on toppling the Ba'ath regime in Syria and threatened Israel with military action. A few weeks later, on 19 May, Israel called up its reserves and three days later Nasser responded by closing the Straits of Tiran, so blocking access to Israel's secondary southern port of Eilat. Most Israeli government ministers saw it as a *casus belli*, but the consensus was that the US should have a go at lifting the blockade by other means. This was contrary to the assessment by the army about these Nasserite moves. The Chief of the General Staff, Yitzhak Rabin, reported to the government on 21 May 1967 that he regarded it all as a 'propagandist move and not yet an aggressive one as the Egyptians have not moved tanks into the peninsula'.[36] At that meeting Rabin correctly analysed the situation, or so it seems in hindsight, and accurately predicted the next move. He still believed Nasser's intention was not to go beyond words, but he would be 'entangled in events beyond his control'. Namely, Israel would exploit the situation better than it had in 1960:

> We are now ready to hit him, if we want . . . there is no preparation for a war in Iraq or Jordan. I do not believe they are preparing an attack. The north is quiet, no dramatic developments [there]. We are equal in number of troops and tanks to Syria and Egypt together.

In fact, until the day Israel launched its attack, 5 June 1967, Rabin consistently reported that the Egyptian force in the Sinai was not sufficient for staging a war against Israel. In his book *Fateful Triangle*, Noam Chomsky cites several quotations to show that in retrospect Israeli generals and politicians admitted having been the aggressive party in the 1967 war. One of them was Yitzhak Rabin, who told *Le Monde* as early as 28 February 1968, 'I do not think Nasser wanted war. The two divisions he sent to the Sinai would not have been sufficient to launch an offensive war. He knew it and we knew it.'[37]

This is a crucial point of historiography. The common narrative of these events, spun by both the Israeli Foreign Ministry and recounted by the most recent and more neutral Israeli historians, is that Israel fought a war of self-defence in order to pre-empt an all-Arab attack. This is not what I read in the documents that have recently been released. No one in Israel in a position of command at that time attributed genuine aggressive intentions to either the Egyptians or the Syrians, and definitely not to the Jordanians.

In the prevailing narrative, nonetheless, Nasser's closure of the Straits of Tiran, the entry of Egyptian forces into the Sinai and the bellicose rhetoric in the Arab world are all proof that the Arab world was on the point of going to war. This suggests Israel's attack as an act of self-defence. But this portrayal of the 1967 war is a false historical reconstruction. All these actions, very typical of pan-Arab politics on the Palestine question, with the exception of the 1973 war, were arguably *reactions* to aggressive Israeli rhetoric and military activities that could understandably be seen as preliminary preparations for attacking Syria at any given moment. The difference from the past was the intensity and escalation of the Israeli assault in the east and in the north, and not Nasser's repetition of his 1960 act, which was intended as a deterrent rather than an attack.

The notion that Nasser repeated his 1960 script was also raised by Abba Eban, the Foreign Minister, in the cabinet meeting in the wake of the Egyptian actions. He referred to the 1960 episode and found out that the only difference was a foolish response by the UN Secretary General, U Thant. The latter refused to accept that it was Nasser's intention merely to show his commitment to Palestine, rather than to act on that commitment. Eban told the government that Nasser's actions in 1960 were motivated by the need to maintain face (the cabinet minutes refer to Eban saying 1962; either he got the year wrong or the typist did). On that occasion, Nasser had asked the previous UN Secretary General, Dag Hammarskjöld, to concentrate UN forces in several places rather than spread them along the border with Israel, and in 1960 the UN had obliged; Nasser sent troops to the peninsula and withdrew them a month later. Eban suggested that, left to his own devices, Nasser would do the same, but he commented: 'U Thant made a mistake by telling Nasser we [the UN] do not concentrate [elsewhere,] we either go or stay'. Nasser's reputation was on the line, he added, and suddenly there was a 'vacuum' nobody expected or knew how to deal with.[38] U Thant asked Eban to allow Nasser time to bring the episode to an end instead of what he saw as warmongering on the side of Israel: 'your embassies around the world create the impression that an Israeli attack is imminent', he complained to the Israeli Foreign Minister.[39]

Eban seemed to think that it was all rather a minor affair, and that only if Israeli ships were attacked would Israel be allowed to activate

Clause 51 of the UN Charter, that of the right to self-defence, which was the official American position. He also ridiculed the panic among the Jewish communities around the world, and especially in the US. He warned that this unwarranted response from international Jewry could prove to be more detrimental to Israel's power of deterrence than Nasser's action. 'We are portrayed as the lamb among the wolves', a strange image, he felt, 'as we know that the forces in the Sinai are not a huge Armada'. The Minister of the Interior too was alarmed at the level of panic in the US, which was worse than in Israel: 'Can we not control it?' he asked.[40]

In many ways Rabin confirmed Eban's analysis. As already mentioned, he also asserted that Nasser did not expect the UN to cower and 'panicked when he realized there were no UN troops in Sharm el-Sheikh and therefore sent paratroopers there' (in other words, Nasser was worried that Israel would pre-empt this with a similar action).[41]

On 21 May 1967, then, the analysis was that war could be prevented; in fact, it depended solely on the Israeli government. Were these the right conditions for going to war to expand the state? This was the main question the decision-makers were asking themselves.

But it is not clear whether ministers such as Eban knew enough about the level of preparation in the Israeli army for a war. He warned that the Egyptians and the Russians were already deeply convinced that Israel was preparing to attack Syria in the north and that the IDF had already amassed huge forces in the region. But the government minutes do not record any response to that.

A hint as to a different reality on the ground, one in which an army was seriously preparing for war and simply waiting for the politicians to approve it, was provided by Israel Galili, the former commander of the Haganah, the Jewish militia that became the IDF, and the Minister of Information (Propaganda). In a meeting on 21 May he expressed satisfaction that, in his opinion, while the Israeli people were being given a balanced assessment of the fact that there was a serious crisis, they had confidence that the army was fully prepared for this crisis. Galili criticized Eshkol publicly for, on the one hand, giving the impression that Nasser's moves were merely propagandist and then, on the other, for saying that Egypt's policy posed a grave danger to Israel. Galili wanted to keep the people both on the alert and in the dark.[42]

Reading the newspapers and radio broadcast transcripts from that period – as well as recalling it as a teenager living in Haifa– it seems to me that Galili deliberately misrepresented the public mood to the government. He was responsible for passing information to the press and the public, and if one can judge by the way that information was translated into radio broadcasts and newspaper headlines, it is clear that he succeeded in creating panic among the general population with his doomsday scenario. This was a repeat of the 1948 domestic propaganda on the part of the Israeli leaders. Then, as in 1967, they invoked the spectre of the Holocaust and predicted catastrophe, knowing very well that the balance of power was in their favour and there were many non-military options open to them to end the crisis.

The crucial meetings took place in the last days of May. The possibility of an American intervention was still in the air, and given time this would have emerged not so much as a military operation, as the Israelis hoped, but, rather, as a concerted diplomatic attempt to defuse the tension. The government that met on 28 May heard from Abba Eban that President Johnson had promised that the 'USA will, with others, open the Straits [of Tiran]'. His assessment was that they wanted to prevent an Israeli military operation but were concerned that it would take time to build a task force for the mission. Johnson also pointed out that the USSR was showing restraint and made a further comment that was erased by Israeli archivists thirty years later. For that reason we do not know exactly what he said to them that they do not want us to know, but from the deliberations in the government on 29 May it is possible to hazard a guess as to what he said: it was either a plea for restraint or a warning against military action by Israel.[43]

Retrospective CIA documents recently released reveal that the USA was already convinced by the end of May 1967 that if Israel went to war it would easily defeat the Arab armies. The CIA Director, Richard Helms, told the President in a memo entitled 'Who Will Win' that Israel could 'defend successfully against simultaneous Arab attacks on all fronts ... or hold on any three fronts while mounting successfully a major offensive on the fourth'.[44]

Neither was the CIA convinced there was any merit for the Israeli claim of an aggressive Soviet policy:

> The Soviet aim is still to avoid military involvement and to give the US a black eye among the Arabs by identifying it with Israel ... [Moscow] probably could not openly help the Arabs because of lack of capability, and probably would not for fear of confrontation with the US.

This was quite a brave statement on Helms's behalf. At the time Mossad kept insisting in its conversations with US officials that the Israeli military was heavily outgunned by a Soviet-backed Arab war machine. Recent research has shown that the Israelis had their man in the CIA, James Angleton, chief of CIA counter-intelligence. For years, Angleton had been briefed by the Israelis and reported his assessments as his own, without informing his superiors of their origins. As David S. Robage writes, 'that unusual arrangement may have given Tel Aviv a sense that Washington accorded its analyses such special import that US leaders would listen to its judgments on Arab-Israeli issues over those of their own intelligence services'.[45]

Helms was convinced the Israelis were playing games. 'We do not believe that the Israeli appreciation ... was a serious estimate of the sort they would submit to their own high officials'. Rather, 'it is probably a gambit intended to influence the US to ... provide military supplies ... make more public commitments to Israel ... approve Israeli military initiatives, and ... put more pressure on [Egyptian President] Nasser'.[46] In hindsight, it seems the CIA was spot on in predicting the results of the war. Informed by these assessments, President Johnson declined to airlift special military supplies to Israel or even to publicly support it. He later recalled bluntly telling Israeli Foreign Minister Abba Eban, 'All of our intelligence people are unanimous that if the UAR [Egypt and Syria] attacks, you will whip hell out of them.'[47]

Someone who was misled by Mossad was Israel's Prime Minister, Levy Eshkol; in those final meetings before the war he voiced fears that put him in a very poor light in terms of the Israeli ethos of war, as a man both timid and therefore a danger to Israel's security. At the time, his hesitation enraged the Israeli generals and their principal spokesman in the government, Moshe Dayan. Both publicly and privately Eshkol regarded war primarily as a targeted operation in the north to halt Fatah infiltration, but it seems that by the end of the 29 May meeting he was already reconciled to the idea that the Israeli army would go to war in 'two weeks' time'. He tried to convince the government to wait that long as the military preparations were already very costly and he thought more foreign military supplies were needed before any such action should take place.[48] We do not know if he actually believed this or if he was playing for time. This is irrelevant, in fact, since the army chiefs were already determined not to wait longer than a week before launching an attack on all fronts. Eliyahu Sasson, the Minister of Police (previously an office that oversaw the affairs of the Palestinian minority in Israel), one of Ben-Gurion's advisors on Arab affairs in 1948 and a member of the cabal that devised the ethnic cleansing programme in that period, asked that the army not wait for two weeks because this would give Nasser 'time to strengthen his position'. Israel had already amassed a huge force, he said, and yet acts of sabotage continued to be perpetrated in the north. The public, he argued, wanted action.[49]

The decision was taken to mislead the US by announcing that the Israeli government was willing to wait three weeks. The US's position at that point has been analysed by other sources and is not the subject under discussion here,[50] but what concerns me here is how Israeli policymakers reached this decision, given that they had been informed by both the CIA and US army intelligence that they believed

Egyptian policy was in essence non-aggressive. What the Israeli government did not know was that the CIA was already aware on 1 June that Israel had decided to go to war. Helms predicted it would be a few days into June.[51]

Curiously, in response to the news from Washington, the Minister of Justice, Yaacov Shimshon Shapira, argued: 'We should demand from the Americans that they would ensure the end of terrorism, opening of the Straits and the eviction of the Egyptian forces from the Sinai'. This was interesting as it represented a considerably expanded list of expectations and demands from the Americans. One possible explanation, given Shapira's political savvy, is that he wanted to present the USA with a mission impossible and thus ensure American failure, or maybe he believed, naively perhaps, that this was still a feasible option in the eyes of Moshe Dayan and the other trigger-happy ministers.[52]

But there was no desire to wait for that to happen anyway. Dayan, who was pushing for an early military operation, was supported by his arch rival for leadership, Yigal Alon. These two veterans of the 1948 ethnic cleansing had already decided by the beginning of May that this was the historical opportunity to expand, just as March 1948 had been the appropriate moment for ethnically cleansing Palestine. To ensure that ministers such as Shapira would not take the American option too seriously, Alon stated at that meeting:

> We lost our prestige; the IDF lost its prestige in the eyes of the Arab world. We were wrong not to smash the Egyptian forces in the last three weeks. The world was sure we were about to attack this morning [29 May 1967] which would have been a justified act. We should find a way of liberating the US from its commitment to act on our behalf.[53]

Alon took his time at that meeting. Employing the biblical rhetoric of if someone comes to kill you, rise up and kill him first, he said that the war should have been initiated the day before; both the

Mapam socialist Minister of Agriculture, Haim Givati, and Rabin also gave their consent to this approach, as the minutes of the meeting reveal.

The name of Finance Minister Pinchas Sapir is etched in the Israeli collective memory as a dove; he was a man who would always advocate prudence and preferred peaceful to military means for solving problems on the national agenda. In the 29 May meeting he appeared to follow this line at the beginning of the discussions, but after Alon made his remarks he shifted his position to a more belligerent stance. From then on he repeatedly hammered home the same point: 'We should exploit the enthusiasm in the Jewish world for recruiting means and money.'[54]

It was Rabin who first echoed Alon's assertion that the army could not wait two or three weeks, saying that it might be more difficult to attack later (he did not specify the nature of the difficulty). He only assured ministers that the air force was strong enough to hit both the air forces and the armies on the Arab side. Then another 1948 veteran, Minister of Transport Moshe Carmel, who had been responsible for supervising ethnic cleansing in the north, followed suit. Abba Eban felt isolated and demanded the right to make the following statement: 'You do not go to war for prestige. You do not make orphans and widows because of prestige.'[55] But prestige, specifically as a deterrent, was what Rabin and Dayan wanted, and more territory was what Alon and Carmel were after.

The chief of military intelligence, Aharon Yariv, summarized the reports and analyses of the American position in a way that suited the aggressive mood of his fellow officers and trigger-happy ministers in the government. He explained: 'The US will not take any military action and therefore the door is open for an overall Israeli attack.'[56] Pre-empting apprehension about a possible Washington backlash, he added that American Jews would make sure 'the Americans would enthuse about the prospects of a war'. Three days later, he sent a full intelligence report stating that the US administration would actually be very happy with a swift Israeli attack.[57]

At the beginning of June the pendulum of decision-making swung from Jerusalem to Tel Aviv. In an underground bunker, the infamous *Bor* ('pit'), dug in the heart of Sarona, the old German colony built by the German Protestant Templers in the nineteenth century and taken over by the Jewish State in 1948, some of the most crucial decisions about the war were taken. Ministers were usually joined there by the general staff of the army and the heads of the security services. This would remain the headquarters for all future military action against the Palestinians, including the use of the air force to punish collectively the people of the West Bank in 2002 and those of Gaza in 2009 and 2014.

It was in the *Bor* that the heads of the army made their famous outburst against Levy Eshkol on 2 June 1967, attacking him for failing to take military action as he waited until the 5th of the month. The actual decision to go to war was taken on 4 June, after a meeting in the HQ in Tel Aviv.

Ami Gluska, a colonel in Israeli military intelligence at the time, and later aide-de-camp and private secretary to the fifth and sixth Israeli presidents, remarked that even at the height of the crisis it would have been possible for Israel to pursue a very different policy. The most obvious was that of deterrence, which, Gluska said, 'fitted the crisis the way it developed'. But the politicians and generals instead preferred an aggressive policy that allowed them eventually to occupy vast areas of the neighbouring Arab countries, and particularly the West Bank and the Gaza Strip.[58]

All this is corroborated by the recollections of Uri Avnery, the then editor of *Ha-Olam Hazeh*, a weekly opposition magazine (bizarrely, as well as being a serious critic of the State of Israel it contained a nude centrefold). Thanks to his heroic role in the 1948 war, Avnery enjoyed close personal relationships with some of the senior officers in the army. He recalled a meeting with David Elazar, the head of Northern Command, who allegedly told him that every night he prayed that Nasser would concentrate enough forces in the Sinai to justify a war. Avnery remembered that while many journalists around him fostered the sense of an inevitable catastrophe, even that of a second Holocaust, his frequent meetings with the generals persuaded him that no such danger existed, but, rather, that warmongering was all-pervading.[59]

Among the generals there seemed to be a consensus about the need to go to war. Among the politicians there were indications that some were more hesitant, most importantly Foreign Minister Abba Eban. A few weeks after the war ended, the *Washington Post* reported heated debates before hostilities commenced between a hawkish Moshe Dayan and a reluctant Abba Eban. It seems that until 3 June Eban still believed there were peaceful ways to solve the crisis.[60] David Ben-Gurion, who was briefed by Rabin, wrote in his diary on 4 June, 'What is the hurry? I do not understand. Should we not consult the Americans first?'[61]

During the war, not every cabinet meeting took place in the government house; some were held in the nearby Knesset, when West Jerusalem was bombarded in the early days by the Jordanian army, while others took place in Tel Aviv in the underground *Bor*. Given the pace of the Israeli advance and conquest, not many decisions had to be taken. Few strategic decisions were discussed between the government and the army, but two in particular are of great relevance to this account. The first was to occupy the West Bank, and the second, the lesser known one, was the decision to occupy the Gaza Strip.

The mainstream historiography, which ignored the ideological drive behind the decision to occupy the West Bank, blamed King Hussein of Jordan for a fatal mistake. It was made at around ten o'clock in the morning on the first day when he ordered his army to bombard Jerusalem as well as several other central areas in the north of the West Bank, adjacent to the border. In most Israeli history books this is the main reason given for the Israeli occupation of the West Bank.

It is interesting that when Israel decided to pre-empt an attack against Egypt and Syria, this was given widespread acceptance as a reasonable explanation for a historical course of events. However, when King Hussein pre-empted what he and his generals considered an imminent Israeli attack, it was regarded as a fatal historical mistake that led to Israel's attack on the West Bank. The Jordanian generals, it seems, were doing all they could to prepare for a possible Israeli attack. In fact, their preparations for a possible war were more defensive than those of other Arab armies. General Abd al-Munim Riad, the Egyptian supreme military commander who was appointed to lead both the Jordanian and Egyptian forces in the West Bank, was worried that an IDF operation, rather than a war, would allow Israel to occupy part of the West Bank. He was also concerned that the Palestinians would never forgive the Jordanians for such a defeat, and would drive through the Hashemite Kingdom.[62]

The little we know about the Arab plans for war suggests that the Jordanian army was strategically deployed so as to be as visible as possible to the Palestinian population. In reality the fall-back plan was to facilitate a quick withdrawal if necessary in order to focus their forces on protecting the eastern bank from the mountain ridge of the West Bank, close to the River Jordan. This would mean giving up Jerusalem, as noted by the Jordanian Chief of Staff, Habis al-Majali, but such a strategy was authorized by King Hussein himself, though in the end to no avail. As events unfolded, the Israeli army stopped at the Jordan, since this was its primary objective, and because it was halted by military action.[63]

It seems that King Hussein only realized that Israeli aggression was imminent on 4 June. Jordan was bound by its treaty with Egypt to react when Israel attacked Egypt the following morning. This commitment, by a king who was already branded a stooge of the West, was balanced by a famous Israeli warning to refrain from any action. To judge from the past, specifically the case of Palestine in 1948, Israeli promises of immunity during war carried very little substance.

Hussein was looking for some sort of golden compromise, and under pressure from the Egyptian commanders his army retaliated two hours later with the bombardment of West Jerusalem. The Israeli army responded in turn with a heavier bombardment of its own and the destruction of the Jordanian air force – as per the plans drawn up as part of Operation *Moked* (a pre-emptive strike to destroy all the Arab air forces).

Israeli historians describe the two hours between the initial Jordanian bombardment of West Jerusalem and the beginning of the occupation of the West Bank as absolutely crucial, a period during which the nature of the Jordanian attack on Israel was dramatically transformed. In reality it was not; there was no time for any change or, for that matter, much sophistication or planning on the Jordanian side. But it was already a real war.

And yet on 5 June, Eshkol and even Rabin, for tactical reasons, procrastinated about whether or not to occupy the West Bank. In fact, when news came in throughout the day about the successful destruction of the Jordanian air force, Rabin asked aloud, 'Why do we need to occupy territories now?' But his views were overturned. He was seconded for a while by Levy Eshkol, who was not convinced that the options for keeping Jordan out of the war had been exhausted. But these two were not calling the shots. Moshe Dayan and the general commanding the central front, Uzi Narkiss, were. They left it for historians to ask the question just how flexible the situation still might have been, even then. For a long time they had wanted to use every possible opportunity to create Greater Israel, and in the end they accomplished it within two days. This does not mean it was easy or involved minimal costs to the army and the civilian population of Jerusalem. These costs were mainly down to the Arab Legion's desperate defence, but, all in all, in the cynical calculation of generals the price was low, very low.[64]

The US administration was, as noted, hardly surprised by the Israeli success. Within the administration there were those such as the ambassador to the UN, Arthur Goldberg, who worked closely with the Israeli government in trying to win Israel time to complete the full occupation of the West Bank before a UN intervention could be effected.[65]

For the purposes of this book, it is worth adding another comment on the nature of the Israeli 'response' theory, one already made very convincingly by Tom Segev and Norman Finkelstein. If the Israelis wanted to tame the King of Jordan, or even to punish him severely, why occupy the entire West Bank? As Finkelstein put it, 'You could have just defeated Jordan without taking over the West Bank. You simply knock out its air force and disable its army.'[66] As established, on 5 June Rabin shared this opinion.

The decision to occupy the Gaza Strip was discussed at government level and the same few voices that were hesitant about a full-scale war here too failed to accept the wisdom of occupying the Strip. It was once again the generals on the ground who quashed any genuine misgivings and led the government to vote in favour of occupation.

Israel Tal, the commander of Division 84, which in all the war game rehearsals was destined to occupy the Gaza Strip, was the prime mover behind the decision to invade the Strip. If the Israeli army hesitated, he warned, this 'would cause mayhem in the Jewish settlements [alongside the Strip]', and all the other generals supported him.[67] Most vociferous among them was Rehavam Ze'evi, the future founder of Moledet, the party that endorsed the transfer of Palestinians out of the Occupied Territories, and whose supporters were among the most violent settlers in the territories. 'It would be a pity to forfeit the headline "The Gaza Strip is ours"', he said. The only note of caution came from Moshe Dayan: he was worried about the large number of 1948 refugees living there. Eventually, like everyone else, he would 'overcome' this concern by adopting the policy of the mega-prison.[68]

In a matter of three days, the West Bank and the Gaza Strip were under tight Israeli control. The historical context provided in this chapter makes it clear that in 1958 firm international opinion prevented Israeli occupation of the West Bank and that a perceptive UN Secretary General did not allow Gamal Abdel Nasser's brinkmanship in 1960 to turn into a war.

It also shows that there were numerous options open for the international community when the new crisis in May 1967 erupted. But they were discarded thanks to a bold Israeli decision to mislead an *a priori* pro-Israeli American administration. Washington did not wish to contain Israel, and the UN Secretary General was unwilling, or perhaps unable, to understand his potential role in a volatile area where brinkmanship was a move in regional politics that was meant to avert violence rather than engender it. This shift in the previously tougher US approach in the face of an unprecedented Israeli act of aggression was partly due to the growing power of AIPAC, which had already existed for more than ten years by that stage.

Michael Oren claims that AIPAC's clout was only felt in the mid-1970s,[69] but the Johnson administration was already aware of its presence. Isaiah 'Si' Kenen, who founded AIPAC, was already boasting in 1973 that AIPAC ensured the generous American aid to Israel of around $1 billion a year. This came up in the congressional inquiry into the way AIPAC destroyed the career of Senator J. William Fulbright, who opposed the very idea of AIPAC.[70] But it is true that it was not merely the power of AIPAC that reoriented American policy. The presence of heavy Soviet armaments supplied to the Egyptian and Syrian armies turned Israel into an ally in the Cold War. The impressive Israeli triumph in the 1967 war reinforced this image in Washington.

Another important difference was the absence of the reformed Ben-Gurion, who might have been able to contain the warmongering manoeuvres of Moshe Dayan and Yigal Alon, both of whom had been minor players during the 1958 and 1960 crises.

Moreover, in 1967 the Israeli army was even better equipped to finish the job – hundreds of aircraft, more than a thousand tanks and almost a quarter of a million soldiers were thrown into the battlefield, a force unprecedented in the history of the region since 1945. Finally, the Israeli leadership in 1967 was far more committed ideologically than any previous government to creating the Greater Israel. The Mapai-led government of 1960 was more limited in its ideological scope and too weak politically to venture a dramatic transformation of the geopolitical reality in historical Palestine.

Taking the larger historical picture, the various key moments mentioned in this chapter – 1948, 1957, 1958, 1960 and 1967 – can be seen as stages in a continuous colonialist project meant to Judaize Palestine and de-Arabize it. In 1967 there were no existential threats against Israel, nor were Nasser's manoeuvres different in kind or scope from his previous actions. A less aggressive Israeli policy on the Syrian border could also have calmed the situation on that front. It is still surprising that even critical and thoughtful historians today regard the Israeli war in 1967 as self-defence and a no-choice war. Yet it was more than anything else a continuation of the 1948 ethnic cleansing and the overall dispossession of Palestine. As in 1948, it had two fronts: one against the neighbouring Arab states, who once again discovered that war and war rhetoric are not the same and who were once again defeated on the battlefield. And the second front was the 22 per cent of historical Palestine that Israel had decided against occupying back in 1948 but which now, in 1967, offered it the chance to rectify, in its eyes, a historical mistake.

Chapter Two

Devising the
Mega-Prison

The [UN] General Assembly characterized Israel's occupation of
the West Bank and Gaza as a denial of self-determination and
hence a 'serious and increasing threat to international peace and
security.'

John Quigley, *Palestine and Israel: A Challenge to Justice*

On 11 June 1967 the Israeli government met for the first time to
discuss the new geopolitical reality that unfolded after the war. After
three days of fighting, Israel was in control of all of historical Palestine
and ruled over one million Palestinians in the West Bank and 450,000
Palestinians in the Gaza Strip, of whom 315,000 were refugees (in
another account provided for the Israeli government in June the
number of refugees in Gaza was stated to be almost 400,000).[1]

Three days earlier, ministers were still locked in the bunker of the
Knesset, and when they resurfaced on 8 June Prime Minister Levy
Eshkol declared that the new united Jerusalem would be Israel's eternal capital. Towards the end of the month, on 23 June, he announced
in the Knesset that the West Bank and the Gaza Strip would remain
under Israeli control and there would never be any military presence
on the part of Palestinian or any other Arab military force on its soil.
Israel, he promised, would normalize the lives of the people in these
territories.[2]

For the next week it was the exclusive prerogative of the senior ministers, convened as 'the ministerial committee for defence affairs', to try to find a consensual policy towards the newly occupied territories; but they drew a blank. By the end of that week the issue was transferred to the full quorum of the thirteenth government of Israel, and surprisingly it was this huge body of ministers that succeeded swiftly in deciding on the strategy that has remained the cornerstone of Israel's policy ever since.

FOUR CRUCIAL DECISIONS

Within a week of the occupation, the Israeli government had to answer four fundamental questions about the future of the remaining 22 per cent of Palestine that Israel had failed to occupy in 1948, which was now under its full control. The first was what would be the fate of the territories? Should Israel retain the territories or contemplate only a limited stay there (pending a political agreement with Jordan, the former sovereign authority in the West Bank, and with Egypt, the former ruler of the Gaza Strip)?

Since this question was answered early on in favour of a permanent stay, it was discussed in conjunction with a second question: what was to be the fate of the people living in the West Bank and the Gaza Strip? Since it was decided not to opt for a massive expulsion, the policymakers discussed the various ways of ruling the people without expelling them and without granting them citizenship. Early on, a distinction was made between areas that would be ruled directly and those that would be monitored indirectly. So in a way the solution to that problem was to partition Palestine once more – always a favourite tactic of the Zionist movement with regards to Palestine – and thus the West Bank and the Gaza Strip were divided into a 'Jewish' space and a 'Palestinian' one.

As the years passed, and as this book and others show, Israel exerted pressure and pursued a policy that caused people in the West Bank and the Gaza Strip to leave. Thus, when I articulated the second decision as opting against ethnic cleansing, I meant that the resolution was not to enact a massive expulsion on the scale of 1948. Even when it transpired that there are ways of downsizing the population, and these methods were implemented intentionally, it was clear that a significant number of Palestinians would remain under Israeli rule.

Whether directly or indirectly, as will be seen in the following chapters, you could be punished by not being allowed to leave and, equally, you could be punished by being expelled. The decision depended on what the 'inmates' wanted most: if they wanted to leave they would be barred from doing so, and if they wanted to stay they were threatened with expulsion. Such a methodology was nothing new, it was a rehash of old practices that were extrapolated from the past: a carrot and stick policy was suggested – reward and punishment – for those accepting or rejecting whatever Israeli rule would be imposed on them. The language taken from the world of husbandry is not mine. 'Carrot and stick' is how Israeli policymakers have described their options since 1967.[3] The main demand placed on the local population was to accept that they had no say whatsoever in determining their future, and, should they reject these new circumstances, they would find themselves incarcerated in a maximum security prison. However, should they cooperate they could enjoy an open prison run autonomously by them. As we shall see, this policy was already being carried out in June 1967.

A third question was how to market this generous idea of an autonomous open prison as a peace proposal while hiding the unilateral establishment of facts on the ground. This question was insistently put by the Foreign Minister, Abba Eban, but seemed to concern other members of the government much less.

Finally, there was the question of domestic consumption: how to market the new reality to the Jewish public, which at least at that stage was not entirely convinced that the occupation would work as a long-term strategy.

Let us now look at how the Israeli government addressed these four issues in the months of June and July 1967.

DECIDING THE FUTURE OF THE
TERRITORIES AND JERUSALEM

This discussion began with a consensual point of departure. Both the limited ministerial committee and the expanded government endorsed the statement by the head of the ministerial committee, Prime Minister Eshkol, that Israel's security border would have to be the River Jordan. A week later, on 18 June, this subject was raised again by Yigal Alon, who stated that not only the river but also the Jordan Valley alongside its banks on the western side should always be part of Israel. It meant, as Eliyahu Sasson noted at that meeting, that both the Jordan Valley and the Jerusalem area were excluded from any potential negotiations with the Jordanians.[4]

Anyone visiting the river today would have a hard job imagining how this creek could be considered a natural obstacle to a bunch of Boy Scouts, never mind a modern army. Even in those days, it was ridiculous to suggest that this extremely narrow waterway was a natural border – and yet it was a major strand of Israeli logic for the strategy they created for themselves and others as to why Israel should keep the West Bank.

Only one liberal minister, Moshe Kol, suggested that any insistence on keeping the Jordan as Israel's future border would lead to a bi-national state all over historical Palestine. The Prime Minister, however, was not worried about this and was mainly concerned about what his Foreign Minister, Abba Eban, who was in the UN at the time, should tell the world about Israel's intentions, if this indeed was the strategy. How could the Jewish State be seen to be committed to peace, while in practice it had decided unilaterally that both the West Bank and the Gaza Strip were to be under Israeli control for ever? Israeli diplomacy has been attempting to square the circle on this issue ever since.[5]

There were separate discussions in the 11 and 18 June meetings about whether the Gaza Strip was a different case from the West Bank. The Gaza Strip in those early days is mentioned jointly with the West

Bank whenever the question of the territories' fate comes up. And it was assumed, if not articulated, that whatever was decided about the one applied to the other. Indeed, until the 2005 decision by Ariel Sharon to disengage unilaterally from the Gaza Strip, it was treated in the same way as the West Bank. Although from the very beginning the discourse on Gaza was less messianic and euphoric, it was still considered, in the words of one of the ministers, Eliyahu Sasson, as a 'liberated area'. It was Menachem Begin, Minister without Portfolio, who wondered aloud whether the Strip should not remain under some sort of Egyptian control. 'It is our responsibility now,' was Eshkol's reply.[6]

When the full government reassembled on 18 June, it continued to meet daily as it had during the war. On the second day of that intensive week, 19 June, the full gathering of Israel's political leaders decided, without a single objection, to exclude the West Bank and the Gaza Strip from future negotiations. As was already clear in the previous week, this would necessitate a dual language, one for domestic and international consumption – the discourse of peace – and one for the bureaucracy of the occupation – the language of annexation and control.[7]

This position was clarified by Prime Minister Eshkol himself. He explained to ministers why he had made comments to this effect in a press conference he gave the day before the meeting. In that encounter with the press he talked about an Israeli readiness to withdraw from territories in exchange for peace: 'I did not mean the West Bank and the Gaza Strip,' Eshkol reassured his ministers.[8]

Moshe Dayan, in many ways the chief policymaker in those days and probably more transparent than any other politician at the time, spoke it as he saw it both in and out of government. Speaking in 1969, he gave the game away:

Our fathers had reached the frontiers which were recognized in the UN Partition Plan of 1947 [56 per cent of the land]. Our generation reached the frontiers of 1949 [78 per cent of the land].

Now the Six Day Generation [of 1967] has managed to reach Suez, Jordan and the Golan Heights. This is not the end.[9]

In the background to those June meetings were also some domestic political developments that solidified the consensual inclination to view the 1967 occupation as a historical opportunity for expanding the Jewish State. That same month, Ahdut Ha'avoda, a splinter party within the Labour movement headed by Yigal Alon that cherished the idea of a Greater Israel, commenced negotiations with the ruling party, Mapai, which eventually created the new Labour party that we know so well today.

A final decision on the fate of the people of the Occupied Territories was never taken. Instead a dialectical process left autonomy as the main option. Expulsion was ruled out early on, and annexation of part of the West Bank to Jordan, while a serious option, would become unfeasible once King Hussein declared in 1988, with tears in his eyes, that Jordan ceded all its ties and affiliation to the West Bank. To be fair to him, he was never offered the whole of the West Bank in any case. I am not sure expulsion has finally been rooted out from the list of possibilities but it does seem that a system for allowing a certain measure of autonomy was the main preoccupation of Israeli strategists at this time.

So Israel was about to swallow up the areas of historical Palestine it had failed to take over in 1948. The next, inevitable, question was what would be the fate of the people living in those areas?

DECIDING THE FATE OF THE PEOPLE

On 18 June ministers began to debate the future of the people, not just the territories. The Prime Minister was aware very early on that any kind of annexation from a Zionist, and in particular a socialist or liberal Zionist, point of view posed a real danger to the Jewish nature and identity of Israel. He therefore toyed with the idea of concentrating all the Palestinians in one place, 'a canton with autonomy'. He also wanted assurances from his advisors and experts that the problem was not that huge and demanded a census in order to ascertain the precise number of Palestinians now under Israeli control.[10]

All the ministers were acutely aware of the interplay between geography and demography. This is why in those early days of the occupation the idea of transferring the population was also considered:

> We cannot expel the Palestinians of Jerusalem, 70,000 in number, but we have to understand that we are dangerously increasing the number of Arabs in Israel. We are also getting 200,000 refugees. There are 400,000 Palestinians in the Gaza Strip – we should negotiate with Jordan their transfer to Jordan.[11]

The minister who made this suggestion, Eliyahu Sasson, was convinced that this was a win-win situation:

> What a boost to Jordan if they would come, it would be its source of living, and there will be more money from UNRWA [United Nations Relief and Works Agency for Palestine]. Dayan told us that local notables . . . are willing to discuss it. We can only do it if Jordan is willing, if not we will have to solve it.[12]

If need be, added Sasson, the Jordanians could be tempted with certain parts of the West Bank; as long as the River Jordan remained the border of Israel this would have been an ideal solution. As it transpired, the Jordanians did not play along, but it is interesting to note that only Menachem Begin objected to the very thought of transferring people.[13]

Begin, however, succumbed quite easily to the ingenious solution of 'non-annexed annexed territories'. He would stick to this formula even after his term in office as a Likud prime minister in 1977 and, despite his public commitment to annexing the territories, while he was the leader of the opposition. Thus, those who supported him loyally on the Israeli right, and wished for a historical *de jure* annexation of what they deemed 'the heart of the ancient homeland', conceded that annexation in practice – but not in theory – was a brilliant idea.

Others with reservations would follow suit. If they had reservations about the wisdom of annexing the territories, they nonetheless liked the idea of saying little while in fact incorporating the West Bank, at least through a sort of creeping annexation. This is how one of the most vociferous opponents of direct annexation, the Mapai party's Minister of Education, Zalman Aran, believed he could solve the problem. He is recorded as demanding that the government avoid any step that would be regarded as indicating an Israeli desire to stay permanently in the Occupied Territories. When he was assured that no such official declaration would be made, on the grounds that the territories would be quietly absorbed, he accepted that the new formula was obscure enough to satisfy him as well. In any case, Aran was not consistent in his position, and for some bizarre reason he also demanded the *de jure* annexation of the Gaza Strip.[14]

Pinchas Sapir, the Minister of Finance, was more consistent in his rejection of any act of annexation, but he never bothered to explain how the problem could be solved. To the end of his life, he seemed to be troubled by the demographic reality that an everlasting 'temporary' occupation created on the ground, and over the years he argued that either total separation from the territories or their full incorporation were really the only two viable options. In practice, he tried to prevent the integration of Palestinian workers into the Israel labour market, but as he did not offer an alternative his views were ignored. Sapir was not powerful enough to override Dayan, who wanted the Palestinians to work inside Israel as day commuters so as to provide them with a source of livelihood. Sapir eventually supported not only the entry of Palestinian workers into Israel, but also the abuse of this 'benefit' by disallowing them to work in Israel whenever the various governments decided to inflict collective punishment on the local Palestinian population.[15]

One would have expected the most leftist of the ministers, those belonging to the Zionist socialist party Mapam, to share Aran's concerns, but it seems that they not only embraced the new idea of the Minister of Justice to have a non-annexed annexation, they even went further in imagining it. Their leading representative in the government, Housing Minister Mordechai Bentov, saw the whole issue in terms of 'psychological warfare', explaining that the best means of proceeding with the agreed policies was to declare that there would be no Israeli withdrawal from the territories before a peace treaty was concluded. What is bewildering about his contribution is the openness with which he linked the conversation about peace with psychological warfare. The enigmatic 'peace treaty' as a pre-condition for withdrawal would from then on be the main Israeli rationale and pretext for consolidating the occupation and refusing further compromise with whomsoever represented the Palestinians. At the time, on 18 June 1967, all the other ministers concurred with Bentov that this was the best propagandist line they could adopt. Moshe Carmel, the Minister of Transport, assured them there was no prospect for peace in the near future anyway, unless perhaps with Syria, but even this was doubtful, he added.[16]

In a way, there were two different discussions when the fate of the people was debated: one concerned those who lived in the West Bank and the other the inhabitants of the Gaza Strip. Absurdly, the conversation about Gaza was more forthright – ministers spoke candidly about the need to expel people from there – but little was done. The discussion on the West Bank was more guarded, but far more West Bankers were uprooted in the end. Gaza was singled out in such a way as to be depicted from very early on as a uniquely hostile Palestinian spot, probably because it had been the first front on which Palestinian guerrilla fighters had attempted to launch a war of liberation against Israel in the early 1950s.

The discussion on Gaza was closely related to the conversation about the fate of the refugee camps there. The first decision was to allow UNRWA to remain the sole agency responsible for running these camps. From such an arrangement Prime Minister Eshkol saw an opportunity for a profit to be made on the side for the state, and proposed that Israel should be the sole supplier of food and other essential commodities to the Gaza Strip. However, a decision on this was initially deferred and later forgotten: UNRWA's responsibility remained the same as it had been before the occupation.[17]

A more alarming development, and one that illuminated the past and future Israeli fear of and animosity towards the Gaza Strip, was revealed in the next government meeting on Gaza on 18 June. In the main not much was decided – more than anything else it was a specu-lative conversation about how to deal with a population that was deemed hostile and unwanted. Disturbingly, all the ideas put forward in that discussion had one thing in common: a wish to reduce the refugee population in Gaza to a minimum. The three main proposals were push them into Egypt, settle them in the West Bank or in Jordan. Eshkol wanted to send them to Iraq. The socialist Mapam minister Bentov suggested resettling them in the Jordan Valley, to which Menachem Begin objected: 'Is it wise to have a strip of Arabs between us and the River Jordan?' he asked rhetorically.[18]

Ministers oscillated between resettlement of the refugees by force and trying to induce them to leave. We have since come to under-stand that 'voluntary transfer' is just another name for ethnic cleans-ing, and so it is not surprising to learn that this conversation was led by Moshe Carmel, a leading figure in the 1948 operations. He suggested: 'We should take the initiative on the question of refugees by encouraging their emigration out of Palestine and resettlement in Sinai; that is why we should keep the Sinai for a while. We should get international and Jewish money for it.'[19]

Quite a few ministers liked this idea; even the Prime Minster became briefly excited and for a while allowed his imagination to run away with him, outlining a new project of transfer and resettlement. Eshkol was Israel's number one expert on water, so naturally he began by explaining the water infrastructure that would be required for such a project. For some reason he thought the refugees could, like

Moses, extract water from the desert. This would be feasible, he commented, 'especially if they find water there as they did recently in the Sahara Desert'. He reminded his ministers of the Zionist El-Arish plan at the beginning of the twentieth century. This was one of the early attempts of Theodor Herzl, the founder of the Zionist movement, to persuade the British government in Egypt to support the Zionist colonization of Palestine. A Jewish Gaza, instead of a Palestinian one, irrigated by a sweet water canal from the Nile to Gaza. At the time, Lord Cromer, the Governor General of Egypt, rejected the plan and it did not materialize.[20]

But Eshkol's monologue soon lost its momentum, vision and optimism. Israel needed the territory, he agreed, somewhat despondently, but what if resettlement did not prove feasible? What could be done? he asked. Israel needed the territory but the 'heart sours' (*mar balev* – a Hebrew saying that connotes a most troubling and unpleasant sensation) that these coveted territories should include 400,000 Palestinians. He did not go as far as the Minister of Finance, Pinchas Sapir, who described the Gaza Strip as a 'snake pit' – something, according to Sapir, he had already noted in 1956 when Israel occupied the Strip for the first time – but the Prime Minister was not far from using this kind of racist language. Given typical Palestinian birth rates, he noted, they would be uncontrollable.[21]

Every now and then during the debate Sapir attempted to explore the possibilities of transferring the population, which he proposed should be presented to the world as a population exchange. 'Like Greece and Turkey,' concurred Menachem Begin. 'Exactly, no harm done, we are not doing it in the dark, we say this is our land and we have ousted them.'[22]

The actual policy decided upon when these deliberations were concluded in the summer of 1967 was to divide the West Bank (and to a lesser extent, as we shall see, the Gaza Strip) into two basic areas: 'Palestinian' and 'Jewish'. The West Bank is 124 kilometres long and 30 kilometres wide and its topography and demography played a crucial role in determining the Israeli decisions on the ground. The most populated areas – the 'Palestinian areas' – sprawled over the mountainous ridge that cuts the West Bank through the middle and where the main cities are located, Hebron, Jenin, Nablus and Jerusalem. The mountainous Palestinian areas were the only part of the West Bank that proved a problem for Israeli strategists. The rest of the West Bank was conceived in one way or another as an integral part of the future enlarged Jewish State. Those who were unfortunate enough to be in the more 'problematic' areas in 1967 waited for their fate to be determined by Israel.

This cartographic vision of the West Bank as an area divided between annexed regions and 'populated' spaces informed the colonization and Judaization policies of Israel from 1967 onwards. Thus, as early as 1967, the drive was to determine by a fait accompli which areas would be directly annexed to Israel and which would form Palestinian enclaves. At that point – and as remains to this day – the Jordan Valley, Greater Jerusalem, Hebron and Gush Etzion were deemed, and developed, as part of the greater future Jewish State. Ten years later, there were already thirty-two well-established Jewish settlements in these areas, not including the so-called neighbourhoods of East Jerusalem that are still designated as settlements even by the US State Department.

Settling Jews was the main method of redefining what was 'ours' from what was 'theirs' and it was first tried out in the Greater Jerusalem area. The fact that this operation in Greater Jerusalem is still going on today, even as I write, testifies to the Palestinian steadfastness in the face of a very determined and systematic policy of Judaizing their lives and surroundings. This Greater Jerusalem colonization effort consisted of three rings, each one of them a Palestinian space targeted as an area for Jewish settlement. The inner ring was the Old City of Jerusalem, the middle one was the pre-1967 Palestinian suburbia in the east and the outer was West Jerusalem.

It was the inner ring that first received the attention of Israeli strategists in 1967, and the specific aim was to downsize the number of Palestinians inside the Old City. Within a few days of the occupation, the Old City was covered with posters inviting any Palestinians willing to be transferred to Jordan to register at the city's courthouse. There, anyone interested enough to find out more was given five days to volunteer for transfer. They could not know then that some of them would be forcefully evicted, even if they decided to stay. They were the first to learn that parts of the West Bank were already deemed to be purely Jewish, even if Palestinians still lived there.[23]

Whether it concerned territory or demography, the rhetoric in those early meetings was messianic and euphoric, but the outcome was nonetheless very practical. The balance between the decision to remain in the territories and Israel's need to be regarded internationally as a peace-loving nation was immediately put to the test in the case of Jerusalem.

MARKETING THE NEW REALITY: VOLUNTARY AMERICAN BLINDNESS

Ministers knew there was a wide consensus about Jerusalem and therefore it was the first topic on the agenda. No dissenting voices were to be heard amid the paeans of praise for the new liberated and unified Jerusalem, the eternal capital of Israel. The problem was – and this made the discussions somewhat urgent – that the international community did not seem to share this messianic enthusiasm. It was feared that some governments, agencies and Christian denominations would offer to be caretakers of the city pending a solution – a development that could have prevented the Israeli annexation of the city. Interestingly, the pressure to take unilateral action on Jerusalem was pushed by those ministers who, at least in Israeli collective memory, are depicted as 'doves'; namely, politicians who seek compromise with the Palestinians. This reflected the extent of the consensus on the city's future from both sides of the political spectrum. The consensus remained the constant variable in the city's future and explains why, regardless of any political changes in governments in years to come, the city was not only united but kept expanding until it would take over almost a third of the West Bank by the end of the twentieth century.

It took the Israeli government longer than intended to settle the issue of the *de jure* annexation of Jerusalem. The Minister of the Interior, Haim Moshe Shapira, who understood early on that after the occupation the government would have to get used to double talk vis-à-vis the international community, suggested that, rather than rushing out official declarations, they should quietly speed up establishing facts on the ground. But most ministers were deeply convinced that in the case of Jerusalem there was no need for any double talk – it should be declared, from the outset, as an issue that would always be outside any future negotiations. So in those early days the Knesset was asked to pass a law that recognized Israel's undeniable right to be for ever the only sovereign in the holy city.[24]

The one insistent voice of caution was that of Haim Moshe Shapira. He saw no logic in attracting unnecessary attention to the imminent annexation and Judaization of Jerusalem. He particularly failed to understand the urgency of legally formalizing the process. Shapira (not to be confused with Yaacov Shimshon Shapira, the Minister of Justice) saw no difference between the way Israel had annexed and Judaized the areas of Palestine originally designated as an Arab state in the UN 1947 partition Resolution 181 and the forthcoming project. A veteran politician, he had supervised the 1948 takeover of dozens of Palestinian towns and hundreds of villages forcibly evicted during the ethnic cleansing of Palestine. In the meeting he claimed: 'I annexed Jaffa to Tel Aviv without any law.'[25]

These legal deliberations, which continued, as we shall see, until the end of the month, did not in any way slow down the annexation of the 1967 Palestinian part of the city. Jerusalem's airport was already used for domestic flights; streets were renamed – either by Hebraizing Arabic names or by honouring famous and not so famous Zionist leaders. This was not a new praxis – similar renaming had taken place in Palestine after the 1948 ethnic cleansing. Now, in 1967, the old

Palestinian, Muslim and international street map disappeared within a day, and history was instantly rewritten with the help of that quintessential local ambassador of Zionism – the tourist guide. Soon after the occupation, Israeli tourist agencies began encroaching on the territory of their competitors in the Old City. Everyone chipped in: the atmosphere was such that there was not a single dissenting voice from the public about turning Jerusalem into Israel's eternal capital and an essentially Jewish city.[26]

Even those who early on (and there were some) doubted the wisdom of keeping the territories demanded that Jerusalem remain under Israeli control. One of the unexpected voices of assent was the founder and foremost leader of the state, David Ben-Gurion, now out of touch and with no political influence. 'We should keep Jerusalem and create an autonomous Palestinian state, under the UN trusteeship, with strong economic ties to Israel,' he suggested.[27]

But despite such confidence, caution was still called for with regard to Jerusalem since the American position on the city had not yet been clarified. The US had still not accepted the way Israel had abolished the international status of the city after 1948, and hence located its embassy in Tel Aviv. These were in fact quite tense days as far as the bilateral relationship was concerned – in the background was the unprovoked Israeli air assault on the American navy intelligence and surveillance ship USS *Liberty*.

This is not the place to dwell on the *Liberty* incident in full, only within the context of Israeli apprehension about American retaliation for the unilateral policy in Jerusalem. The USS *Liberty* was flying the Stars and Stripes and its identification was clearly indicated in large white letters and numerals on its hull when it was destroyed by Israeli torpedo boats on 8 June 1967.[28] George Lenczowski assumed that 'Israel clearly did not want the U.S. government to know too much about its dispositions for attacking Syria' while it was clear that Syria was about to accept a ceasefire.[29] Another scholar believed that the idea was to kill everyone on board to make sure that this ploy would not be discovered.[30]

This episode meant that the Israeli government needed to proceed cautiously when it decided to mislead the Americans further, this time concerning Jerusalem. But that concern did not last long, because even then ministers were quite confident in their ability to orient American policy towards unconditional support for the State of Israel and its policies of occupation. This is not as obvious as one might think. As recently as 1964, just a few years earlier, it was not at all clear that Israel was America's blue-eyed boy in the region. But this changed after the assassination of President Kennedy and the appointment of President Johnson. In a stroke a new era began that continues to this day, in which Israel is regarded as a member of a unique club of states in whose policies the USA does not as a rule interfere but instead offers only polite protestation when, in the eyes of the rest of the world, they have gone too far.[31] Or, put more diplomatically by the Jewish State's super-diplomat, Abba Eban, he anticipated a non-critical policy to develop in Washington. He predicted even then that in the long run the US would endorse, or at least would not reject, the unilateral decisions Israel took about the territories in general and Jerusalem in particular.[32] With the hindsight of fifty years, it is quite astonishing to see just how accurate his prediction was.

The American policy towards Jerusalem over the years had three particular features: there was and is no American embassy in Jerusalem; there is a separate American consulate in East Jerusalem; and there is an ongoing commitment by senators and presidential candidates to one day move the American embassy from Tel Aviv to Jerusalem. These three contradictory positions conveniently obfuscated for all concerned any principled US stance on the issue. But this is our understanding only in hindsight. The question is, why did Abba Eban feel so confident in 1967, given that the US administration made it clear on every possible page that it opposed these policies, first when they were announced on 19 June 1967 and then when they began to be applied on the ground on the 28th of that month?

President Johnson said on 19 June that 'in our view there . . . must be adequate recognition of the special interest of three great religions in the holy places of Jerusalem'. On this principle he assumed that before any unilateral action was taken on the status of Jerusalem there 'will be appropriate consultation with religious leaders and others who are deeply concerned'.[33]

The Department of State was even clearer when it declared on 28 June: 'The United States has never recognized such unilateral actions by any of the states in the area as governing the international status of Jerusalem'. And the American ambassador to the UN, Arthur Goldberg, informed the General Assembly on 14 July:

> With regard to the specific measures taken by the Government of Israel on 28 June, I wish to make it clear that the United States does not accept or recognize these measures as altering the status of Jerusalem. My Government does not recognize that the administrative measures taken by the Government of Israel on 28 June can be regarded as the last word on the matter, and we regret that they were taken. We insist that the measures taken cannot be considered as other than interim and provisional, and not as prejudging the final and permanent status of Jerusalem.[34]

One possible explanation for Eban's foresight and powers of prophecy, or at least for his confident position, was the pivotal role he played in establishing AIPAC in the 1950s when he was alarmed, as Israel's envoy to the UN at the time, by the anti-Israeli shift in the Eisenhower administration. By 1960 the lobby, as it became known, could boast its first significant success: the political destruction of the powerful Senator J. William Fulbright, who wanted to expose the illegality of AIPAC's activity and paid dearly for his efforts: his political career was permanently ruined.[35] The American ambassador to Israel, Walworth Barbour, would be one of many ambassadors in Tel Aviv who were completely ignored by Israeli governments, and consequently Washington would send a succession of pro-Israeli ambassadors *a priori* who played only marginal roles in shaping the bilateral relationship between the two states.

A telling remark by Eban at the meeting indicated just how double edged was the message the Israelis were trying to convey both to the American people and administration. The people were being urged to support a small Jewish David living constantly in grave, existential danger of another imminent Holocaust, while the administration was led to accept the invincibility of Israel as an asset in its Cold War – and later in its twenty-first-century 'War against Terror'. Eban complained about what he called an 'unwise' demonstration of 40,000 Jews in Washington 'crying about poor Israel', after 'we defeated seven Arab armies and drowned an American warship'. President Johnson, reported Eban, was very upset by this demonstration.[36]

Small successes increased the appetite for territorial gain and emboldened the state's willingness to test further American tolerance towards a policy that in the main was indefensible on the international stage. Since it seemed that nothing would stand in Israel's way in the making of the Greater Jerusalem, not even the Americans, some ministers suggested including Bethlehem in the new annexed territory, but the majority of ministers rejected this idea.[37]

The same concerns about Jerusalem were relevant to the discussion about the fate of the territories as a whole. Israeli policymakers were unsure whether the Americans should be notified about the strategic decisions the government took in 1967. They decided against such transparency, although they were aware that eventually Washington would notice the developments on the ground and thus a different dilemma presented itself: how to present that transformation in a way that would not alarm the US.

On 19 June the government discussed how much the USA should be told about their internal decisions. The way forward was proposed in the afternoon session: the government would on the one hand deflect attention from the Palestinian areas while on the other show serious commitment to the attempt to reach peace with Egypt and Syria. The ministers' confidence was such that some of them suggested publicly declaring that the West Bank and the Gaza Strip were non-negotiable, but this idea was eventually abandoned. There was some apprehension on 20 June ahead of the speech by President Johnson, who presented a rather vague American peace plan consisting of five points, none of which contradicted the Israeli policy on Jerusalem or on the refugee question. It was all about the priority of peace before any withdrawal or other settlement, precisely the line Israel wanted the USA to follow.

American documentation reveals that Washington was not easily deceived and even by 1967 they understood that what they had been told had little relevance to what was happening on the ground. On 25 June 1967 the President requested that the Israeli government should not officially annex Jerusalem. This was the first use of a formula that would be employed again and again, and, one should say, that would be perfected over time and it is still in use today: a firm American request not to annex or colonize is followed by an unequivocal promise to take this position on board, while the planned annexation or colonization goes ahead anyway.

The tactic for dealing with the explicit American request not to annex East Jerusalem was devised and successfully trialled the next day, 26 June. Prime Minister Eshkol interpreted this message, while admitting it was an angry one, as a warning that such a unilateral action by Israel could lead to the creation of an anti-Israeli bloc in the UN that would demand a unilateral Israeli withdrawal. But he added that American anger was about the timing of the decision and not about the decision itself. With these assurances, the government proceeded to annex Jerusalem.

It is worth dwelling for a moment on how this was achieved. Bypassing US objections did not prove as easy as the government had expected. While there was, of course, an active pro-Zionist lobby in Washington, the challenges there were quite formidable when it came to the question of Jerusalem. The Israeli embassy in Washington reported, and American documents reaffirm this in retrospect, that there was a growing unease in Washington about Israeli declarations to annex East Jerusalem. So when the government met on 25 June, Eshkol wanted first to discuss any policies towards Jerusalem in the light of US concerns about it. Always the pragmatic Mapaynik, he stressed the need to act without making any open declarations to the international community. 'We should move on with the annexation [of East Jerusalem], without changes in the law.' He was annoyed that the otherwise obedient print media had highlighted ministers' wish to annex and unify Jerusalem, which embarrassed Israel in Washington. 'We should meet the editors in chief despite the fact that [Gershom Schocken, the editor in chief of *Haaretz*] will complain, but it would be all right.'[38]

There was an urgent need to meet with these senior editors because with the wish to annex Jerusalem came the simultaneous desire to soothe the Americans, thus necessitating a delay between the actual decision and its implementation. So the final decision to 'unite' the two parts of the city was taken on 26 June 1967. However, since the likely American reaction was not yet clear, it was decided to delay the official declaration until clarification arrived from Washington. The problem was that newspapers were keen to cover an event of such historical importance, but as Israel Galili, the Minister of Information, put it, the move 'would attract unnecessary global attention to it'. It was the liberal Minister of Tourism, Moshe Kol, who suggested once again that 'we should meet with the editors of the newspapers and ask them not to publicize it'. Great minds think alike and he was told by Shapira, the Minister of Justice, that he had already met with them and that, apart from one, all 'were very sympathetic'. But he added that in the case of the stubborn *Haaretz* editor, more pressure would be needed to force him to toe the official line.

Eshkol had no qualms about resorting to a familiar ploy, one which Israeli governments had used in the past and would use in the years ahead when they wanted to hide certain policies from the Israeli media: 'I can declare this is a meeting of the "ministerial committee for defence matters" and thus it will be closed to the public or public knowledge.'

LAYING THE FOUNDATIONS FOR THE PEACE CHARADE

So by ensuring an obedient press, which is seldom difficult even today, the government was free to focus on how best to manage the interplay between actual policies on the ground and marketing them to the USA. In a meeting on 27 June, Abba Eban assessed that the Americans would prefer that any announcement on the intended law of unification be delayed. He reminded ministers that the UN was still debating a Soviet draft resolution calling on Israel to withdraw to the 4 June 1967 borders. 'Such a promulgation could not help,' he told them. The other ministers understood better than Eban how things stood with Washington. In reality, there was nothing to worry about there; it might be a nuisance, they said, but not a crucial issue and despite the Foreign Minister's protestations they gave the green light to the members of the Knesset to activate the process of legislation that would unify Jerusalem as one Israeli city and Israel's official capital. The only concession they made was promising Eban that they would ask Knesset members to tone down the debate; what that meant exactly nobody bothered to explain.

Eban was not satisfied. The following day he told the government that the Americans, including the President and the Secretary of State, Dean Rusk, were furious. In addition he was worried, needlessly it may be said in hindsight, that the UN could still exert pressure on Israel, since there was now yet another attempt, a joint Yugoslav–Indian initiative, to pass a resolution that would call on Israel to withdraw unconditionally to the 4 June borders. The debate in the Knesset could therefore severely undermine efforts to counter this initiative. In retrospect it would appear that the Knesset was more important than the UN in determining the fate of the Palestinian territories.

But no one was alarmed, not even Prime Minister Eshkol, who called it 'a small misunderstanding of timing and pre-information'. In fact, if there was still any uneasiness in American–Israeli relations this revolved around the aforementioned *Liberty* affair; it seems that the US administration did not accept the Israeli version of events. It established a commission of inquiry that concluded that the Israeli air force had clearly identified the ship as a US navy vessel but attacked it nonetheless. Nor did the Vatican express concern, as it transpired from that government meeting on 26 June. According to Eban, the Israelis were told by Pope Paul VI that he no longer insisted on the internationalization of the city, and only wanted the Vatican to have a say in the running of the holy places for Christianity, something the Israelis had themselves suggested in 1952.

It was over those two days in June therefore that the dichotomy between what official Israel said and what official Israel did was clearly laid out as policy. Not everyone in the government engaged with this issue in the same way; but, all in all, the consensus was that the Americans, and certainly the Western world as a whole, could be ignored. The Minister of Defence, Moshe Dayan, comes across as the most arrogant minister in this respect, and did not seem remotely concerned about the packaging and marketing of a policy that, *prima facie*, would be unacceptable to the West:

> For me the important issue is our internal decision, not what we are going to broadcast outside . . . we have to operate on the basis of principles: Jordan River is the border, the 1,250,000 in the West Bank are not going to be Israeli citizens and '*yerushalayim hash-lema*' ['unified Jerusalem' in Hebrew; he meant it should always be unified] . . . They [the inhabitants] should be administered by a military rule until further decision. After that they should run their lives in an autonomy, and if this does not work, I would rather have them as Jordanian citizens than Israeli ones. Running their lives under military rule, as long as the River Jordan is our border is also not a bad option.

It was more than 'not a bad option' – it became the only policy in town for the next fifty years, and it was transformed into stark reality on the ground. In a similar vein, Dayan summarized the debate about the refugees and how to market Israel's stance on this question. 'We have a problem,' he stated in the closing minutes of the meeting on the afternoon of 19 June 1967: '800,000 refugees are now under our responsibility, after years of the world shouting at the Arab states to do something about it.' But this did not mean, Dayan asserted, that Israel had to initiate any constructive policy: 'It is not an issue now, let us not raise it. We shall deal with it later . . . We should be thankful for the fact that UNRWA still takes care of them.' This stance by Dayan put an end to further attempts by Eliyahu Sasson in those meetings to persuade the government to prepare a comprehensive Israeli plan for the resettlement of all the refugees in various Arab countries.

Yigal Alon's objections to Dayan's position, which were rooted more in personal animosity than ideological differences of opinion, were also easily overcome. Alon asked: 'If the USA asks you what will you do with the refugees, what do you answer?' Dayan responded, 'That we will in due course take care of it.' The last words on the issue were more like a conversation between the two grumpy old men in *The Muppet Show* than a serious discussion. Eshkol: 'I wish the whole world and the Arabs would take them.' Dayan had the last word, finishing in his usual nonchalant way: 'This is a problem beyond peace agreement with the Arab states. After peace with them, we will still have the problem', predicting an Israeli policy that over the decades would altogether exclude the refugee problem from any peace negotiations.

His words would be the bedrock for the future Israeli stance on the issue: in order to let the problem die down the Israeli government should not initiate any discussion on the refugees. 'No need to awaken sleeping dogs,' Dayan added. For internal consumption only, Dayan reminded his colleagues that Israel bore no responsibility for the refugee question. By that he meant not only historical accountability but also the need to care for them in the present. It was UNRWA's realm of authority, as Dayan chose to describe it, and Israeli ministers should not challenge it. 'Egypt did us a great service running the refugee camps with UNRWA in the last nineteen years. We should keep it in UNRWA's hands.' Dayan agreed with Sasson that this reality of refugeehood in the UN camps could be sustained for a very long period, and therefore there was no need for talk about resettling the refugees in the Arab world.

It was left to the more 'sensitive' ministers of the Zionist liberal or socialist left to devise the language and approach necessary to propagate the new policy. In time these linguistic cover-ups would ensure Israel's immunity from retribution for any of its transgressions of international law or human rights. In those days, it was the Minister of Education, Zalman Aran, of the ruling Mapai party, and the Minister of Tourism from the liberal party, Moshe Kol, who did most of the work in this field. Aran is quoted in the minutes as saying: 'We should say something, not necessarily mean something.' What he meant was that they should say something about their wish to seek peace, but not really mean it.

Kol and Aran also wanted to assist in marketing Israel's leading diplomat, Abba Eban. In the meetings they devised a formula for him, which meant, when in the UN, making vague references to Jordan as Israel's main interlocutor on the future of the West Bank and the Gaza Strip. Eban's principal problem was that in those early days after the 1967 war (and this is perhaps not the case today) the USA still attached great importance to the UN, and the only real proposal on the UN table was a Soviet call for an unconditional Israeli withdrawal. It took a while, but eventually the Israeli government succeeded in pushing the Americans towards accepting the formula they favoured: withdrawal would only be possible after a comprehensive peace agreement had been reached. This would become the official Israeli and American position for years to come, thwarting any real chance for peace and reconciliation, and allowing the Israelis to continue with their policies in practice under the pretext that as long as peace had not been achieved they were committed to their security, which meant settlements, military rule and control.

Israeli ministers offer us a variety of angles on this question – how best to market worldwide the decision to create unilaterally a huge open, or if necessary closed, prison for the inhabitants of the West Bank and the Gaza Strip. Although they all say the same thing, some of the personalities involved are worth revisiting because of the important role they will play later on in the so-called peace process. One such voice was that of a junior minister belonging to the National Religious Party, Mafadal, Yosef Burg. Later he would become a long-serving Minister of the Interior in several governments, and would lead the futile Israeli–Egyptian discussions on autonomy for the Palestinians in the late 1980s and early 1990s. It seems that he invented this magical concept of the need to retain the Occupied Territories until such time as peace was established, in 1967. Egypt's President Anwar Sadat and US President Jimmy Carter would adopt it as a basis for a permanent peace solution and for about five fruitless years would discuss it until it petered out. It was one of many rounds of diplomatic discussion that had little relevance to the reality or to the way Palestinians lived under occupation since 1967. In June 1967 Burg echoed Dayan in making a clear link between the idea that there would not be peace, or, as he put it, there would never be 'a partner for peace', and the justification for Israel's unilateral policies on the ground. 'No partner for peace' became quite a common slogan, one used by future Israeli politicians for excusing hostile actions against the Arab population. As the veteran Zionist Burg put it: 'We are going to have to hold on to the territories for a very long time, while claiming outside we wish to make peace.'

In those June meetings, a few final touches were added and some quite innovative ideas floated as to how best to move between marketing the policies in one way, while carrying them out in exactly the opposite way. Eshkol, for instance, suggested not overusing the term 'annexation', even when the future of Jerusalem was being discussed. He came up with a better Hebrew word, one that he hoped would translate adequately: *hachlala*, meaning 'incorporation'. He wondered aloud if perhaps with regard to Gaza the government might use the word 'annexation', speculating that since Gaza contained such a large Palestinian population nobody would object.

Government minutes are dry documents at the best of times and very rarely can one extract from them the tone in which declarations were made, or fully sense the prevailing atmosphere in the room. But in this case one cannot miss the air of superiority that pervaded these discussions about Israel's relationship with the rest of the world. The men seated around the oval and rectangular tables felt powerful: they feared no resistance from the Palestinians, cared little about the Arab world and were confident they could manipulate the rest of the world, and in particular the USA.

However, towards the end of June 1967, other countries could occasionally be heard voicing more explicit criticism and demanded answers that could potentially embarrass the government. As a result, the officials of the Israeli Foreign Ministry requested that the army consult them on major decisions on the ground. Assurance was given, but one doubts whether it was ever kept. There was thus constant tension between what Dayan called 'our internal decisions' and the hectic diplomatic activity in the UN where a formula for peace was being sought. The prime movers behind the scenes at the UN, apart from the USA and the USSR, were Britain and France. There were worrying signs in the last days of June that Britain would adopt a tough position that echoed the Soviet call to end immediately the Israeli 'policies of annexation and expansion'. But in the United Kingdom there was already a growing pro-Zionist lobby and pressure was duly exerted on the British Prime Minister, Harold Wilson, who forced the Foreign Office to reappraise its initial stance.

At times, the Israeli press was harder to satisfy than some Western governments. Generally, the press was very loyal, but now and then it put a more humane perspective on Israeli actions and had to be hauled back into line. Ministers complained that the Israeli press unnecessarily showed pictures of the new refugees from the June war, or the first demolition of houses that were targeted either in response to sniper fire or as part of the early plan to create a new state of affairs in several West Bank towns. Eshkol warned, 'This could damage our image in the world.'

Other culprits suspected of damaging the image of Israel were discussed in the meeting, among them foreign diplomats in Israel and in neighbouring Arab countries. The Italian ambassador in Amman was singled out in particular. He reported constantly to his foreign ministry that the Israelis were expelling people or that others were forced out because they had no food or work in the West Bank, and that an alarming new refugee problem was developing. He also accused the Israeli army of widespread looting, something that quite a few soldiers recalled later on in interviews and oral histories. The ambassador in Amman also initiated a European call for an international committee to investigate the situation in the occupied areas, a move Israel rejected out of hand.

Even the Americans expressed their misgivings about the Israeli policy of expulsion. We do not know how exactly they phrased this concern as the censor has erased much government discussion on the subject. However, we do have the comments of Yaacov Shimshon Shapira, the Minister of Justice, on the American message, and they seem to have been articulated in tones of regret: 'We could have waited two or three weeks with the expulsions, especially in Eastern Jerusalem.' So the language must have been quite harsh. But the whole affair alerted ministers to the possibility that the policies on the ground could also be monitored and not simply their declarations and statements.

It was Moshe Dayan who laid the foundations for future attitudes towards foreign journalists at times when Israeli forces were carrying out operations that he did not wish the world to know about. In those early days he did not mince his words: 'A main concern is not to allow any journalists into the West Bank; it should be a closed military area.' Dayan wished to prolong this state of affairs for as long as possible, but even he understood that it could 'only' be done for certain fixed periods ('fixed periods' that could be quite long, as we learned during the Israeli Operation Cast Lead in the Gaza Strip in 2008–2009, when it lasted more than two years). The policy was shaped at that meeting with the help of the Director General of the Foreign Ministry, who suggested issuing licences instead of a sweeping prohibition. 'Oh,' said Dayan, 'then you will get untold horror stories.'

So the press was domiciled, the world indifferent and the Americans willingly misled. Israeli ministers had little concern for either US condemnation or support for Israeli actions. Every now and then condemnation of a sort would be heard, but it did not alter the Israelis' determination to continue their efforts to create the facts of a new reality on the ground. One crucial issue was the arms embargo that had been imposed by the Truman administration back in 1948 and was still in place in the early days of the Johnson administration – but not for much longer. Years of building a pro-Israel lobby in America began at last to bear fruit. The sinking of an Israeli warship, *Eilat*, was the trigger the lobby needed to realign US policy. At the beginning of October 1967 that lobby began pressuring the new Special Assistant for National Security, Walt Rostow, who proved more susceptible to these pressures and the embargo was lifted. About a year later, the first shipment of the most up-to-date aircraft arrived in Israel. Israel was now America's favourite son and could continue to do whatever it wanted in Palestine.[39]

The world, then and today, was divided into two groups of observers and opted for two types of engagement. The political elite in the West and in most of the rest of the world accepted the two models Israel offered between autonomy and imprisonment as a necessary evil in order to preserve Israel's national security – at least until the conclusion of a final peace solution that would allow some sort of Palestinian independence in some parts of the West Bank and Gaza Strip. In principle this legitimized the Israeli structure of control for as long as the Israelis deemed it necessary. The more conscientious segments of global civil society saw the Israeli policy very differently – as a protracted and long-term programme of colonization. At first only a minority subscribed to this view, but in this century an increasing number of people have also come to adopt it. Some were affected by a particular Israeli policy; most of them formulated their views after visiting the places concerned.

While the political and military elite of Israel framed clear guide-lines for controlling the fate of the areas the IDF occupied in 1967 within a matter of days, with very little internal dissent, outside the halls of government the public debated that future in a livelier and less consensual manner. But this had very little impact then, and later, on the policy actually implemented.

THE CHARADE OF A PUBLIC DEBATE

The debate about the future of the territories that raged in the public arena commenced, in many ways, the moment the troops moved into the Palestinian territories. The first letter by a future and famous settler, Eliakim Haetzni, was published on 7 June, warning against the withdrawal of Israeli forces and arguing for the resettlement of the Palestinian refugees in neighbouring Arab states.[40] Those who followed his lead probably intentionally published their articles and op-eds alongside the obituaries of soldiers killed in the war. The question of withdrawal or annexation of the Occupied Territories would be the signifier that would map the Israeli political scene in a new way. On the right were all those who called for annexation of the territories; on the left were those calling for a withdrawal in return for peace. As one scholar put it, it was a discussion between the 'redeem-ers', who believed the ancient homeland was finally under full Jewish control, and the 'custodians', who believed the territories could be traded for a bilateral peace with Jordan or the Palestinians. This latter viewpoint was first promulgated by the Israeli Communist party; it demanded an unconditional withdrawal from the very first day of the occupation. Non-Communist members formed their own lobby led by a new outfit named the Israeli-Palestinian Federation, which included luminaries such as Amos Elon, Uri Avnery, Abie Nathan, Dan Ben-Amos and Uri Zohar (the last two were the best-known bohemians in the 'state of Tel Aviv'). Their means were limited, which is why they aired a few, infrequent advertisements in favour of an immediate withdrawal. At the very margins of Israeli society, anti-Zionist groups such as Matzpen were hoping, in vain, for an even more profound discussion on the essence of Zionism and the outcome of the 1948 war.[41]

The politicians, however, while subscribing to this new public discourse and positioning themselves accordingly, in practice differed very little among themselves about the strategy hitherto defined in this book, only disagreeing about which tactics to employ.

Where politics and the street met in agreement was on the issue of Jerusalem. The press reported public opinion as wishing to exclude Jerusalem from any future negotiations, as the politicians vowed to do. This explains the press's jubilant reaction to the news about the renaming and re-signposting of the streets and alleys of the Old City of Jerusalem and the Hebraization of most of them.[42]

The collective memory of the Zionist left, which is also reflected in academic discourse on the period, is of a political system and a public mood that were basically in favour of withdrawal; and, had it not been for a cynical usurpation of the political process by the settlers' movement later on, Israel would have exchanged the territories for peace.[43] This would be the line of argument of the left until this political force disappeared as a significant player on the local stage in 2000. The right wing, on the other hand, pointed to Arab intransigence as the main reason for the failure of this peaceful initiative. However, it is important to realize that even if the public mood was pro-withdrawal, for which I have found no convincing evidence, it had no impact whatsoever on government discussions at the time. Ministers debated the future of the territories in the belief that the public was happy and wanted them to consolidate the military achievements for Israel's long-term advantage. There was no pressure of any kind to withdraw or to enter into significant peace negotiations with the Arab states, let alone with the Palestinians.

The international community, and more importantly the American administration under President Johnson, and later under Richard Nixon, behaved as if such a debate was ongoing, but never provided, internally or externally, any explanation as to why this debate had not produced a genuine Israeli peace effort. The idea of a complete Israeli withdrawal only appeared in American documentation, whether these were official government initiatives such as the two Rogers schemes, or support for the UN initiative (the Gunnar Jarring Mission). It was sometimes mentioned when individuals in the USA were trying their luck with peace, as in the case of Senator Fulbright's peace initiative in the first three years after the war (as mentioned, his standing and career were already significantly undermined when he was targeted by AIPAC). He advocated a total Israeli withdrawal. To all these initiatives the Israeli responses were negative and the American reaction indifferent.[44]

So there were no domestic expectations of any dramatic decisions in the first two months after the occupation, but there was international activity, especially in the UN, that demanded government reaction. The Israeli politicians navigated these moves adroitly by giving the impression that they were seriously discussing the options for peace and withdrawal, while at the same time taking a series of decisions that demarcated clearly the West Bank and the Gaza Strip as future mega-prisons controlled by Israel.

One section within Israeli society, however, was stirred into action and was profoundly affected by the new reality created by Israel. This was the Palestinian community inside Israel. Their initial response was a wish to be reunited – with family members and parts of their homeland from which they had been separated for nineteen years. At first the Israeli Security Service, and especially the internal security agency, the Shabak, tried to disrupt this unification. The first Palestinians from Israel who went to the West Bank and the Gaza Strip were arrested. Later, by the beginning of the following month, they would be released and allowed to enter. But as in all other aspects of life, the Palestinian minority in Israel had no impact whatsoever on Israeli policies in general and towards the Occupied Territories in particular.[45]

Notwithstanding, the public debate reflected a reasonable optional policy to the one the government pursued at that time and later. And maybe this is the reason why some of the bureaucrats conducted a dialogue that might have opened the way for a different history. They met, with the knowledge if not the blessing of Moshe Dayan, with a group of Palestinians who had been trying to represent the issue of Palestinian refugees in the UN, an agenda they had been pursuing since the spring of 1949 when they had tried in vain to offer a new peace plan for Palestine. They formed a committee chaired by the Palestinian lawyer Aziz Shehadeh and a group of public figures who suggested that the Israelis establish a Palestinian government and an autonomous entity under Israeli rule that would eventually negotiate a final settlement with Israel. They were hopeful that this would be based on Resolution 181, the partition resolution from November 1947, and Resolution 194 from December 1948, which called for the return of the refugees.[46]

While some officials did take this suggestion seriously, the government never gave it any credence and thus we can only speculate what might have happened if such a proposition had carried more political weight. Quite a few of the Palestinians who knew about it regarded it as collaboration with the occupation, and most Israeli policymakers believed that whatever negotiations were needed to finalize the unilateral Israeli actions on the ground, the partner, in those days, was the Hashemite Kingdom of Jordan and not some Palestinian body.

The PLO, incidentally, was totally opposed to this initiative, something that also contributed to its failure. What is interesting is that it laid the ground for a West Bank minority stance that might be developed into a more mainstream option in the future. The gist of this position was best articulated by the current president of Al-Quds University and public figure Sari Nusseibeh.[47] On numerous occasions in the last fifty years he has suggested that if Israel does not allow Palestinian independence to develop on the ground, the Palestinians themselves should ask to be fully annexed into the Jewish State and demand full civil rights. But, as noted, Palestinians in the Occupied Territories had so far made no such impact on their fate; the best they could do was resist, or at least, as was suggested by Aziz

Shehadeh's son, Raja, remain resolute and show *sumud* ('steadfast-ness') – staying put on a land Israel coveted and envisaged without any Palestinians on it.[48]

As a general rule, the lives of people in the Occupied Territories would not greatly concern the Israeli Jewish population at large until the first Intifada in 1987 brought it to their attention. In June 1967 the consensual government of Israel could rely on the widest possible support for any decision it took. The euphoric mood lasted for the entire month, but in one way or another it actually lasted until October 1973 when the army was almost defeated by the Syrian and Egyptian forces. The victory of 1967 was seen by many Israeli Jews in much the same way as *Haaretz* described it at the end of the short war: 'An event as monumental as the creation of the State of Israel in 1948.' The paper itself played its part in this euphoric legitimization of the occupation of another people and their lands. In a bid for new subscriptions, the newspaper reminded its readers that it had pressed the government to go to war as early as the middle of May, and even supported the occupation of the Golan Heights.[49]

By the end of June an overall policy towards the new reality was agreed upon, a debate which sealed the fate of the territories, the status of their inhabitants, the question of their expulsion and the future of Jerusalem. What the government did not discuss, or at least it does not appear in the records, was the actual setting up of the mechanism to control the lives of the people in the West Bank and the Gaza Strip. It was left to the army to manage these people, who at a stroke became stateless and without any recognized international legal standing that could protect their basic civil and human rights. In many ways, this is still the case today. And thus on 16 June, the Chief of the Central Command, General Uzi Narkiss, took over the control of the West Bank and appointed as 'Military Governor of East Jerusalem, Judea and Samaria' the Irish-born future Israeli President, Chaim Herzog, who had served as the main spokesperson for the thirteenth government on the wireless, effectively calming down or intensifying the panic, as the government wished, on the eve of the war. Governors General were appointed all over the West Bank and the Gaza Strip, and the bureaucracy of the occupation began its daily routine of maintaining the mega-prison of Palestine.

It was in the Greater Jerusalem area that all these attitudes and practices were put into effect in the first month of occupation and, following their success, expanded to other parts of the West Bank and the Gaza Strip.

Chapter Three

The Greater Jerusalem as a Pilot Project

The delineation of a Palestinian space, enclosed within several colonized Jewish areas, was the result of a concerted effort that gave the mega-prison its final shape. When examining it closely as we do here, colonization can become very tedious. So let me warn the reader: this chapter contains a long list of the names of colonies, numbers of dunams[1] confiscated and urban spaces created. Let me also urge the reader to study it closely. It describes the meticulous planning and the swift implementation of this plan within the first year after the end of the 1967 war. Long before Israel tried to justify the colonization of the West Bank and the Gaza Strip as a necessary security response to terrorist activities or a unilateral act in the face of a long-standing diplomatic deadlock, the West Bank in particular was fated to be bisected, settled and Judaized in such a way that from the outset any notion of turning it into an independent state was doomed.

The politicians made the decisions, and they were, as we have already seen and will see again here, determined to establish the facts on the ground that would keep both the West Bank and the Gaza Strip as part of a new and larger Israel. But it was the bureaucrats who were busy charting the new geographical and demographic maps of the Occupied Territories. They were supervised by a group of experts, including some of Israel's leading academics of the day, men of great international repute such as the economist Dan Patenkin, the sociologist Shumel Noah Eisenstadt and the demographer Roberto Bachi among others.[2] So in 1967, politicians, academics, generals and civil servants set about turning the West Bank and the Gaza Strip into a mega-prison – the biggest ever seen on earth.

There were two principal enterprises, one external and the other internal. The external one was the slicing up of the West Bank and the Gaza Strip by driving colonized wedges into them. The internal one was a constant, never-ending issuing of decrees, the purpose of which was both to expropriate Palestinian land for future colonization and to limit the natural and organic growth of the Palestinian communities by preventing new building and expansion. A very similar method was used before 1967 and after in relation to the Palestinian minority inside Israel.

The basic idea was clear: some of the Occupied Territories were to remain 'Palestinian'; the rest had to be controlled directly. Apart from Jerusalem, where such control meant *de jure* annexation, in all other areas it was done through Judaization, primarily in the form of settling Jews, as soldiers or civilians, on Palestinian land.

JERUSALEM FIRST

In the typical Israeli way, the dramatic transformation of the urban and rural landscape of Jerusalem and its environs was depicted as urban planning. However, what began in 1967 and continues to this day is an ethnic cleansing operation based on land expropriation. Back in 1967 and 1968, this so-called urban planning was a military operation par excellence. It was therefore entrusted to the Chief of the Central Command, General Rehavam Ze'evi (who replaced Uzi Narkiss in the summer of 1968). This veteran of 1948 was nicknamed Gandhi, not for his peaceful policies – in every respect his philosophy was the exact opposite of the Mahatma's – but due to his dark complexion. He would later form the first political party in Israel that openly advocated the transfer of the Palestinian population to Jordan. He was assassinated during the second Intifada by the Popular Front for the Liberation of Palestine (PFLP),[3] in the Hyatt Hotel in Jerusalem, built on land he had helped to expropriate in 1967.

The boundaries Ze'evi helped to establish as a municipal space for Greater Jerusalem are the current boundaries of the city. As the Israeli journalist Leslie Susser pointed out, the line Ze'evi drew 'took in not only the five square kilometres of Arab East Jerusalem – but also 65 square kilometres of surrounding open countryside and villages, most of which had never had any municipal links to Jerusalem. Overnight they became part of Israel's eternal and indivisible capital.'[4]

In order to establish settlements in the occupied areas, Israel used the same legal practices it had employed in Israel itself from 1948 to 1967. It was executed in a very direct and obvious way in East Jerusalem, since this area was officially annexed to Israel and thus Israeli laws were applicable there from 1967 onwards. In addition, in 1970, the Israeli government re-activated a Mandatory law from 1943 that had already been used to expropriate land inside Israel, and now applied it to the area of occupied Jerusalem annexed in 1967. Thus, 17,000 dunams were confiscated under the Ordinance of the Law (acquisition of land for public use) – all previously held in private ownership by Palestinians. On this land, the government developed the *shechunot* ('neighbour-hoods'), a euphemism used to describe the new Jewish colonies built in East Jerusalem so as to single them out as part of the new post-1967 Israel. It was through land robbery by the state, endorsed by all the Zionist parties, that these urban sprawls were created. A very thorough and exhaustive study by the Palestinian researcher Khalil Tafakji enables us to follow this process very carefully, facilitated by the helpful way he lists the names and locations of the new settlements. This act of recording is extremely important, as only a handful of Israeli Jews within the consensus, including the Zionist peace camp, would recognize these neighbourhoods as settlements.

The massive land expropriation in Jerusalem began in earnest towards the end of 1968. Most of the residents were not compensated for this expropriation, while those who were found the compensation ridiculously low. The 17,000 dunams that were commandeered included buildings such as schools and hospitals. In December 1967, when the requisitions commenced, the Prime Minister's Office was instructed to publish positive information, such as the presence of Palestinian patients in Jewish hospitals, in order to distract attention and stifle criticism.[5] However, as the expropriation gathered pace, it became clear that the world was already reconciled to the annexation of East Jerusalem to Israel.

The principal means used to expand the East Jerusalem wedge were systematic land robbery, colonization, the designation of certain areas as green spaces, the ecological lungs of the new metropolis – namely no-go areas for Palestinians – house demolitions, and a repeated refusal to allow extensions to existing buildings for Palestinians. Another means of extending this wedge was a disinclination to invest in any infrastructure for future Palestinian housing and habitats, although the Palestinian citizens paid the same taxes as the Jewish settlers. Tafakji's research tells us that only 5 per cent of the taxes were invested in the eastern part of the city in the second half of the twentieth century. This wedge now has a name, 'The Greater Jerusalem Municipal Area', an amoeba that grows by the day and swallows whole areas, de-Arabizes them and colonizes them. Palestinians were forced exponentially out of the newly expanded amoeba as it swelled over years, and eventually by the beginning of this century it had cut the West Bank in two.[6]

Within a decade of occupation, the composition of the Jerusalem wedge comprised up to fifteen huge newly colonized areas. The most significant was the Jewish quarter in the Old City, built after the occupation and which grew to become one-fifth of the Old City (116 out of 668 dunams). On the day of the occupation, 6000 Palestinians who lived in three out of the four ancient quarters – the Mughrabi quarter that was totally demolished, al-Siryan and al-Sharf – were summarily expelled from the city to Jordan. At one time there had been five mosques, four schools, a historic market and a commercial avenue dating back to the Mamluk period in those quarters. Judaization swept it all away.

The enormity of the wedge and its impact on Palestinian life became apparent when in 1993 the municipal borders of Greater Jerusalem were officially drafted. Later on, when the Oslo peace process petered out in the 1990s, successive Israel governments claimed that any new settlements built in the West Bank in general and in Jerusalem in particular were in retaliation for 'Palestinian terrorism' (mainly suicide bomb attacks). In reality, this settlement policy had nothing to do with 'retaliation' and began long before any suicide bombing commenced and continued throughout the years of occupation – it was simply presented this way, mainly for domestic consumption. Again there was nothing new in this line of argument: it was used to justify the early stages of the 1948 ethnic cleansing, then not to colonize Palestine but to uproot the people.

So while the ink was still drying on the Oslo Accord, Greater Jerusalem was reinvented as an area consisting of 600 square kilometres, which included 15 per cent of the West Bank (just one block of it, Maleh Edumain, is nearly 1 per cent of the West Bank).[7] Satellite settlements in areas adjacent to this new Greater Jerusalem were built with the future intention of serving as land bridges between Greater Jerusalem and the rest of the Israeli colonies in the West Bank.

This expansion soon covered the ancient hills of North and East Jerusalem with a new urban sprawl of modern housing dressed up here and there with orientalist façades that resembled the very houses demolished to build these new 'neighbourhoods'. As Eyal Weizman elucidated so clearly in his book *Hollow Land*, the 1968 master plan for Jerusalem was committed to both a colonial and oriental heritage dating back to the British urban planning of 1917 – with two huge differences. The British redesign and beautification of the city was not done through the demolition of old houses and the eviction of the indigenous population, and did not involve covering Greater Jerusalem with the concrete monstrosities that characterize the new Jewish 'neighbourhoods'.[8] By 2005, 200,000 Jewish settlers lived in this area. Many more are expected to join them in the present century.[9]

I will now describe the way the greater Jerusalem wedge developed. In essence it was made of fifteen colonies, which the Israelis immediately called neighbourhoods. The first colony, already discussed, is called the French Hill. The second one is Neve Yaakov, established gradually between 1968 and 1980, and the third wedge colony is Ramot, which necessitated the expropriation of more than 4000 dunams of private Palestinian land, and is now home to about 40,000 settlers.

A fourth colony is the ever-expanding settlement of Gilo, which was established in 1971 on confiscated land of around 2700 dunams, making it now the biggest colony in South-east Jerusalem. This discordant eyesore is a familiar landmark for anyone making their way from Jerusalem to Bethlehem, on the western side of the road. It is a huge complex towering over Beit Jala, Bethlehem and Jerusalem.

A fifth is East Talpiot, built in 1973 over 2240 Palestinian dunams, hosting about 15,000 settlers today. Together with Gilo it comprises a Jewish colonizing belt in the south-east of the city. Part of the land was designated no man's land prior to 1967, and it was the UN that gave up an additional 2000 dunams to allow the expansion of this colony, which, like all the others mentioned here, is referred to by all Israeli Jews as a neighbourhood.

The sixth is Malot Daphna, built in 1973 on 7000 dunams of land owned by Jerusalemite families, hosting, in mainly impoverished conditions, North African Jewish settlers. It was built in the heart of the Palestinian East Jerusalem neighbourhoods in order to cut their territorial contiguity. The Police and Border Police Headquarters moved there to emphasize the Jewish presence.

The next is the Hebrew University, built in 1924 on land bought from the village of Issawiya. More land from that village was then expropriated by the university in 1967 for a new campus. Now a mammoth labyrinth, it took me hours to find my way from my class to my office when I taught there for a short while. The Hebrew University is now part of the complex of what is called the French Hill and Mount Scopus neighbourhoods, colonies established in 1967 along with an eastern extension added later comprising Givat Hamivtar and Ramat Eshkol both discussed below. The French Hill, the western slope of Mount Scopus, was one of the first colonies built on land belonging to the people of Shua'fat. It covers 800 dunams, hosting today 12,000 settlers in 5000 units. The university stretches over 740 dunams, built as a modern-day fortress towering above North Jerusalem with its Palestinian villages.

The eighth colony is Ramat Shlomo, first established as a green zone on 1000 dunams expropriated in 1970. The trees planted by the Jewish National Fund (JNF) in 1970 were razed in 1990 to make way for a settlement of more than 2000 houses for Orthodox Jews. This colony has now expanded so much that it enjoys territorial continuity with Neve Yaakov and two new colonies that complete the colonizing belt: Pisgat Ze'ev and Pisgat Omer. These two new colonies were built on land belonging to the villages of Beit Hanina, Shua'fat, Hizmah and Annata. Comprising altogether 3800 dunams of Palestinian land and ultimately hosting about 100,000 settlers, it completes the north-eastern strangulation of Greater Jerusalem.

Then there are Ramat Eshkol and Givat Hamivtar, the first two colonies established to connect the western with the eastern parts of the city. Built on land expropriated from private Palestinian owners in 1968, it stretches over 3300 dunams and hosts 60,000 settlers. They were the first bricks in the 'neighbourhood wall' surrounding the Palestinian neighbourhoods and villages in eastern and southern Jerusalem. There are gaps in this ring of Jewish colonies (the outer ring excluding Palestinian areas, and inner rings separating Palestinian areas from each other) but they are quickly being filled with new Jewish settlements in the twenty-first century.

You can add to this list the Atarot industrial zone on 1200 dunams of land requisitioned in 1970 near the old airport built by the British during the Mandatory period, and mention should also be made of Givat Hamatos, built on land expropriated from the villages of Beit Safafa and Beit Jala of about 170 dunams. Givat Hamatos was only built in 1991 (a more sensitive year, which necessitated the charade of first erecting a temporary caravan that later was gradually replaced by about 5000 building units). Together with the colony of Gilo, it is part of the south-eastern colonizing belt meant to prevent Palestinian territorial integrity and continuity. So the Palestinian neighbourhoods that were incorporated into Greater Jerusalem after 1967 were later besieged by Jewish colonies hemming them in on all sides.

The last of the fifteen colonies – and I apologize to the reader for this checklist but its importance cannot be overstated – were clusters and pockets of colonization that appeared later in the day. They mushroomed sporadically in the Old City and to the south and north of the city of Jerusalem. On the southern end, Har Homa (Jabal Abu Ghanaim) was the most famous of them because of the attempt of one man, Faisal al-Husseini,[10] to stop the stealing. In 1990 Israel bulldozed almost 2000 dunams of land belonging to the villages of Sur Baher, Um Tuba and Beit Sahour in the same area, to the south and south-east of the city. Around 6500 units were built there, a project completed in 2011, and together they completed an urban sprawl that completely cut off these Palestinian villages from Bethlehem and Hebron.[11]

Finally, in addition to the expropriation of land and the erection of substantial new neighbourhoods in the West Bank, particularly in the area around Jerusalem, we should mention the crime against aesthetics that took place over the years in one of the city's most beautiful neighbourhoods, Mamilla, opposite the Jaffa Gate (Bab al-Khalil). It was a buffer zone between the Israeli army and the Jordanian Arab Legion between 1948 and 1967 but survived the skirmishes, exchanges of fire and the 1967 war relatively unscathed, but not the colonizing zeal of the occupiers. If you are, like me, a connoisseur of the city's photographic history, you have seen countless photographs of this neighbourhood, which was home to some of the finest hotels in the city in the early twentieth century. These gems were replaced by a new eyesore – an indecipherable complex of garden houses and American-style condominiums. Work on the complex commenced in 1970 on 130 confiscated dunams.

To the aesthetic crimes against the city of Jerusalem can be added those of culture and religion. One of the most important parts of the

Mamilla area was its Muslim cemetery dating back to the seventh century. The graves were removed at night so that no one could witness this, and in their place the Simon Wiesenthal Foundation built a Museum of Tolerance! To ensure that Muslims could not reach this sacred site, it was surrounded by an electric fence.[12] Desecrating Muslim graveyards for new constructions was nothing new, however: the old cemetery in Haifa, al-Istiqlal, was desecrated in a similar way when a highway was driven through it, scattering the gravestones to either side.

The municipal master plan set for completion in 2020 includes filling the gaps in the colonizing outer ring by the takeover of the village of Wallaja's land of 2000 dunams and the building of a new colony, Givat Yael, west of Gilo, comprising 13,000 houses for 55,000 settlers, which will create a huge wedge from Gush Etzion to Jerusalem. With regard to this it is important to stress that the building of 'neighbourhoods' such as Gilo is considered a war crime under international law. The Rome Statute of the International Criminal Court of 1998 defines 'the transfer directly or indirectly of the Occupying Power of parts of its own population into the territory it occupies' as an indictable war crime.[13]

Now might be a good moment to look at the Israeli violations of international law that were already evident in the first year of occupation but were ignored by the international community.

Acquiring land by force after hostilities have ended is illegal under international law. Military action and occupations are legal only if they are for self-defence, or for the direct benefit of the indigenous population. From the very beginning it was clear that Palestinian land was acquired for the purpose of *de facto* annexation. In this Israel violated the second article of the UN 1945 Charter. The first settlement built on the Occupied Territories was a violation of the Fourth Geneva Convention, Article 49(6) (1949). It is illegal to colonize occupied land or transfer a non-indigenous population to that land.

All these colonies are regarded, even by most liberal Zionists – many of whom live in these colonies – as Israeli Jewish urban neighbourhoods that are completely excluded from any future negotiations. In terms of the law, the international community does not distinguish between 'legal' and 'illegal' settlements, but it seems that quite a few Western governments, and most certainly the various American administrations, accepted such a division and included in the former category these new 'neighbourhoods'.

They had become part of Israel and had been excluded from the West Bank during the 1950s in a process similar to when Israel annexed areas allocated to the Palestinians in the 1947 UN General Assembly partition resolution – without seeking international approval. The world was simply presented with a fait accompli.

So these 'neighbourhoods' became part of 'Small Israel', which for many liberals in Israel and in the West represented the moral and ethical state, prior to the occupation of the West Bank and Gaza Strip. Such areas, even in the eyes of the Israeli peace camp, were non-negotiable, as would transpire with the Oslo Accord when their fate was discussed for the first time. So while, in the eyes of more enlightened observers, 78 per cent of Palestine was non-negotiable prior to 1967, after the occupation this exclusion spread over 85 per cent of the land. By this I mean that while the West Bank and the Gaza Strip were 78 per cent of Palestine, the parts of the West Bank that all the Israeli governments declared as non-negotiable had left only 10 per cent of Palestine as a possible territory for Palestinian rule; this10 per cent was spread all over the West Bank, divided by settlement blocs and military bases.

In time, with the full support of the West, the efforts of the Israeli peace camp to draw a line between the 'immoral Israel' of the settlers and the 'moral' one of the pre-1967 state will dwindle, and with it any hope of solving the conflict by a two-state solution.

While the government delineated the boundaries of the 'new Jerusalem', one politician in particular took it upon himself to draw more clearly the boundaries between a future Jewish State and the Palestinian West Bank and Gaza Strip. This man was Yigal Alon.

Chapter Four

The Alon Vision

Beyond Greater Jerusalem and the need to delineate the new acquisitions in a way that would satisfy Israel's territorial appetite and allay demographic fears, there was a need for a more structured and, in a way, visionary approach. Such an approach was offered by two figures familiar in the pantheon of Israeli heroes: Yigal Alon and Moshe Dayan. In the crucial early, formative stages it was primarily Alon who orchestrated the policy. Dayan would chip in whenever he was interested in more long-term planning, but he was really a man of ad hoc, short-lived projects. Long-term planning was not really his forte.

Alon rose to power early. At the age of thirty, he already commanded the Palmach, the Zionist elite units, and as such was responsible for the cleansing of Palestinian villages and towns in various parts of the country in 1948. His loyal Zionist biographer Anita Shapira has described him as the 'cleanser of the North' in 1948, and indeed he was. He was the epitome of the new – almost Aryan – Jew that Zionism craved as the antithesis of the 'exilic' Jew. Handsome, charismatic and brave, he shone as a future leader of the Zionist movement, but he did not live up to that promise. More cynical and sophisticated politicians marginalized him over the years and he never played the leading role that he and his admirers wanted him to play.[1]

After the 1948 war he became a member of the Knesset, later attempting but soon abandoning D. Phil studies at St Antony's

College, Oxford, under the supervision of the illustrious Elizabeth Monroe (a chair – a real, physical one – in the JCR still commemorates his time there). When he returned to Israel in the early 1960s he joined the government, for most of his time there serving as Minister of Labour. The occupation of the West Bank and Gaza Strip provided an opportunity for him to regain past glories that had dimmed in the post-1948 years when he was out of the military establishment.

He was not particularly interested in the Ministry of Labour and immediately after the 1967 war focused all his attention on the colonization efforts in the Occupied Territories, which became his main interest in life.

His efforts in this area are usually characterized by scholars as an attempt to find a solution to the conflict. Initially he was presented as the father of the 'Jordanian option', namely trying to reach a territorial compromise on the West Bank and the Gaza Strip between Israel and Jordan, which he later revised by replacing Jordanian sovereignty with Palestinian autonomy.

In July 1967 Alon had presented to the government his famous Alon plan, 'The Future of the Territories and of the Refugees'. It was never officially adopted but became more a blueprint for where to colonize and less a template for a peace agreement with Jordan. Apart from blocs of Jewish settlements, the rest of the West Bank would be autonomous or under a Jordanian demilitarized sovereignty.

The first principle of the plan was that the River Jordan would form the eastern border of Israel. Jordan would possess a sliver of land near Jericho that would give it a land bridge to the mountainous areas of the West Bank. Alon singled out the areas around Hebron, Jerusalem and the Jordan Valley for future Jewish colonization.

To the credit of the Jordanian government, it was among the first to recognize that this was intended to ease Israel's preoccupation with demography and had nothing to do with preventing another conflict, which did indeed come a few years later. The American embassy in Amman succinctly summarized the Jordanian take on the Alon plan:

The Israelis seem unable to grasp that the Alon plan and its varia-
tions are not only unacceptable to Jordan but that it also repre-
sents the kind of arrangement that would perpetuate hostility.
Similar arrangements elsewhere during the twentieth century
have demonstrated they are more likely to breed subsequent trouble and irredentism than to guarantee security.[2]

This is to my mind a distorted historiographical picture of the man
and his deeds in 1967 and onwards. He was not seeking a compromise but expansion. Alon was the first to think of how best to use
Jewish colonization in a way that would secure the space without
incorporating the people – which became the eternal Israeli problem
and preoccupation since the inception of the state in general and with
regards to the West Bank since 1967 in particular. He imagined and
put in place a chain of Jewish colonies that would separate Palestinians
from Palestinians and essentially annex parts of the West Bank to
Israel. The concept of wedges would be perfected and in a way
completed by Ariel Sharon both as Minister of Housing and National
Infrastructure in the 1980s and as Prime Minister in the twenty-first
century.

Alon's initial colonization plans were 'modest' compared to those
that his successor Ariel Sharon would drive into the heart of Palestine.
As early as July 1967 Alon had devised a plan for the colonization of
the Jordan Valley and of the slopes of the eastern mountains of the
West Bank, effectively slicing out part of the mountains of Jerusalem,
Bethlehem and Hebron that were adjacent to the pre-1967 border.
From very early on it was clear that creating the colonized spaces in
the West Bank or Gaza Strip would cause a de-Arabization of these
particular areas.

For a very short while, in the first years after the occupation of the
West Bank and the Gaza Strip, Yigal Alon dominated the Israeli
government's strategic thinking and left his mark on the cartography
of the occupation. Although his plan was not adopted as a blueprint,
it did suggest an informal protocol for how to rule both the West

Bank and the Gaza Strip. The modus operandi he devised would inform Israeli policy up to the present day. In essence it was a suggestion to rule densely populated Palestinian areas indirectly while striving to annex in one way or another all the rest.

His broader perspective helped the government throughout the remaining months of 1967 to better contextualize its own practical and brutal annexation of Greater Jerusalem. The already Judaized part of the city and its environs were now part of the space that would be annexed to Israel, regardless of who might be its partner for peace or when the final lines of its borders would be drawn. Other areas included Khalil (Hebron), Bethlehem, the Jordan Valley and various smaller enclaves in the small West Bank, leaving the rest for either a future Palestinian entity to be supervised by Israel, or annexed as demilitarized zones to Jordan. The latter was Alon's first preference, but he was also open to the former option and would come to prefer it as the years passed. Alon's afterthoughts were sometimes more telling than his more structured presentation. Exploring further the issue of a possible Palestinian mini-state as a reward for Palestinian good behaviour, he highlighted the negative demographic impact of the refugees and suggested resettling them all in the Sinai.[3]

These thoughts were aired for the first time in the meetings in the middle of June 1967, and were articulated even more explicitly during July. He steered the government towards considering a way of having the territories, without annexing the people or expelling them. It was clear to him that the key word was control. In hindsight, the language he used at the time did not include the prison terminology I am employing in this book, but it was not far from it as he constantly referred to the policy of 'carrots and sticks'. The 'carrot', the open-air prison, was in Alon's example the opening of a post office in Hebron, and the 'stick', the maximum security prison, was the collective punitive action against Nablus in July 1967 in response to an attack on a military convoy: mass arrests, vicious house-to-house searches, curfews, disconnection of the telephone system, which are all war crimes. On the one hand, the provision of normal services, a given duty of the occupier under international law, became a reward for good behaviour; on the other hand, resistance – even non-violent forms – was met with collective punishment of which, as Tom Segev rightly commented, humiliation already played the most crucial part in the Israeli repertoire in 1967.[4]

Alon focused entirely on the West Bank, and like all the other ministers hesitated to express clear-cut opinions about the Gaza Strip. But a certain pattern of thinking developed, and although it took time to mature it can be seen that Alon's vision also applied to the Gaza Strip. Even though the Strip is a very small piece of land, as long as it remained within Israel the same policy of dividing it between 'ours' and 'theirs' was executed here as well.

Alon's vision was translated into two major strategies that would shape life in the Occupied Territories for years to come: a physical strategy that demarcated clearly which parts would be Judaized and colonized; and an administrative reality that determined the rewards and punishments for either accepting or rejecting Israeli rule.

Alon was assisted by a group of bureaucrats who were veteran colonizers. Given both the disregard they all had for the basic imperatives of international law and their religious adherence to the consensual Zionist impulse to integrate the occupied space – but not its people – these colonizers found it easy to associate their 1967 endeavours with earlier Zionist colonization efforts going back to 1882. The chief bureaucrat was the Prime Minister himself, Levy Eshkol. In previous stages of his political career he had been a junior Zionist activist during the Mandatory period, when he was immersed in colonization projects. He later rose to more prominent ranks in the state through party politics and hard work as an efficient technocrat.[5]

From the 1930s to 1967, he played a crucial role in the colonization of historical Palestine. On the official website of the Israeli government, he is presented as someone 'who determined the general framework for the largest settlement operation in history'.[6] This 'largest operation' was planting Jewish colonies in the heart of the Palestinian countryside; these spots were originally far apart from each other, but in 1948 they would be integrated into one single Jewish space by cleansing all the territory between them of its native Palestinian population.

As Prime Minister in June 1967 he emerged as the leading figure in the colonization effort at the heart of the bureaucracy the government established to run the areas that Israel occupied in the war. This new effort was coordinated and supervised by the settlement department of the Jewish Agency. Previously this had been the domain of Yosef Weitz, who was very active in the 1948 ethnic cleansing of Palestine. Now it was handed to his son, Raanan Weitz, a man as active as his father in realizing the dream of turning Palestinian areas into purely Jewish ones. His father was still there in the background, but playing a far more marginal role in shaping the new reality.

The vision of Alon and the pragmatism of Eshkol meant that even domestic debates about the future legal status of the Occupied Territories would not hinder their colonization. On 20 August 1967 the government in full quorum wanted some sort of overview of the colonization effort. This was an important meeting, from which Alon understood that the question of the legal status of the Palestinians within the Occupied Territories did not have to be associated with the question of how much territory to colonize. There were quite a few ministers in this meeting who argued that if the West Bank and the Gaza Strip were to be annexed, Israel would have to consider giving the residents there full rights (whereas in June most of the ministers objected to this idea). How to have the cake and eat it, therefore, was the question. The answer was to decide on continued colonization while leaving the question of the status of the Palestinian residents open for a future meeting, which never happened.[7]

The colonization effort was a triple enterprise: the constant grabbing of land, moving Jewish settlers into new colonies and limiting by force any natural growth of the Palestinians inside the Occupied Territories.

The grabbing of land began with a series of decrees, within the context of the emergency regulations. They were issued in 1967. The first was decree No. 25, which declared that every land transaction had to be authorized by the 'official authority'. The next significant decree, No. 59, proclaimed the same year, stipulated that any land owned by the Jordanian government (160,000 dunams in total) was now to be transferred to the State of Israel. State pillaging within the context of this decree was based on an 1855 Ottoman law whereby any uncultivated and non-private land would become state land.[8]

THE ALON WEDGES

The concept of Jewish wedges that would bisect and prevent Palestinian spatial continuity and geographical integrity was not confined to Greater Jerusalem; it was applied to the West Bank in general and it was Yigal Alon who oversaw the implementation of this enterprise in the early years of the occupation. Alon's first wedge was made up of scattered Jewish colonies that spread the length and breadth of the Jordan Valley, coupled with the annexation of additional parts of the eastern West Bank. This wedge was completed by 1971. It was executed in exactly the same way that Zionist colonization had operated in Palestine since the very beginning of the project. The first step was to colonize a distant point and then claim all the area between Israel and that new Jewish settlement as exclusively Jewish, as well as applying the same exclusionary rule to the roads leading to it. The new stretch of land had to be protected; this was achieved by the erection of military camps that were hurriedly built on yet more expropriated land. The last such point in Alon's wedge was Mitzpe Shalem on the Dead Sea. Built by the socialist kibbutzim movement, it began the production of Ahava Dead Sea cosmetics, which even today, when the European Union prohibits the buying of products from the Occupied Territories, are displayed in many fashionable shopping malls in the West.

This wedge expanded to the north and the west, and by 1977 consisted of twenty-one colonies Judaizing the Jordan Valley of the West Bank. These colonies today remain at the heart of the Israeli consensus, and are never referred to by the Israeli media as '*hitna-chluyout*', namely colonies beyond the 1967 borders, as liberal Zionists would, for instance. In 1976 Yitzhak Rabin, then Prime Minister, declared on a visit to these colonies in the Jordan Valley, 'these settlements will be here for a very long time. We do not build settlements to evacuate them.' Almost two decades later, in a speech to the Knesset on 5 October 1995, he stated: 'Israel would always remain, with the fullest meaning of the verb in the Jordan Valley.'[9] Any space that could be carved out by aligning the initial isolated colonies with one another was to be included in the Jewish State in any prospective peace deal. Ironically, the pace of colonizing that part of the West Bank slowed down when the Likud came to power in 1977, as the new government was interested in channelling resources into colonizing other parts of the West Bank. Alon's map for colonization, dictated largely by demographic considerations – namely, not to annex densely populated Arab areas – was replaced with a colonization plan motivated by the ideology of Greater Israel, which allowed for the annexation of any area coveted by Israel.

In truth, there was little left for the Likud government to bite into. The eastern and western parameters of the mega-prison were already Judaized and annexed in one way or another to Israel by the time Eshkol's successors, Golda Meir and Yitzhak Rabin, had completed their terms in office (1969–1977). The western border consisted of blocs of urban settlements that the international community would accept as part of Israel in any future negotiations. The eastern one was clearly announced by Prime Minister Levy Eshkol in 1968 as part of the Jewish State when he declared, 'The River Jordan is the security border of Israel.'[10] The colonization of this wedge intensified throughout 1968, and the Minister of Propaganda, Israel Galili, begged the Prime Minister that summer not to make public announcements ahead of the colonization programme for fear it could cause international uproar. He was wrong, of course.[11]

Alon's second wedge drove right into the heart of the West Bank. It engulfed the city of Nablus and centred on the two colonies of

Kedumim and Eli, and later on the town of Ariel. The third wedge connected 'Jewish' Jerusalem with the northern tip of the Dead Sea and the city of Jericho. It developed incrementally and began with the establishment of Ma'aleh Adumim, a colony that attracted the less fortunate Jewish dwellers of Jerusalem, and grew to such a size that it strangled Abu Dis and other neighbourhoods of East Jerusalem. The Israeli plan in 2012 to extend this sprawl from East Jerusalem to the Dead Sea, and in so doing cut the West Bank into two inaccessible parts, caused the EU – for the first time in the history of the occupation – to use less than diplomatic language in its condemnation of Israel, and to threaten sanctions. The Israeli political elite was probably right not to get too agitated about this change of tone and language – not much has happened in the international arena, while quite a lot has occurred on the ground to consolidate this physical partitioning of the West Bank.

It is interesting to note that, in 1967, Alon and Dayan were contemplating the possibility of dividing the West Bank into northern and southern cantons but eventually decided against this option. But the two cantons, the north and south of the West Bank, divided by the wedge stretching from Jerusalem to the Dead Sea, became a fait accompli as the occupation progressed. Fifty years into the occupation and the two cantons were each divided into eleven counties controlled by the Israeli army and separated by a network of 'apartheid roads' and settlements and strangled by wide no-go areas for Palestinians, blocked physically by the army.

The colonizers' butchery of land did not end there. Early on in the occupation, on 26 June 1967 to be precise, a different kind of bisection took place: the separation of Jerusalem itself from the West Bank. The tearing up of the economic, religious, cultural and social heart of the West Bank was finalized in a series of daily cabinet meetings at the end of June 1967.

In the interplay between demography and geography, the exclusion of Jerusalem from the West Bank created a problem. Any Israeli *de jure* incorporation of land tipped the demographic balance in favour of the Palestinians. Ministers noted that the new plan for the unification of Jerusalem added 70,000 Palestinians to Israel's population. They were not deterred by this. It could be offset by the immigration of Jews and the purchase of private Arab lands, Prime Minister Eshkol reassured his cabinet. A more sinister plan, which was eventually implemented, was offered by the socialist Minister of Agriculture, Haim Givati. He had overseen the covering of destroyed Palestinian villages in 1948 with Jewish National Fund forests, and considered using the JNF to complete the act of dispossession once again – this time in another way. He suggested allocating some of the newly dispossessed lands to the JNF, since, according to its charter, it is not allowed to sell or let land to non-Jews. He must have been delighted when Eshkol responded by saying: 'Ergo, we should give money to the JNF to also buy the private Arab land.'[12]

The area annexed in East Jerusalem was exclusively Palestinian prior to 1967. A year later, only 14 per cent of the land remained in Palestinian hands: 46 per cent was owned by the state, and the remaining 40 per cent was designated green areas.

Alon's fourth wedge was driven into the south of the West Bank, separating Bethlehem and the Hebron Mountains and surrounding area from the rest of the West Bank.

Alon was less influential in determining the colonization policy in the Gaza Strip, but the same methods were applied there as well: slicing, bisecting and then cantonizing the territory. Here it was mainly Yitzhak Rabin who proved to be the moving force behind the bifurcation of the Strip. He called it the 'five fingers' plan. The five fingers materialized as the *Gush* ('Block') of Jewish colonies that remained until their eviction by Ariel Sharon in 2005 (known later as Gush Katif). From May 1968 onwards, Rabin and Alon persuaded the government of the day to establish two colonies as a wedge between – as Alon put it – Gaza City and the south of the Strip, and added that 'it is highly important from a security point of view to have a Jewish presence at the heart of Gaza'. Prime Minister Eshkol retorted that Gaza had belonged to the Jewish people since the days of Samson.[13]

Because of the small size of the Strip, the early violations of Israel's duties, as far as international law was concerned, were more obvious in their bluntness. This forced the government to justify in 1967 its total disregard of the law and in particular of the Geneva Convention. What the government came up with would serve them later in the expansion of Jewish settlements in the West Bank: the Jewish colonies in Gaza were presented as a form of retaliation against the actions of the nascent resistance movement that appeared in the first year of the occupation, before it was crushed by Ariel Sharon, then serving as the head of Southern Command. The climax of that ruthless campaign was a military invasion of the refugee camps of Jabaliyya and al-Shati in July 1971, which ended with the forced transfer of more than 15,000 people out of the camps to the city of Gaza, El-Arish and the West Bank. According to a UN report, more than 6000 homes were demolished in this operation.[14]

By the end of 1967 the first band of colonies appeared south of the Israeli city of Ashkelon (which now incorporates the evicted 1948 Palestinian town of al-Majdal) and stretched as far as Gaza's northern outskirts. This was the first 'finger'; the second separated Gaza City from the town of Deir al-Balah (located 14 kilometres south of Gaza). Two others became the famous (or infamous) Gush Katif, the main Jewish settlement block in the Strip. The fifth never materialized; intended to penetrate the Sinai Peninsula, thanks to the bilateral peace agreement with Egypt in 1979 it was never completed.[15]

The size of the Gaza Strip also meant that the options for bisecting it were never the same as in the West Bank. When they were completed, the colonies made up a relatively small zone of Judaization, which made it easy for Sharon to evict in 2005 in the hope that it would enable him to annex the West Bank. The intense preoccupation, from 1967 to the present day, with delineating and re-delineating the space in the West Bank shows that this region did indeed have a different place in the Israeli strategy from that of the Gaza Strip. The only reason it was not overrun along with the rest of Palestine in 1948 was the different role the international community played in its affairs

– through the so-called peace process – and the demographic dilemma that each new Palestinian territory coveted by the Jewish State posed for Zionism.

This intensive preoccupation paid off. From 1967 onwards Israel used the bureaucratic decrees of military rule to take over 41 per cent of the land of the West Bank; by 1985 it already controlled 52 per cent. In 1991 this had risen to 60.8 per cent. This process ended with the establishment of 130 settlements in the West Bank and sixteen in the Gaza Strip. By the end of the twentieth century 200,000 settlers lived there, in addition to the same number living in the Greater Jerusalem area.

It also paid off as a strategy to thwart any future chance of creating an independent Palestinian state next to Israel by constructing irreversible facts on the ground, a point argued convincingly by Meron Benvenisti and Shlomo Khayat.[16] The two-pronged strategy of territorial continuity between the settlements and territorial discontinuity between the Palestinian villages, towns and cities assured this scenario. Instead of a state, something else was on offer: a level of autonomy as a carrot for good Palestinian behaviour, or ruthless retribution as a stick against Palestinian resistance.

Were the wedges legal? Surprisingly, the Israeli government did ponder this question. The new colonization reality required a legal infrastructure – not for the sake of international consumption but for the sake of an orderly and well-regulated system of governance of the stateless people of the West Bank. The easiest thing to do would have been to annex *de jure* all the coveted territories. But *de jure* annexation was impossible for demographic reasons. Very early on, the Minister of Justice, Yaacov Shimshon Shapira, demanded that his colleagues be aware that the law of the state, of Israel, did not apply as the law of the land, Eretz Israel (apart from Jerusalem) – that is, in the West Bank and the Gaza Strip.[17]

On 18 June, Shapira was entrusted with constructing the legal infrastructure for the new reality. He laid the foundation of what would later be a more elaborate Israeli attitude, informed and fed by the wish to hold the territories without officially annexing them. He told the government on that date that Israel would have to declare military rule over the West Bank and the Gaza Strip in accordance with the demands of international law, but he assured his colleagues that this 'is only platform not substance'. Therefore he proposed a committee of senior ministers to oversee the construction and policies of such a rule.[18] The fact that Israel decided to designate it a military occupation while at the same time refusing to respect the international laws that should govern such a move has had a major impact on the suffering of the people in the West Bank and the Gaza Strip from 1967 up to the present day.

In essence, he explained, there would be two kinds of 'territories': some would be annexed and would become like 'the 1948 Galilee', and the rest would be 'administered territories', the status of which would be decided later. Moreover, he noted, at this point the government could basically choose to annex essential areas, and as an example he pointed out the possibility of annexing the city of Qalqilya to the nearby Jewish city of Kfar Saba.[19] This proposal never materialized, but the power of the new masters could not be mistaken. In hindsight, from our vantage point at the beginning of the twenty-first century, it is easy to see how this foundational policy shaped the geopolitical map of the Occupied Territories over the next fifty years.

It was in the meetings of 18 and 19 June that the government discussed more specifically how this division between annexed and non-annexed areas within the West Bank would work, and what would happen to the areas not directly ruled by Israel. It was there and then that the formula of autonomy was first spelled out and the model of an open prison was introduced as the best option for the Palestinians. It was Yigal Alon who first advanced these ideas, at least according to the minutes of these meetings: 'I am willing to give them autonomy, provided they are part of the State of Israel,' he declared pompously, but hastened to add the proviso that this should be done hand in hand with widespread Jewish colonization. He called that colonization effort the establishment of '*Uvdot Hitayshvuityot*

ve-Hukiyot', or 'legal and colonizing facts' on the ground.[20] He specifically identified the need to annex the Hebron area to Israel, along
with the city itself and the mountains around it, while leaving the
refugee camps and the rest of the southern West Bank to a future
autonomy.

He was more generous than those who took on the task of implementing his plans many years later. He believed every Palestinian in
an annexed area should become an 'Israeli Arab'; namely, upgraded,
if indeed this was what it was, from an inmate in the mega-prison to
a second-rate citizen in Israel. He prompted protests based on demographic apprehension among his colleagues: 'Together with the Arabs
in Jerusalem we can still deal with them demographically' (that is,
tolerate them). As we now know, his 'willingness' to grant Israeli citizenship to the newly annexed Palestinians was only offered in part of
the Greater Jerusalem area. The offer to be a citizen and the threat of
losing this citizenship became a cruel tool in the hands of the future
occupiers.

But this was not Alon's legacy. It was, rather, the colonization
plans he offered that became realities on the ground: creating settlements all over the West Bank without granting basic civil rights to any
of the Palestinians living there. He laid, as mentioned, the foundations for the protocols of ruling. An example of its application can be
seen in a passing remark he made about the need to drive a wedge
between the Palestinians living in the West Bank and those who were
Israeli citizens living in Wadi Ara. The Wadi, which consisted of
fifteen villages, used to be one solid region but was cut in two by the
armistice agreement with Jordan in 1949 (under an ultimatum of
war). The Israeli strategic thinking and tactical argument about this
particular community reveal the absurdity and cruelty that the racist
'demographic discourse' produces in the realm of planning and politics. Until recently, there was a wish to follow Alon's ideas and ensure
the Palestinian community in Wadi Ara (who were Israeli citizens)
was not reunited with the Palestinian community in the West Bank.
Two villages – Baqa and Barta'a – out of the fifteen in Wadi Ara were

in fact cut in two as a result of this strategy. The climax of this separation was the construction of the wall at the heart of these and other villages. Then came the twenty-first century, and with it the conception of new ideas. Ariel Sharon wanted to Judaize Wadi Ara altogether and built colonies in the midst of the Palestinian villages in a programme called 'The Seven Stars' – each star representing an exclusive gated Jewish community. Avigdor Lieberman went further and repeatedly suggested the annexation of Wadi Ara to the West Bank, very much as his colleagues in the government did for much of Greater Jerusalem in the twentieth and twenty-first centuries, 'demoting' people who 'enjoyed' Israeli citizenship back to the non-citizen status of a West Banker.[21]

Alon was also at the forefront of discussions about the prospects of life for Palestinians under Israeli control. By pointing to the Jordan Valley and Hebron as possible annexed enclaves, he began to flesh out the differences of life within areas directly and indirectly ruled by Israel. Indirect rule, he clarified, meant autonomy – an almost magical word that would be used until the onset of the Oslo Accord in 1993 as the best the Palestinians could hope for. Direct rule meant the prospect of being forcefully transferred in the future into indirect rule areas.

The reframing of the West Bank and the Gaza Strip as an Israeli space did not go unnoticed by the local population. The policymakers and those on the ground offered inducements to stifle resistance and reacted harshly when resistance indeed appeared immediately after the occupation. This economic carrot and punitive stick policy is examined in the next chapter.

Chapter Five

Economic Rewards and Punitive Reprisals

Within a single month, June 1967, Israel laid the foundation for a new reality in the West Bank and Gaza Strip that would last until today. Within that month the economists among the politicians hoped to facilitate a smooth transition by also creating a new economic reality that would benefit the new colonizers and appease the indigenous population. The main discussion, as we shall see, was how the new territories could benefit Israel, but the basic assumption was that a by-product of a sound economic policy would benefit the local population as well. The difference between the two sets of interests was that from the outset the policymakers treated the economic needs of the local population as a reward for 'good behaviour' and means of punishing it as retaliation for 'bad behaviour'.

THE ECONOMY OF OCCUPATION

The first aspect discussed in June 1967 was the economic dimension of the occupation, although the debate within the government was not economic per se. The ability, and the need, to create a new economic reality was discussed as part of what Israelis called, falling back on their distorted imagery of ruling the Palestinians as husbandry, the 'carrot and stick' policy towards the people of the West Bank and the Gaza Strip.

There was another key economic aspect to the Israeli strategy for the Occupied Territories. By the end of July 1967, the first economic and financial regulations gave early indications that Israel had long-term ambitions for the West Bank and the Gaza Strip. The government decided that only the Israeli pound (the lira and later the shekel) would be the legal currency in the territories its army occupied. This decision on the currency was swiftly followed by an intensive Israel campaign around the world for foreign and Israeli investment in the territories, and later that month it encouraged Israeli companies to use local firms in the West Bank and the Gaza Strip as fronts for exporting Israeli goods to the Arab world – an attempt to break the Arab trade boycott on Israel.[1]

The ideological imperative was to keep the territories; the economic logic was that it might be too expensive. In order to minimize the expenditure of creating a new reality on the ground foreign aid was necessary; this was eventually forthcoming, in particular from the American taxpayers' pocket and later almost solely from the EU. No less important was the need to ensure economic dividends in the form of Israeli monopoly in the territories and, later on, the recruitment of a cheap labour force from the Palestinian society.[2]

This kind of consideration indicated that there was never a 'pure' economic or financial policy towards the Occupied Territories, and this is why decisions were not left in the hands of the Minister of Finance, Pinchas Sapir, as impressive as he was (at least in the collective memory of Israelis). Decisions were mainly taken by the Minister of Defence, Moshe Dayan. Sapir troubled his colleagues, as he seemed to be one of the few ministers who genuinely contemplated a unilateral withdrawal from the Occupied Territories. He was particularly anxious about a prolonged Israeli presence in the Gaza Strip. In one cabinet meeting he commented that remaining in Gaza was wrong because of the natural birth rate there (muttering something about how no Arabs could be trusted apart from the Druze) and added, 'we should get rid of the West Bank and give it to King Hussein if possible.'[3] Otherwise, he warned, Israel would have to integrate the

Palestinians into the Israeli labour market as equally paid workers. In practice his views had no impact on the government, and, more importantly, his ministry implemented a policy that contradicted the reservations he constantly expressed in cabinet meetings. The areas were annexed economically and the Palestinian labour force was never paid as much as Jewish workers, nor did it enjoy any of the rights and protection workers in Israel had. It was essentially a captive labour market for Israel, presented as an Israeli reward for 'good' Palestinian behaviour, a reward that was denied Palestinians during uprisings or resistance.[4]

Thus economic annexation was based on two movements. It consisted of a flow of Israeli goods into the Occupied Territories, and in the opposite direction a supply of cheap Palestinian labour inside Israel.[5] The first movement was enacted immediately – a smooth transfer of goods was ensured just a few days after the military occupation was completed through the currency monopoly; it took a while for the second one to materialize. The efficient movement of commodities and workers needed the support of the general trade union, the Histadrut. By the end of June 1967, the Histadrut had already worked out guidelines that would allow Israeli industry, much of it owned by this trade union, to dominate the marketing of goods in the West Bank and the Gaza Strip. It would act, or rather *not* act, in a similarly swift manner to allow industry to employ Palestinians without providing them with basic workers' rights.[6]

THE STICK OF PUNISHMENT

While this economic policy was in the main meant to serve as the 'carrot' of the occupation, or as the inducement for the local population to cooperate, the 'stick' was not primarily economic. It entailed a comprehensive blow to the dignity, freedom and, quite often, life, of a person in response to any individual or collective act that was subversive or was deemed to be so by the new rulers of this part of Palestine.

Retribution and punishment were seriously contemplated because some of the policymakers knew all too well that, historically, occupation was often met with resistance. Government protocols, for what they are worth, reveal Alon once more to be the main thinker and speaker on these issues. He did not anticipate significant resistance from the Palestinians, and for this reason even envisaged granting them a kind of puppet state. If they 'behaved themselves' – in other words accepted their fate with only a modicum of resistance – he considered allowing them to have their own state in the West Bank, provided the colonization and annexation programmes had been completed. However, he warned that Israel could not wait too long, as 'they [the Palestinians] will have a national movement', and then it would be unwise to offer them a state as this might turn out to be a real one.[7] This became the bane of the liberal Zionists, forever asking the rhetorical question: why did we not build a subordinate state in 1967 when the Palestinians were weak and lacked a clear sense of nationalism?

Moshe Dayan viewed things quite differently. As with Alon, in the days immediately after the 1967 war he was very much in the public eye and basking in the attention and admiration. But his, of course, was a particular case and explains his arrogant overconfidence that nothing should stand in Israel's way, and definitely not the Palestinians. He was, after all, the national saviour who had been called in at the eleventh hour before the 1967 war to be Minister of Defence and lead the nation to victory, replacing the insecure and hesitant Levy Eshkol.

He told the government he did not anticipate the Palestinians being able to raise a national movement, and constantly referred to them as a disparate collection of religious sects (*edot* in Hebrew) rather than a single community or people. Alluding to the Palestinians merely as Muslim, Christian or Armenian was the way the British Mandatory authorities related to the Palestinian population prior to the 1936 Arab uprising. This perception of the local population as an agglomerate of communities determined Dayan's basic philosophy towards them. It enabled one to choose at will, at any given moment, which group among the Palestinians one wished to communicate with. Dayan took the lead on this issue and reported constantly to the government on his regular meetings with the heads of the local religious sects and, less frequently, with the local mayors.[8]

But as Minister of Defence, Dayan knew better than the rest of his colleagues that the Palestinians, particularly in the Gaza Strip, were already acting as a national liberation movement and the Israeli army, and in particular General Sharon, were channelling all their energies into suppressing these initial attempts to liberate the territories. With Dayan's full knowledge, Sharon was the first to employ the method of collective punishment in response to the early resistance in the Strip. Sharon's policy included the demolition of houses, mass arrests without trial, long hours of curfew and violent break-ins into houses and huts.

In 2008 an official website commemorating Sharon's life and achievements was established, in which, rather than hiding his role in Gaza in those days, it proudly lauded it:

Sharon participates in these searches himself. He orders the soldiers to perform a full body search on all males and sometimes imposes curfews on refugee camps in order to conduct a search. The clear goal of the mission is finding terrorists and killing them. The soldiers have orders not to try and capture the terrorists alive. Sharon instructs them to be rough with the local population, to perform searches in the streets and even to strip suspects naked if necessary; to shoot to kill any Arab who holds a gun; to shoot to kill any Arab who does not obey a Stop! call; and to diminish the risk to their lives by employing a big volume of fire, by uprooting trees from orchards which makes it difficult to capture terrorists, by demolishing houses and driving out their owners to other houses in order to pave secure roads.

Haider Abd al-Shafi, Senior Palestinian leader, says: 'Sharon took a decision to open roads in Al Shateya camp and in Rafah for security. That led to removing houses, the houses of refugees, which is an action not to be taken lightly, but there was no objection neither from Dayan nor from the Israeli government. They let Sharon realize his aim and he really destroyed a lot of refugees' houses.'

Eli Landau, political ally and a friend of Ariel Sharon, says: 'He was a very senior officer going with the troops from house to house, from bunker to bunker, from orange grove to orange grove, to explain what he meant. Three months later, Gaza was quiet. The terror was crushed with an iron fist, with a vicious hand. He cast fear in Gaza, he was feared.'[9]

The manner and detail of the retaliation were based on British military counter-insurgency methods employed against the Palestinians during the Arab revolt in the 1930s; it seems that the new rulers of the West Bank and the Gaza Strip were highly impressed by this ruthless methodology. In the case of the British this pattern of inhumanity was in place for three years; in the case of the Palestinians it has lasted for more than fifty years.[10]

On a smaller scale, the army was testing the punitive options in the West Bank as well very early on. A ruthless policy of searching Fatah 'suspects' was carried out in the very first week after the military occupation, more as a show of strength than a strategic move to undermine Fatah, which was not regarded as a force to be reckoned with at that time. Less than a year later, in April 1968, Fatah stepped up its resistance significantly, launching a series of terror attacks on civilian targets in Israel. As a result, the Israelis expanded their actions in what the military correspondent of *Haaretz*, Ze'ev Schiff, called 'counter terrorism', which, he wrote, 'increases the damage done to innocent people but it is worth considering [as the right policy]'.[11]

The *Hashud* ('suspect') came to refer to any Palestinian the Israeli disliked; he was the 'bad Arab'. Being a 'suspect' already meant guilty until proven otherwise even in those early days, and therefore a 'suspect' was someone who was likely to be arrested without trial and then remain listed on a kind of 'criminal' register that would then bar him or her later on from working in Israel, passing through checkpoints, getting permits to open a business and all other normal aspects of life. The only way of avoiding this, or of being taken off the register, was by becoming an informer for the internal Israeli security service, the Shabak.

The main mission of Israel's elite units in those days was to capture 'suspects', even when in many cases they turned out to be either innocent civilians or young boys whose crime was throwing stones. The army still kept its best units for some more significant operations, such as the assassination of PLO leaders in revenge for the 1972 Munich attack on the Israeli Olympic team and delegation, and the release of the kidnapped Air France aeroplane in Uganda in 1976, and in between the rescue of a whole radar unit from Egypt and similar operations of a more military nature. But after 1976, being an elite solider in the IDF meant spearheading the occupation's most vicious policies.

One of these elite units was the commando group Haruv ('Carob'). Its heroism was celebrated in a famous song from the 1970s that topped the popular music charts. It is a love song to a soldier in the unit, and his lover describes his daily assignments:

Monday and Tuesday he did reconnaissance work,
This is a secret and say no more
But we can say that because of his love of Zion
He caught many 'suspects' in the Shomron [Samaria in Hebrew].[12]

The brutality of the Israeli army in the early 1970s escaped the attention of the Western media, for these were supposedly years of intensive peace initiatives that went on in parallel with these operations. These initiatives began with the despatch to the area of Gunnar Jarring, a UN Special Representative, followed by two missions carried out by the American Secretary of State, William Rogers. However, the fate of the occupied West Bank and the Gaza Strip were very marginal to these agendas, which were mainly focused on the Sinai Peninsula and the Golan Heights.[13]

This frantic and ultimately fruitless diplomatic activity created the illusion to the world at large, and inside Israel itself, that the fate of the West Bank and the Gaza Strip was still negotiable. But what this futile activity achieved for Israel was the immunity to continue with its unilateral bisection of the territories in such a way that would ensure Israeli control over it for decades to come.

So far we have seen that within one month, June 1967, crucial decisions were taken demarcating the possible partition of the Occupied Territories into 'Jewish' and 'Arab' spaces, with the help of wedges and a belt of Jewish colonization. In addition, the methodology of how to deal with resistance and how to try to pre-empt future resistance were experimented with in that month. Finally, it should be noted, and as the next chapter illustrates, that month was seen as the last chance to downsize the population before becoming reconciled to the idea that the Jewish State would now control the lives of millions of Palestinians.

Chapter 6

The Ethnic Cleansing of June 1967

DOWNSIZING THE POPULATION

The Labour party policy in the first decade of occupation had an even more sinister side to it. Before 1967, the settler colonial project of Zionism, very much like other similar projects, displaced and replaced the indigenous population. There was no reason not to contemplate and even implement this method as well after 1967. As noted in the Preface of this book, large-scale ethnic cleansing[1] was ruled out because of the particular circumstances unfolding after the war.

Although the decision was taken not to repeat the massive expulsions of 1948, Israel nevertheless carried out ethnic cleansing operations in the areas it occupied in 1967; with the basic view that downsizing the population in the immediate aftermath of the war was a viable and opportune modus operandi before the dust settled and the 'peace process' commenced.[2] The first group targeted were the inhabitants of the old Jewish Quarter in the Old City. They were ordered to leave and on 18 June 1967 those who did not leave the quarter voluntarily were forcibly expelled. Here is how *Haaretz* reported it on that day (in its inside pages, one should note): 'Many Arabs living in the Jewish quarter were ordered to leave . . . many women, children and men were seen, with their belongings, moving out of the quarter.

They carried clothing and furniture on their shoulders. Most of them are 1948 refugees or their descendants.'

This should not be mistaken for a lament or a sign of compassion; it was an 'objective' piece of reportage. This report was not noticed by the chief military correspondent of the paper, who stuck to the government's propaganda line of denying all such acts when he wrote about a massive 'voluntary' flight of Palestinians out of Jerusalem over the damaged Allenby Bridge on the River Jordan. Such double speak was to be a feature of Israeli media coverage that still pertains today: correspondents on the ground reporting one reality, that of wrongdoing and abuses, while the editorial summaries of the same events describe them as acts of self-defence, as benign policies. Introspective, critical Israelis have become more aware of these fallacies, but this praxis still continues. It was particularly prevalent during the second Intifada, as was fully exposed by a former deputy editor of one of Israel's most important dailies, *Yedioth Ahronoth*, in a book he wrote a few years later.[3]

Diplomats and foreign journalists voiced some concern and an all-too-familiar pattern emerged. Blatant lies were told without blinking an eye and an instant newspeak developed. For example, Chaim Herzog, the Governor General of Jerusalem and later the President of Israel, talked about Palestinians' desire to be united with their families in Jordan. At the same time, *The Times* of London and some British MPs were already discussing the creation of a new refugee problem. As in 1948, disturbing news about Palestinian refugees was not taken seriously: the governments of the West left these reports untouched and did not bring them up in their basic dialogue with the Jewish State.[4]

Everything now seemed possible and Israel Yeshayahu, the Minister of Postal Services, the representative of the Yemenite Jews in the government (heading a party that had been incorporated into the Labour party to secure the votes of the Yemenite Jews), wanted his own poetic justice. He heard that the Palestinians who were expelled by Dayan and Herzog from the Old City were being relocated in

Silwan, the Palestinian village on the south-western slopes of the Old City. He claimed that Yemenite Jews had lived there until 1934 but had fled because of the growing tension with the Palestinians in Mandatory Jerusalem. He therefore wanted these Jews to be settled in Silwan instead of the expelled Palestinians; in other words to expel the expelled once more.[5]

It should be said that Yeshayahu got his history wrong. This beautiful village on the southern slopes that fall away from the Old City into the Judean Desert had always been a Palestinian place of habitation – for centuries, if not longer. The Yemenite settlers inhabited a nearby location they believed to be the biblical location of the Shiloah, the water spring of Jerusalem. But this part of the story was, of course, immaterial. Eshkol promised Yeshayahu he would look into the possibility of creating a Jewish centre there.[6] This did not transpire. However, in recent years, with the government's blessing, Jews began to settle in the village, encountering a campaign of steadfastness by the people of Silwan. Jewish settlers and a systematic policy of house demolition have not as yet succeeded in depopulating this Palestinian village.

On 19 June 1967, the head of UNRWA in Jordan reported that 100,000 new refugees had arrived from the West Bank, most of whom were second-time refugees.[7] They had been refugees in 1948 and were being expelled once again by Israel in 1967. Many more would join them, while the government began to settle Jews in their place in the Greater Jerusalem area. Dayan told *Haaretz* that the 100,000 who left would, in his words, not be allowed to return as they were enemies of the State of Israel.[8]

The sheer magnitude of the expulsions can be deduced from the reports from Jordan. As early as 19 June they pointed out that the local government had to build new refugee camps to cope with the influx of expelled Palestinians. Eventually, within a year, seven new refugee camps were erected in Jordan – Souf, Baqa'a, Husn, Irbid, Jerash, Marka and Taibeh – to accommodate both the new refugees and the overflow of the 1948 refugees who were living in three older camps there. A quarter of a million new refugees were housed in the new camps.[9]

In the Gaza Strip, as in the West Bank, the combination of depopulation and colonization as initial shapers of a new geopolitical reality took place, but on a smaller scale. It took a bit longer for the Israeli colonization pattern to take shape in the Strip, but the construction of an infrastructure of control over the Strip entailed expropriation of land and the transfer of people even before 1967 was out. June saw hundreds of people forcibly moved to Egypt by the Israeli army.[10]

The discussion over Gaza took up only a small part of the government's meetings. Most of their consultation was devoted to the fate of the refugee camps in the West Bank as a whole, but the same approach and method was applied to Gaza. Here, too, ministers seemed convinced that mighty Israel could send and resettle these refugees whenever and wherever it wished – Iraq was the preferred destination (as it was in 1948). However, Yaacov Shimshon Shapira, the Minister of Justice, rejected the idea, 'because they are the inhabitants of this country, you cannot take them out to Iraq. When Jordan was controlling the West Bank, it was something else.'[11] In other words, in 1948 you were entitled to push them from Palestine into the West Bank. He did not believe that a mass expulsion was an option in 1967 as it had been in 1948. Something had changed in the Israeli political elite. In 1948 there was not one voice objecting to the ethnic cleansing of the land. However, in 1967 it was not a small cabal that discussed the ethnic cleansing but a fully attended cabinet.

And yet people were expelled in Gaza, even though it was on a smaller scale. The operations there were not limited to evicting people from their homes but, as in 1948, included other atrocities and brutalities as described in the previous chapter. This repertoire of barbarity would be repeated whenever the Palestinians rejected the open-prison model offered to them by Israel. In the newspeak of this century the Israeli military and political elite would call it *Bank Ha-matarot*, the 'Bank of Targets'. I leave it to the reader to work out this particular metaphor.

However, the government's discussions on 25 June are particularly revealing in this respect. This was, ironically, the same date on which the government eventually decided to leave the West Bank refugees in their camps. We have very few other sources that record the inhumanity that raged in those early days, both in Gaza and the West Bank. The human rights organizations that would industriously and faithfully collect such evidence would only appear on the scene much later, and Palestinians did not, in those days, write books and articles about the early years of occupation, and thus the government minutes are an important and almost exclusive source (together with the UN 1971 report) for these criminal policies.

From the government and the UN archival treasure trove five horrific cases stand out: the massive demolition of houses in Qalqilya; the deportation of large numbers of people from Tul Karem; the mass deportation of around 50,000 people from the Jericho area; the destruction of three villages in the Latrun area; and finally the demolition of two villages in the Hebron area. In addition, other villages were expelled, such as Beit Awa with its 2500 inhabitants and Beit Mirsim with a population of 500. These atrocities and others are listed in a unique UN report prepared by the Secretary General's Office in October 1971. This was the result of a special committee established to investigate Israeli violations of human rights, which included deportation, annexation, colonization, demolition of houses and the 'eradication of villages'. Four years into the occupation, the international organization accumulated enough evidence to deem it necessary to summarize them in a report titled 'Report of the Special Committee to Investigate Israeli Practices Affecting Human Rights of the Population of the Occupied Territories'.[12]

The American consulate in Jerusalem reported the expulsion of 7000 Palestinians from Tul Karem and the UN reported that, under Dayan's orders, 850 of Qalqilya's 2000 houses were intentionally demolished.[13]

'The destruction we wreaked in Qalqilya can destroy us, we should change our conduct,' retorted the Director General of the

Foreign Ministry when the issue was discussed in the government for the first time.[14] He usually addressed such statements to Dayan, who quite often ignored him. As foreign diplomats and journalists continued to ask questions about the demolition of houses in Qalqilya, all Dayan was willing to say in the government meeting was that it was not clear who gave the order to demolish the houses and that the General Chief of Staff, Yitzhak Rabin, was looking into it. It was possible, he said, that half of Qalqilya's houses were destroyed, and in this case the town was now empty. He also conceded that this had happened elsewhere in the West Bank, such as in the villages in the Latrun area. Altogether at that time in June, there were, Dayan estimated, 20,000 displaced persons as a result of Israeli eviction policies.[15]

It is not clear why in that particular meeting Dayan was somewhat discomfited (to judge from the dry records at least) and even, at times, unnerved by the criticism directed at him. Perhaps a probing question by one of his colleagues or an inbuilt defence mechanism led Dayan to say, 'Look, we did not execute anyone, we did not rape anyone and some of them would not be allowed to return because this was a war.'[16]

In Qalqilya, he explained, this was a punitive action in response to sniper fire directed at soldiers. As for the reported disappearance of young men from Tul Karem, Dayan was again only willing to focus on the question of 'who done it' and reported that he still did not know which unit took the men. The young men were taken to a prison camp in Atlit, a former 1948 Palestinian village south of Haifa that became a Jewish settlement, and Dayan estimated their number as being around forty.[17]

Unintentionally, he admitted that a thousand such young men had been abducted from all over the West Bank. They would, he assured ministers, be returned after interrogation. Thus we see, already occurring in the very first days of the occupation, the first of the endless procedure of arrest without trial for as long as was deemed necessary by the security forces. The benefit of ruling without any international scrutiny or supervision became obvious to Dayan and his successors in the seat of absolute power over the Palestinians under his control: Rabin, Sharon, Mofaz, Ben-Eliezer and Ya'alon, to mention but a few.

What these early discussions exposed was that Dayan took for granted the omnipotence of Israeli wardens of the new mega-prison Israel created in 1967. He informed his colleagues that the army did not exactly wait for instructions. But there were limits even in this new fiefdom. Dayan told the government that he allowed the people of Qalqilya to return to their homes because of the UN presence in the area. But as we know, from then onwards the presence of international emissaries would not inhibit the army from carrying out any policy it deemed necessary.[18]

The government approved the policy Dayan wanted to pursue. And Dayan hastily informed the press that the government had decided not to allow the repatriation of the 100,000 West Bank refugees in Jordan. In so doing he ignored a promise he had made to the Director General of the Foreign Ministry in the meeting not to publicize the anti-repatriation policy. In the meeting the following day, the Minister of Education protested that this was a very liberal interpretation of a government decision that was intended to deal more with permitting the army to encourage the departure of Palestinians than prohibiting their return. Dayan rejected the notion that he was in the wrong and his colleagues had to publicly reaffirm his interpretation of the new government policy.[19]

The events of Qalqilya were less important in the context of Israel's overall strategy of punitive action – they would be discussed within a broader and more chilling perspective. Each such local action was part of a systematic attempt by the Israeli government in the early years of the occupation to downsize the local population. This is why the two issues of punitive action and forced transfer were always discussed jointly in government meetings at the end of June 1967. Prime Minister Eshkol viewed the issue of downsizing the number of Palestinians in Qalqilya or Tul Karem not as a retaliatory tactic but, rather, as a response to the demographic concern of the nearby Jewish towns and settlements. The settlers in the kibbutzim near Qalqilya impressed upon him that 1967 provided a golden opportunity to get rid of the people of that town. 'We should oblige them. There will be no good relationship,' he explained to his ministers, and he pondered whether a voluntary deal would be struck with the local people to convince them to leave.

The Minister of Finance, Pinchas Sapir, objected to this callous approach on the grounds that Qalqilya was too close to Israel and would probably be part of Israel sooner rather than later, and moving the people out from there would have no bearing on the demographic balance (as this was not a sizeable community): 'it will create a lot of noise,' he warned, for nothing.[20]

While Qalqilya was not in the end significantly depopulated, other villages were not so lucky. The three villages around Latrun – Beit Nuba, Imwas and Yalo – were hit worse. The residents were expelled on 7 June in order to remove all Palestinian presence near a new road, Highway 1, from Tel Aviv to Jerusalem. A rare film can be seen describing the destruction of Beit Nuba, which offers eyewitness evidence from both sides.[21] Today when you drive along this highway, through one of Palestine's most scenic panoramic views, you can only imagine the beauty of the villages that once surrounded the impressive late nineteenth-century Monastery of the Silent Monk nestling in this ancient valley between the mountains and the sea. More than 10,000 people lived in these three villages. They were expelled on the day of the occupation, and the houses were destroyed over the next three days.

Marie Thereze, a Catholic nun, wrote in her church's paper: 'Here is what the Israelis do not want us to see. Three villages destroyed systematically by TNT and bulldozers.'[22] She noted that the villagers were forced to leave in a hurry, unable to take anything with them. Their fields were deserted in the middle of work and she could see 'tractors from nearby Kibbutzim that were quick to cultivate the villages' lands'. An Israeli journalist, Amos Kenan, had also witnessed the expulsion, but his report was only published thirty years later in *Haaretz*. Kenan was one of the soldiers who took part in the demolition of Beit Nuba, and he wrote: 'We were told the three villages have to be destroyed for strategic reasons, and also as a revenge for them being a launching pad for terrorist attacks in the past, and potentially so in the future.'[23]

The very last moment of Beit Nuba's existence comes to life in his articulate writings (Kenan would become one of Israel's foremost novelists in later years):

> Elegant stone houses, orchards of fruit trees around each house – olives, peach and vine trees – and next to them cedars. All the orchards nicely cultivated and maintained ... In the morning the first bulldozer arrived and demolished the first house. In ten minutes, the house, the orchard and the trees were all gone. The house and its contents were destroyed ... After the third house was destroyed, the refugees' convoy began to make its way towards Ramallah.[24]

The three picturesque villages are now hidden by Canada Park – a pine forest of the kind planted in the aftermath of the 1948 ethnic cleansing as a means of covering such atrocities, and part of Beit Nuba's land now forms a new colony named Beit Horon.

INTERNAL CRITICS

The expulsion was discussed by the Israeli government. The socialist Mapam minister Mordechai Bentov took an exceptional position and pleaded with Dayan to allow the Latrun villagers to return, saying: 'I heard they are not far away, in Ramallah.' Dayan and the Minister of the Interior claimed it was enough that the government had offered to resettle the expelled elsewhere. One after another ministers lined up behind Dayan and retrospectively approved the expulsion of the three villages in the Latrun area.[25]

Equally unfortunate were 65,000 Palestinians who were targeted in the area of Jericho. Most of them were eventually expelled. They were 1948 refugees, residing in UNRWA camps, and one can only imagine the trauma and the pain of experiencing the same catastrophe, less than twenty years later. The government had to discuss their fate as well, as the foreign press, of course, could not but notice such a massive depopulation. Dayan claimed this was a 'voluntary flight' – a familiar Israeli euphemism for the ethnic cleansing of 1948 in which Dayan had played a major role. The censor has erased from the protocol an afterthought of Dayan's in which he refined this categorical rebuttal. He began to explain that the 1948 Palestinian refugees in the occupied areas consisted of three categories: those who left voluntarily, those who stayed and those 'we force to leave'; here the rest of his survey disappears under the censor's eraser.[26]

Ministers concurred that it must be a voluntary flight after all since, unlike in 1948, they had not actually decided on a mass expulsion. Once again it was the voice of conscience spoken by Bentov that prevented the government from glossing over this issue so easily. He quoted the new Governor General of Jerusalem, Chaim Herzog, who estimated that a thousand Palestinians a day were leaving. The army admitted that it was not always as a result of a 'voluntary flight' but quite often because of the pressure it was applying on people to leave. 'One military commander bragged about the fact that he intimidated the population under his control to the extent that the area was totally emptied,' Bentov told ministers. He added that he did not find it hard to believe, as he had witnessed the army expelling the Golan Heights' population at first hand.[27] Bentov made a rare demand that all the Palestinians who had left the West Bank should be repatriated and that the army should cease expelling them. His words speak powerfully of his moral calibre. To some extent, after 1968, most of his friends at the top concurred with him, not on moral grounds, but on the practical grounds that there was no need for further mass expulsions. They found a different formula for ensuring the ethnic purity of the Jewish State: the containment of the Palestinians in their own areas as 'inhabitants' – not citizens.

Israeli strategists discovered that if you want to implement ethnic cleansing by other means, the alternative to expulsion is not to allow people to leave the places where they live – and thus they can be excluded from the demographic balance of power. They are contained inside their own areas, but do not have to be counted in the overall national demographics since they cannot freely move, develop or expand, nor do they have any basic civil and human rights. Glenn Bowman has a word for this strategy: encystation. This is the process of enclosing something within a cyst, and here the Palestinian communities were encircled within territories over which Israel claimed sovereignty.[28]

Bentov was not alone on this occasion. Abba Eban was even fiercer in his criticism of the army's conduct. Facing the Prime Minister directly he said:

> I would like to bring the following item to the government's atten-
> tion. The international press brings horror stories on the extent of
> the flight from the West Bank and the terrible suffering it causes.
> As these descriptions are to be found in our press, I assume this is
> an accurate picture. The worst seems to happen within the territo-
> ries we hold. Israel is being portrayed in the international commu-
> nity and among world Jewry as pursuing an immoral and inhu-
> man policy. The problem is not in the way we represent this policy,
> but in the wisdom behind the policy itself.[29]

Under pressure from Eban, Dayan said, 'I can confirm that 50,000 refugees left Jericho'; and they will be allowed to return, added Eshkol.[30]

Old habits die hard and it seems that, since many of the senior army commanders were veterans of the 1948 ethnic cleansing, they were falling back on the same methods they had used before when occupying villages. Dayan had to issue a special order to the army to stop dynamiting evicted villages – common practice in 1948 that was meant to prevent the return of the villagers to their homes. The Zionist left ministers of Mapam, a movement that was very active in the 1948 ethnic cleansing, reappeared in 1967 with moral sensitivities and a conscience that had been absent in 1948. They felt, as they told the Prime Minister, that they represented in the government the members of various kibbutzim that were located next to West Bank villages. One of them told Dayan that the 'astonished' members of 'our Kibbutzim', such as Kibbutz Nachshon in the Latrun Valley, were bewildered to find out that villages with which they enjoyed cordial relations were depopulated by force. Dayan's insistence that he agreed with the consensual position of the government against massive eviction and that these represented unauthorized exceptions was more or less accepted. However, the Minister of Tourism, the liberal Moshe Kol, noted that regardless of the government's stance, the foreign press gave the impression that Israel had created a new refugee problem.[31]

These reservations voiced in the meetings at the end of June were to be the last of their kind. For many ministers the main worry was the large number of 1948 refugees within the Occupied Territories. Yaacov Shimshon Shapira, the Minister of Justice, said, 'We should establish a ministry for refugees with the purpose of encouraging their emigration . . . especially the young elements because they are very dangerous and they are the worst.'[32] He argued that Israel should demand the 'exclusive right to solve the question'. However, he concurred with Bentov that, as for the 100,000 who 'left', in his words: 'We cannot repeat 1948 [the anti-repatriation] policy . . . we should give them a month to return and if 5000 would return [this is] not a big problem and we would have a different image in the world.'[33]

Not everyone agreed. Israel Yeshayahu, the Minister of Postal Services, objected to repatriation. Haim Moshe Shapira, the Interior Minister, suggested allowing repatriation only for those who were expelled, but the Justice Minister did not want to see such a distinction being made. Bentov, very much aware of the way the military mind in Israel worked then, as it does today, stressed that the only way to ensure that the enthusiastic expellers among the officers ceased their operations would be to let them know that everyone who was expelled would be allowed to return.

Dayan was also unable to relinquish completely his desire to downsize the population. He objected to repatriation and wondered just how terrible it would be if the army expelled Palestinians here and there: 'This is a good process; we convince them to leave, we give them transportation, and Jordanian cars wait for them on the other side.'[34]

The problem, said Menachem Begin, was that it did not quite work like that. According to the London *Times*, he said that, in almost all cases, when people were seen leaving their houses the army fired in the air. This, he insisted, had to stop. Dayan defended the army, saying that in most cases the soldiers 'assisted' the people to cross (over to the other side of the River Jordan). 'We were both there and saw it,' he said, turning to the Minister of Tourism, Moshe Kol, for confirmation. Kol concurred but, unlike Dayan, he began to qualify this with 'but it was shocking . . .' but then stopped. Did he mean it was better when they acted barbarically by firing above people to encourage them to leave rather than pretending to help them? We will never know. What we do know is that there was unease about the enforced transfer of people that took place. The ministers of the liberal and socialist (Mapam) parties were still anxious to promulgate the myth of a voluntary flight. Maybe, they suggested, they could ask UNRWA to assist with the 'transfer'? Dayan vehemently objected. Interior Minister Haim Moshe Shapira disliked what he felt was an unnecessary discussion. 'People move because we force them to move,' he insisted. 'Do we want to adopt a policy that if Palestinians stay quiet they can stay?'[35] This was indeed the crux of the matter: the most elementary rights of human beings, protected by international law, were conditional on an Israeli approval of the enigmatic term 'good behaviour'. In only one context anywhere in the world was such a connection made: the modern prison.

But Dayan did not let go that easily. It seems in retrospect that his main 'achievement' was to divert what began in the first meeting of June 1967 as a discussion about a solution to the 1948 refugees into a debate about how many 1948 refugees in the West Bank and the Gaza

Strip should once more be expelled. He had already successfully established a policy of expulsion even before this particular meeting, which to his mind struck just the right balance between the impossibility of a mass expulsion and the need to downsize the population. He was not looking for a massive expulsion either, but refused to reverse the ethnic cleansing that had already taken place after the end of the 1967 war by adopting a policy of repatriation. No future Israeli government would engage in any thorough discussions about the 1948 refugees, apart from a brief, unsuccessful attempt by Yossi Beilin, when a minister in Ehud Barak's 2000 government, to slightly modify Israel's inflexible anti-repatriation policy.

In those days in June, the international press, on the other hand, was full of hollow promises by Israeli diplomats vociferously declaring their wish to convene an international consortium with the Western powers for the resettlement of the refugees. Dayan, the ultimate Mapaynik (i.e. someone who was mentored by Ben-Gurion on how to manipulate domestic and international public opinion), was in the meantime pursuing the real policies on the ground. He was particularly proud of the policy he and Chaim Herzog initiated of prompting people to leave 'voluntarily', induced by money. So when Prime Minister Eshkol pleaded with him, 'But can we be assured that in 99 per cent of the cases pressure is not applied?' he replied, 'Of course. It is now in the hands of the mayors of Hebron, Nablus, Jenin, Bethlehem.' They could, he suggested, follow the example of Jerusalem: 'We organize it there [in Jerusalem] so that there is always a bus near the Nablus gate until it fills up completely ... recently something wonderful is happening: one thousand Palestinians leave daily.'[36] Why were the mayors so important? Dayan explained: 'The best is to get a person to sign that he is willingly leaving; the second best is for the mayor to sign for him.'[37]

The rather pathetic resistance of the liberals and socialists in this government can be seen from the way Bentov reacted. He began by referring directly to the bus option as inhuman but, perhaps fearing Dayan, he quickly added, 'All I suggest is that we stop it for a while, so there will be nothing [for the foreign press] to photograph.' This fired up the Director General of the Foreign Ministry, and he exclaimed: 'We can organize a tour for the Red Cross!' Dayan as always detested the idea of any such tours, and he reported to ministers that the Red Cross had gone on such a tour but the army stopped it because the international organization broke the rules. All in all, Dayan was furious with the way the Red Cross was trying to interfere.

Dayan in fact persuaded the government to bar the International Red Cross from any involvement in the affairs of the people of the West Bank and the Gaza Strip. He ordered their removal from the bridges on the River Jordan connecting the West Bank with Jordan, which were the main conduits for removing Palestinians from the West Bank.

Under his guidance, the government rejected Red Cross demands, according to the Geneva Convention of which Israel was a signatory, to provide food distribution for the population, protection from expulsion and supervision of the application of pre-occupation laws. The government's legal advisor, Yosef Tekoah, confirmed that all this was indeed according to the letter and spirit of the Geneva Convention. But Tekoah shared Dayan's concern. He explained that acceptance of the Geneva Convention in relation to the West Bank and the Gaza Strip would mean Israel acknowledging that Jordan and Egypt were respectively the sovereign states there.[38] Not one minister was willing to risk such a development; there was and is now only one sovereign state – Israel – and nothing will change it in the years to come, not even the UN General Assembly Resolution in December 2012 that granted Palestine the status of a UN Observer State.

In general, throughout the June 1967 meetings Dayan shrugged off any complaints that originated from Red Cross sources, or for that matter any source that was not his. Thus, he refused even to respond to the concern expressed by the Education Minister, Zalman Aran: 'What we are doing in Abraham's Cave in Hebron [*Maarat Hamachpela* in Hebrew] is scandalous! The Muslims maintained the place in a much better state than we did.'[39]

All in all, according to UN sources, Israel expelled nearly 180,000 Palestinians in those early days.[40] In summing up this period in Palestine's ethnic cleansing, I want to return to some of the plans that were not executed, or at least to one that might, unfortunately, still be relevant in the future should Israel ever have the power, the will or the need to massively depopulate the occupied population in order to satisfy what it would deem its strategic and existential requirements. This is the idea of moving the people of the Gaza Strip, or at least the refugees there, into the West Bank.

This was discussed seriously for the first time in July 1967 by one of the army's most respected and senior officers, Mordechai Gur, who was invited by the government to present his plan. He proposed to absorb the Gaza refugees in the West Bank:

> We need to create the circumstances that would induce the people to leave. We need to pressure them, but in such a way that would not cause them to resist, but to leave. This should be encouraged among both refugees and permanent residents so that they would feel there is no hope in the [Gaza] Strip from an agricultural aspect ... Furthermore, when UNRWA would complete a new census it would become clear they would not have enough food portions for the refugees ... these could have severe security implications ... we should freeze all development there [so as to encourage transfer].

The proposal for such a transfer was raised once more in November 1967. It came from the head of the settlement department of the Jewish Agency, Yosef Weitz, who wrote in the daily *Davar*, the mouthpiece of the ruling Labour party (then still Mapai), of a proposal to 'transfer' (the word he used) the refugees from Gaza to the West Bank. He was then invited to meet the Prime Minister to discuss this. The government then considered his plan and it was endorsed by the Director General of the Ministry of Agriculture: 'We can move a large number [of refugees] to the Jordan Valley.' The military officer coordinating the government's policies in the Occupied Territories, Colonel Shlomo Gazit, suggested a more selective and gradual process, i.e. not to include everyone, that might end in their final removal from Palestine altogether: 'Moving them to the [Jordan] valley can lead to their move to the east; we should create an atmosphere of population transfer.' The legal advisor to the occupation, Zvi Dinstein, added to this: 'We should move them to places where they can have work . . . the main question [being] can one transfer a population in the open?' There is no record as to how this question was answered. Apparently you could not undertake such an operation in the open and hence that particular scheme collapsed.[41]

So a sizeable population remained and, when the thirteenth government ended its term after the war, the fate of the territories and its people depended now on Mapai, the Labour party, which would rule them for the next ten years.

Chapter Seven

The Labour Legacy, 1968–1977

This first decade in the history of occupation, 1967 to 1977, has been portrayed in more than one Israeli publication as the enlightened decade – ten years of opportunities for peace and progress for the Palestinians that they themselves later destroyed.[1] A more focused look also reveals another reality – that of consolidating a unilateral rule that incarcerated the people of the Occupied Territories as inmates for life – them, their children and their grandchildren. From the first day of this decade, their life was governed by a bureaucracy that would deem them a potential threat and source of danger unless they succumbed totally to its whims and demands.

The responsibility for deceiving the world during that decade lies solely with the Labour party (and, within it, also the late Shimon Peres, who after his death in 2016 was hailed as the champion of peace). The thirteenth government shrunk somewhat after the euphoric years of 1967, and decision-making was transferred back to where it was before the war: in the hands of the Labour movement, where it would remain until 1977.

On 26 February 1969, Levy Eshkol died and was succeeded as Prime Minister by Golda Meir. Meir led the party to a decisive victory in the 1969 general election. The new leader was as committed to continuing the settlement policy as her predecessor. Meir was a Jewish-American politician who cut her political teeth in the United

States where she had become a committed Labour Zionist, and later as a long-serving minister first of Labour and then of the Foreign Ministry in Israel. She would take very little interest in the fate of the Occupied Territories, leaving that to the bureaucratic inertia of military rule. Peace was not an option for Meir.

By 1969 the Labour movement, still called Mapai, had had a facelift and was given a new name: it became the Ma'arach ('Alliance'). It was a union between Mapai, Rafi (a parliamentary group headed by David Ben-Gurion) and Yigal Alon's party, Ahdut Ha'avoda. The last group to join it was the Zionist left group, Mapam. The 'Alliance' remained intact until its defeat in the 1977 elections to Menachem Begin's own alignment, the Likud.[2]

As previously noted, the unified government had already agreed in 1967 to establish settlers and soldiers in certain areas of the West Bank and the Gaza Strip in order to maintain a strategic hold on the Occupied Territories. Two developments complicated this plan. One was the emergence of the messianic Gush Emunim movement, which sent its disciples to colonize what they considered ancient biblical sites, quite often at the heart of the Palestinian population in the West Bank. The government wanted to settle Jews in less densely populated Palestinian areas.

The core group of decision-makers had a very significant number of '48ers among them who believed that in 1967 they had redeemed the ancient Land of Israel for ever. As government ministers they turned a blind eye when the first group of Jewish settlers moved into Kahlil, Hebron, in the West Bank, on the night of 12 April 1968. The group settled in the Park Hotel at the heart of the city and a few weeks later the government authorized the creation of the Jewish city of Qiryat Arba, overlooking Hebron. There was no international reaction and the US, it seems, moved at that particular historical juncture into a new and upgraded stage in its relationship with Israel: it decided to arm the Jewish State with the most advanced and state-of-the-art weaponry it possessed (fifty Phantom jet fighters were shipped to Israel at the end of 1968).[3]

The endorsement of the first settlers by the Labour government, which remained in power until 1977, was ignored by a world that, fifty years later, would regard the Jewish settlements as the principal obstacle to peace. Every Zionist political party supported the settlement of Jews from the very beginning, at least in limited parts of the West Bank. The first public voice in favour was that of David Ben-Gurion, who wrote in *Haaretz*, on 9 June 1967, that Jews should colonize the old Jewish possessions of 1948, deserted in the 1948 war, and East Jerusalem. He knew when he wrote this that, nine days later, on 18 June, the government would officially decide to 're-establish' Gush Etzion, and at the beginning of July the first settlers were invited by the government to build Kfar Etzion, the Jewish colony in the West Bank. This is an area south of Jerusalem adjacent to Bethlehem in the east and Hebron in the south. Although the invasion into the heart of Hebron nine months later, in April 1968, was not a government initiative, it was approved retrospectively and legitimized.[4]

MESSIANIC COLONIZATION

Gush Emunim, the ideological movement of settlers, had its roots in the early phases of Zionism. The idea of infusing messianic visions of re-enacting the biblical times with the modern project of Zionism was already prevalent in the 1920s. The key figure in conceiving and disseminating this new dogma was Rabbi Abraham Yitzhak Kook, who in many ways can be regarded as the forefather of extreme Jewish fundamentalism. His followers considered him to be divinely inspired. Rabbi Zvi Yehuda Kook, his son and successor, translated the abstract notions into a political plan in the aftermath of the 1967 war. Until his death in 1982 at the age of ninety-one, he gathered about him enthusiastic national religious youth, who regarded the colonization of the West Bank in particular as their main mission in life. This indoctrination was disseminated in an institute called Merkaz Harav ('Rabbi's Centre') where Kook and his colleagues taught generations of students that settling in the Occupied Territories was a divine imperative of the highest order.[5] This very institute was the target of an attack by desperate Palestinians in one of the few operations carried out against civilians in Israel in 2008; it left eight students dead.

The movement was already active in 1968 before it was formally institutionalized in 1974 by Kook, who also gave it its name: Gush Emunim ('the Block of the Faithful'). According to some accounts, his student Rabbi Haim Druckman, still active today in the movement, was the man who coined the term in a meeting held in his house.

The first official act of the movement (as distinct from actions taken by the settlers already in Hebron and Gush Etzion) took place at the end of 1974. This was an attempt to settle in the Nablus area in the old Ottoman railway station in Sebastia – with the intention of creating two settlements that are there today: Alon Moreh and Qadum. Although initially evicted several times, they were eventually granted permission to stay by the Labour government in an agreement that signalled the integration of government efforts with those of the settlers.[6]

Thus by 1974 the settlers' movement had turned into an ideological lobby influencing government policies on colonization and enjoying an increasing presence in the Knesset and in the public domain in general. But while they were not only manipulating, they were also being manipulated. These settlers were used as a weapon, and quite often an excuse, for justifying the confiscation of land and were employed as a demographic tool allowing the state to carry out ethnic cleansing by other means.

This movement was a convenient conduit for implementing those aspects of the colonization policy with which the Labour government did not wish to be directly associated; especially policies that bluntly contradicted international law and conventions. It shifted responsibility from the state to allegedly partisan groups. So after the mega-prison, in whichever version, was delineated geographically and dynamically by the land pillage, it was further tightened and shaped by the map of Jewish colonies. Life within the proximity of the two

communities, the occupied Palestinians and the settlers, only empha-
sized the image of a prison. Each colony, and each colony's block, was
encircled by an electric fence and walls that closeted the settlers
within them, but when combined they enclosed the Palestinians in
scores of mini-prisons within the huge complex of the West Bank and
the Gaza Strip.

It is here that I take issue with the best book written on the subject
of these people, *Lords of the Land* by Idith Zertal and Akiva Eldar,
which claimed that the movement invaded every state apparatus and
authority in Israel in order to implement its ideology of a Greater
Israel. I think it was the other way around: that the ideology and its
upholders, affecting and transforming Palestine ever since 1882,
needed the post-1967 colonies to expand and implement its vision.
The main thrust of the colonization was carried out as part of the
government strategy of settlement. During Golda Meir's government
(1969–1974) it was Shimon Peres who became the principal patron of
the settlers and who worked steadfastly to legitimize their widespread
colonization. It was thanks to his efforts that two future epicentres of
settler activity, Ofra and Qadum, were established at the heart of the
West Bank. Ofra was finally established in 1975, when Yitzhak Rabin
succeeded Meir as Prime Minister and Peres became the Minister of
Defence, and it overlooks Ramallah from the north-eastern corner of
the city; Qadum was authorized as the first Gush Emunim settlement
near Nablus.[7]

The official decision to colonize was a grave violation of international law. The Geneva Convention requires an occupying power to
affect the existing order in the occupied territory as little as possible
during its tenure. One aspect of this obligation is that it must leave the
territory to the people it finds there. Another vital obligation, decreed
in Article 49 of the Geneva Convention, states: 'The occupying Power
shall not deport or transfer parts of its own civilian population into
the territory it occupies.'[8]

Later on, the colonization project continued under the Labour
government (and, of course, intensified under the Likud after 1977).

The Meir government could, if it chose, limit the messianic colonization, but it failed to do so (either because some of its members, such
as Yigal Alon, identified with the colonizers, or others, such as Shimon
Peres, for cynical and opportunistic reasons, saw them as potential
allies in the political game).

RESISTING THE COLONIZATION

The second potential obstacle for the colonization was Palestinian
resistance to it. This was not a meaningful resistance as its success
depended on a regional hinterland in disarray.

The borders of the Jewish State were anything but quiet throughout 1968 and 1969. On the shores of the Suez Canal that year, a daily
war of attrition between the Egyptian and Israeli armies raged. The
Egyptians hoped to force the Israeli army to withdraw from the Sinai
Peninsula, which the latter had occupied in June 1967, and the Israelis
retaliated with raids deep into Egyptian territory hitting, among other
targets, the very infrastructure of the Egyptian economy and
industry.

On the long border between the banks of the River Jordan, a
different kind of confrontation took place. The newly instigated
Palestinian guerrilla movement was trying to send in units to organize a campaign of popular resistance against the occupation. At first
the Israeli army retaliated with the aerial bombing of Palestinian
bases in Jordan, and then decided to stage a frontal assault, which
ended in colossal failure when it embarked on an attack on the PLO
headquarters in the village of Karameh in Jordan. The war of resistance now also included plane hijacking and bombing Jewish areas
inside Israel (the first hijacking of an El-Al plane occurred on 23 July
1968). Israeli retaliation included raids on Beirut airport and the
bombing of thirteen planes belonging to Arab airlines at the very end
of 1968. These kinds of confrontation continued until what became
known as 'Black September' in 1970, when the Hashemite Kingdom
decided to force the PLO headquarters and guerrilla activity out of

the country, and the front of struggle moved to southern Lebanon. The stage for the struggle was now not only an international one but it also included international organizations of resistance and terror. This development culminated in the attack on eleven Israeli team members at the Munich Olympics in September 1972 by the Palestinian group Black September and the massacre of twenty-five passengers at Lod (aka Ben-Gurion) airport in May earlier that same year by Japanese members of the Red Army.[9] The stage for resistance was no longer mainly or exclusively in the West Bank, but extended to other parts of the world. Thus it did not affect the routine of the occupation.

In the Gaza Strip there was no specific hinterland that could become a kind of North Vietnam to the occupied South. Localized initiatives from within the refugee camps therefore formed the backbone of the resistance. This continued until 1971 when it was brutally crushed by the head of Southern Command, General Ariel Sharon.

Thus most of the resistance was outside the borders of the state. Against those actions inside the territories Israel initially responded with collective punishments, but before long added to these reprisals the expansion of Jewish colonization. From very early on, then, resistance and Jewish colonization were intertwined in the minds of the strategists and bureaucrats running the Occupied Territories for Israel. The equation was simple – the stronger the resistance, the deeper the colonization.

It was in the Gaza Strip that, for the first time, Palestinian resistance and Jewish colonization became associated and thus resistance came to serve as a pretext for intensive Judaization of the Strip. The impulse to colonize the territories, in clear violation of international law, was of course not in retaliation for resistance. But for some reason Israeli policymakers asserted that colonization could be justified if it was presented as a means of fighting 'terror'. The right wing of the political system at first rejected this connection and wanted governments to support colonization per se as an act of national redemption. But when even right-wing governments were more careful, under international pressure, to expand the settlement project, the lobby for expanding it was particularly vociferous after acts of Palestinian resistance.

The initial colonization of the Gaza Strip was not pushed forward by the messianic movement of settlers, Gush Emunim, but was championed by one minister, Yigal Alon, and one general, Ariel Sharon.

Yigal Alon was appointed chair of the Ministerial Committee for Settlement [colonization] Affairs in January 1970; shortly afterwards the committee was renamed the Inter-Institutional Committee for Settlement (which in Hebrew would be the correct translation for colonization), since it included not only ministers but also heads of outfits such as the Jewish National Fund, the kibbutzim movement and others. Hagai Huberman, a leading activist in Gush Katif, the block of Jewish settlements in the Gaza Strip, was a member of that committee and in the wake of the Israeli disengagement from Gaza in 2006 he posted the minutes on his website.[10]

What emerges very clearly in these minutes is that Sharon convinced ministers that establishing Jewish colonies in Gaza would send a clear message that Israel would not withdraw from there, and this, as he put it, would dampen the 'impulse for terror'. The first two settlements were decided upon in 1971 and established in 1972. And this would be the theme of the discourse: you settle because it's yours but also as a response to 'terror', thereby providing one explanation for the right-wing electorate and another for the more moderate section of the public, with an eye to the international community.

While the outlines for future Jewish colonization were established by the Labour politicians in the first decade of occupation, the life of the occupied people was in the hands of the bureaucrats. Politicians take decisions at historical junctures; bureaucrats translate them into reality both according to the political guidelines as well as according to their personal judgement, aspirations and foibles.

Chapter Eight

The Bureaucracy of Evil

THE RULE OF BUREAUCRACY

When the essential cabinet meetings were over in June 1967, they ended with the resolution to exclude the West Bank and the Gaza Strip from any peace agenda, to transfer their rule to the army, to authorize some but not massive expulsions, and to incorporate the territories into the Jewish State without formally annexing them, thereby leaving the people there in civil and personal limbo.

It was now up to the bureaucrats to take over. At the top of the pyramid for the initial stages of building the infrastructure for the imprisonment of so many people was the Committee of Directors General, the CDG, in Hebrew *Vadat Ha-Mancalim*.[1] These were the Directors General of all the ministries that were relevant to the Occupied Territories, and it was established on 15 June. There are two volumes comprising thousands of pages recording their meetings.[2]

The first meeting of the committee was chaired by Ya'acov Arnon, the Director General of the Ministry of Finance. Others present included Zvi Zur, a former Chief of the IDF General Staff and in those days a special advisor to Dayan. Others were the Directors General of the Ministries of Trade and Industry, Agriculture and the Interior, along with representatives of the Ministries of Defence and of the army. Diplomacy was not a consideration, hence there was no one from the Foreign Ministry, but, on the other hand, the co-ordinator of the committee was a colonel, Yehuda Nitzan (who was replaced by General Shlomo Gazit in 1968).[3]

From the first meeting the need for absolute secrecy regarding the discussions was stressed. It was decided there and then that each military governor would have a mini-cabinet representing the various ministries, and these civilians would be given both military uniforms and ranks. They would be 'converted' to civilian uniforms once again when military rule was replaced in the 1980s by the Civil Administration, one of the many indications that the transition from 'military rule' to 'civil administration' – hailed by Israel as a move intended to make life easier under occupation – did not cause any dramatic change in the life of the Occupied Territories. Each cabinet minister was asked to recruit local Palestinians to work with them. In the days of the British Empire, in countries such as India and Egypt, a very similar structure was employed whereby the governor had a local advisor shadowing him. The colonial nature and face of the occupation became more and more visible by the day.

The committee produced, as we shall see, two models for the manner in which life would be managed in the territories. One was an open-air prison, which assumed the Palestinians would regard Israeli control as an improvement on the former arrangement and would at least enable them to survive. And should the Palestinians resist that model it would be replaced by the second, a high security prison.

The bureaucracy was able to activate the two models at any given moment. Already by September 1967 this group of officers and officials knew that the occupation would be resisted. In that month, the first cadre of Palestinian informants had eavesdropped on their compatriots and reported the existence of an embryonic resistance movement. Colonel Rehavia Vardi was the officer who reported this to the CDG. Vardi and another colleague were the prime movers in the CDG and their main task was to make clear to everyone concerned about the totality of control granted to the military governors in the lives of the Palestinians.[4]

LEGALIZING THE OCCUPATION

Zvi Inbar, who was part of the legal side of what the Israeli military called 'belligerent occupation', tells us how he and his team became the legislative, executive and judicial authority in the Gaza Strip within a few days:

> Due to problems of communication and a multitude of other problems [arising from the occupation], the military attorney general gave us a free hand. In practice we could legislate any law we wanted and we deemed necessary for managing the occupation ... in due course we established military courts and a complete judicial system.[5]

This reality was created by the CDG whose main mission was to construct a legal infrastructure for the Occupied Territories. The groundwork was already completed in 1963 when the Shacham Plan was devised. It was effectively the British Mandatory regulations that in practice guided the committee in its work after the occupation. The employment of regulations that provided absolute dictatorial powers to the rulers enabled the bureaucrats of the mega-prison to deal with day-to-day management: it provided guidance on both how to offer 'rewards' (the most basic civil and human rights) and how to quell resistance (by the simple act of withholding these rights). In addition to the emergency regulations, certain international laws concerning war and occupation, along with some remnants of the Jordanian legal system, were fused into this infrastructure.

The pace of the Israelis in those early days was mind-boggling for anyone watching from the outside. By 21 June the army's legal experts had completed the establishment of a comprehensive legal system for the West Bank and the Gaza Strip.[6] A team headed by Major Dov Shefi was in charge of overseeing this, with the supervision of the Chief Military Attorney, Colonel Meir Shamgar (later to become a Supreme Court judge and one of the most respected legal minds and personalities in the Jewish State). The rapidity of this achievement was put down to one simple and brutal fact of life: however complex it all sounded, it left the fate of the inhabitants in the hands of the military commanders with very little room for challenge or protest. It was a crude interpretation of the Fourth Geneva Convention (1946) that surrendered executive, judicial and legislative powers into the hands of a military governor – powers that were used, as we only know with hindsight, to grab land, dispossess people, subject them to mass arrests, force them into collaboration and expose them to an ever-increasing process of foreign colonization. Above all, the convention only intended these powers to be in place for a short period.[7]

The people of the Occupied Territories were handed a list of new regulations on the first day when the Israeli army entered their space. In one of the earliest lists – in fact, the second Arabic pamphlet distributed to the people – it was declared that the pamphleted decrees were like the law but could be overruled in the future by the military governors. This particular decree stated, first, that all property previously owned by the Jordanian government would now be taken over by the army, and, second, that all pending taxes would be paid directly to the military governor.[8]

The new rules of the game were not only communicated through the promulgation of pamphlets, but also through operations on the ground. Even before the actual occupation of the West Bank was completed, the army decided to open five military courts (on 7 June) and seven detention centres. This was when the term 'Green Line' was first introduced into the army's, and later into the public, discourse in Israel. On the face of it, the Green Line was the armistice line drawn between Israel and Jordan in the spring of 1949, which delineated the boundary between Israel and the West Bank. However, in reality it was gradually moved eastwards and over time came to define the Israeli/Jewish space that included pre-1967 Israel and any territory that was colonized and Judaized since 1967 (up to half of the West Bank's territory by 2017). Within this space Israeli law mattered, but not beyond the Green Line. In the Palestinian spaces of the West

Bank and the Gaza Strip, the military, and later the pseudo-civil administration, controlled the lives of the people often by draconian methods and according to the whims of the military governors.

From the very beginning, the lawmakers of the Occupied Territories adopted a functional, and cynical, approach to international law. These areas were alternately treated as part of the Israeli legal system and also outside that system in order to serve best the strategy of colonizing them. The imposition of the non-democratic military law was justified as emanating from the duties and privileges that international law granted Israel as an occupying force. However, whenever international law threatened to interfere with the colonization effort – such as preventing Jewish settlers moving into the area and the expulsion of Palestinians from them – then Israeli law was invoked. This elaborate dual system was finalized by the mid-1970s.

The policymakers, in consultation with the senior legal civil servants of the state, decided to put the military court system – set up to run the territories – under the supervision of the Supreme Court. The message to the world was clear: although we do not need to do this, we are taking extra measures to keep an eye on the military handling of justice in the Occupied Territories.

Years later, a famous Israeli jurist would write that it would have been better if this decision had not been taken, since it obfuscated and hid the atrocious military court system that abused the lives of Palestinians of all ages throughout the years of occupation: 'From a radically different perspective, it may be argued that the main function of the [Supreme] Court has been to legitimize government actions in the territories. By clothing acts of military authorities in the cloak of legality, the [Supreme] Court justifies and rationalizes these acts.'[9]

Indeed, it created the charade of an 'enlightened' occupation. Theoretically, and at times also practically, the door was open for Palestinians affected by the military judiciary to complain and appeal to the Supreme Court in Israel. However, since in the vast majority of cases such appeals ended in total failure, the atrocities were legitimized by the most highly respected domestic and international judicial institute in the land.

The most important act by the Supreme Court was legalizing the acquisition of Israeli land pillaged in the Occupied Territories. Palestinians who were victims of land expropriation were not compensated[10] and were advised by their lawyers to appeal to the Supreme Court. The Supreme Court, at least in principle, did not allow anyone but the army to expropriate private land. When the settlers founded companies that negotiated directly with Palestinians who were asked first to buy coveted land, and then sell it to them, in several cases the Supreme Court declared such transactions as illegal and ordered the destruction of the settlers' building (which happened in a handful of cases in the last fifty years). In 2017 the Israeli Knesset passed a law (still to be tested by the Supreme Court) that legitimized all these transactions retrospectively.

On other issues of abuse it was sceptical enough not even to bother – apart from collective appeals such as those concerning the use of torture in the secret service's interrogations (which led the Supreme Court to legalize what it euphemistically called the right of the security services to 'employ reasonable pressure' in interrogations).[11]

One aspect of the land seizures was observed seriously by the legal system: in principle, only land deemed public in the Occupied Territories could be confiscated. Until the early 1970s, expropriation did not distinguish between private and public land, but when one such case was brought to the Supreme Court in the early 1970s, it ruled that only state land could be taken in such a manner and designated for Jewish colonization. This ruling inhibited the colonization efforts for a short while but the legal barrier was removed with the appearance of Ariel Sharon on the political map after the 1973 war, and in particular, as we shall see, after the Likud rose to power in 1977.

However, even under the Labour administration the pillaging of land was quite widespread and intensive. After all, the mainstream

Zionist party had shown great expertise in navigating the legal complexities that allowed them to take over the dispossessed and abandoned property of the Palestinians in 1948. In the Occupied Territories the CDG was in fact quick to implement the same principles of land robbery applied to the huge areas Palestinians left behind when they fled in 1948. This was the principle of custody. In the aftermath of the 1948 ethnic cleansing, the evicted properties in both urban and rural areas were transferred into the hands of a custodian according to a Knesset law from 1950. This government official had the right to decide on the fate of each property. The options were limited: it was either handed over to Jewish citizens or to the various government agencies, including the army.[12]

The application of similar practices to the land looted in the West Bank and the Gaza Strip was not carried out openly; even Israeli officials realized that such a practice in the Occupied Territories would not be tolerated by an international community that otherwise seemed to accept quite a few of the malpractices and abuses there.

So Meir Shamgar, who was soon to become Attorney General, openly declared in November 1968 that Israel's Absentee Property Law was not applicable to the Occupied Territories. However, it was applicable *de facto* until his declaration, as instructed by the CDG, and in any case only related to 8 per cent of the land, much of which had already been taken by 1968. The main significance of the application of this law was for East Jerusalem. There, quite a lot of property left behind by both 1948 and 1967 refugees was 'protected', since 1968, by the Attorney General's declaration. However, in 1977, a limited version of the Absentee Property Law was applied to Greater Jerusalem, and fully applied in July 2004.[13]

With the arrival of the first Jewish settlers in the West Bank and the Gaza Strip in 1968, the decrees authorizing the expropriation of land and the delineation of the Palestinian spaces increased in number and frequency. It began with Decree 291 at the end of that year, which froze any procedures of land registration and rearrangement of water resources so as to prepare for a vast Jewish colonization.[14] This was in many ways a closure for the frustrated Zionist colonizers who in the pre-state period, the last time massive Jewish colonization had taken place, had been heavily restricted by Mandatory laws and supervision. Now they could resume their activities without any interference.

These early land decrees were also used to establish an extensive military presence in the heart of the Palestinian areas. Between 1968 and 1970, the Governor General of the West Bank issued a series of decrees that allowed the seizure of property and land for military purposes. This resulted in the takeover of 50,000 dunams.[15]

Around 1970, both Jewish colonization and military presence were fused into a single means of land robbery: land was first confiscated under the pretext of erecting a military installation, but with the view of later turning it into a Jewish colony. This practice characterized the actions of the Labour governments between 1967 and 1977. When the Likud came to power in 1977, this subterfuge was abandoned and land was expropriated with the explicit purpose of building civilian Jewish colonies on it.

In January 1970 the CDG was incorporated into the Ministry of Defence under the direct supervision and coordination of Shimon Peres, then the Minister of Transportation and Communication. He would later receive the Nobel Peace Prize, as if he had played no part in the colonization of Palestine.

So two years into the occupation, the legal infrastructure was firmly in place, and the last buds of Palestinian resistance seemed to have withered and died. When nothing of note occurred in the West Bank and the Gaza Strip during the 1973 October war, such as a local uprising that could have aided the military efforts of Egypt and Syria, the captains of the Israeli policy were confident they had found the right formula for running the newly acquired territories and the people living in them.

The Palestinians were expected to accept the new reality from the very beginning of the occupation. Resistance of any kind led to immediate imprisonment, as did assisting or hiding anyone involved in resistance. Hiding or assisting a member of the PLO or an activist from the Palestine Liberation Army (PLA)[16] resulted in a fifteen-year prison sentence. Very few chose either option, and it seems that, in the first decade of the occupation, many Palestinians were willing to give the new initiative a chance, but this attitude was not reciprocated by a benevolent Israeli policy and the model soon collapsed.

TOWARDS THE COLLAPSE OF THE OPEN-PRISON MODEL, 1973–1977

Most local people survived this ethnic cleansing and remained in the West Bank and the Gaza Strip under the new rule. That rule in the years leading up to the 1977 change of government in Israel was now entirely in the hands of a bureaucracy that assumed the people living there were reconciled to the new reality and that Israeli interests, however the political elite chose to define them, could be furthered unilaterally without any consultation with the local people or consideration of the sensitivities and laws of the outside world. This self-confidence on the part of the new rulers was fed both by the lack of active resistance from the inside and the absence of any pressure from the outside. As long as this was the perceived reality of the Israeli military and political elite, this system was deemed to be working well, and this situation lasted until the first signs of resentment and resistance appeared in the years leading to the first Intifada. In this book I choose to refer to such a reality, where there isn't major Palestinian resistance and an Israeli crackdown, as the open-prison model.

Dwindling resistance from 1969 onwards contributed to the more 'positive' aspects of the open-prison model. Now that the pattern of Jewish colonization and supremacy was finalized and in place in the Occupied Territories, it was possible to 'reward' the Palestinians for their lack of active resistance.

The first reward was delegating authority to the local municipalities and councils so that the occupation would be felt but not seen.

The second was absorbing the surplus manpower into the Israeli labour market and, finally, keeping the bridges over the River Jordan open to facilitate the exchange of commerce and population, mainly in order to exploit the West Bank as an indirect gateway for exports to the Arab world. It is not surprising that the dynamics described here are of an economic nature. The focus of the open-prison model in its initial stages in the early 1970s was economic more than anything else, as it would be in its most recent incarnation under Benjamin Netanyahu in the twenty-first century when he would talk about 'economic peace'. It was not the Ministry of Finance that took the lead on this question, but, rather, the Ministry of the Interior. This division of labour is another telling indication that the territories were not 'occupied' or temporarily taken, in the official Israeli perception, but were regarded very much as an internal affair.

Indeed, the economic reality of the occupation was meant to be the hallmark of the open-prison model. However, when economic benefits are offered to silence potential resistance to further colonization, their long-term impact is as destructive as some of the features of the maximum security model Israel imposed whenever resistance did occur.

And, indeed, the deep involvement of the Finance Ministry was one indication of how permanent the Israeli presence in the Occupied Territories was in the eyes of state policymakers. The discussion was never about the economic implications of a possible Israeli withdrawal or of that of a 'peace'. Rather, the issue constantly being debated was how to integrate the West Bank economy into Israel without undermining its Jewish demographic majority.

Two personalities at the top clashed on this issue: the Minister of Finance, Pinchas Sapir, and the Minister of Defence, Moshe Dayan. Sapir was a large man and a bald politician whose image is still engraved in popular memory in Israel as something of a peace-loving economic genius (thanks largely to the poor performances of those who succeeded him). He did not like the idea of integrating the two economies and maybe for this reason he was justifiably cast in the role of the 1967 dove who, unlike his colleagues, genuinely wished to relinquish any links to the West Bank and the Gaza Strip, and between Israel and occupation. But his suggestion that the government should encourage Palestinians to work in the Arab world instead, induced by the prospects of sending money back home, was quite ominous. I do not know if he anticipated that his bureaucracy might use this temporary emigration as a means of ethnically cleansing the Palestinians from the Occupied Territories, but, in reality, for residents of the Occupied Territories who chose that option, such a move entailed a calculated risk that they would not be allowed to return.[17]

But in the early 1970s Sapir was not calling the shots. The man in charge was still Moshe Dayan, until he was forced to resign in 1974 after the fiasco of the 1973 war – only to return to Menachem Begin's government in 1977, though in a far less influential position. However, Dayan held power long enough to imprint his ideas in an irreversible manner on the ground, and not even a shrewd and powerful politician such as Sapir could stop him. He shaped the territories as an economic dependency. The Palestinians would now have to rely for their survival on Israeli goods and for their welfare on Israeli permits to work in Israel. The export of West Bank and Gazan goods to the Arab world was still possible, but this was economically insignificant and also dependent on Israel's goodwill. Even more precarious was the option of working in the Arab world and further afield and sending money home.

Dayan brushed aside Sapir's demographic disquiet. The demographic balance he favoured was not only concerned with how many Palestinians there were inside Israel proper but how they were defined. On the one hand, they were to be temporary guest workers with no rights whatsoever inside Israel, and, on the other, their presence there would further advance Dayan's wishes to make the occupation irreversible. Dayan won the day. During the 1970s, a decade celebrated by Israeli historians as a period of Palestinian prosperity under Israeli guidance, the systematic economic colonization was accompanied by neglect of the development of the local economic infrastructure in the

Occupied Territories. The reality was far from a prosperous one – the West Bank and the Gaza Strip were only a source of cheap labour and a captive market for Israeli goods. The official Israeli version marketed a tale of a primitive Arab society that was now being given a golden opportunity to turn over a new leaf in the economic history of the Middle East through the mutual movement of goods and labour between the Jewish State and Palestinian areas. In reality, the movement was in one direction only. It created a one-sided dependency.[18]

Again, despite the sinister long-term policy objectives and the overall negative effect on the local economy, it should be understood that some of these processes would take time to mature and their full effects to materialize. This is why quite a few Palestinians remember the early years as offering opportunities that were not available before, not only economically, but also, for instance, in the realm of education: the Israelis allowed colleges to become universities. And, indeed, the standard of living of the Palestinians who were allowed to work in Israel in that decade rose significantly and the flow of Israelis into the local markets brought business with it.

The open prison seemed to work. From that moment onwards there was no need for direct involvement of the Committee of Directors General or the Ministry of Defence. The army exerted its rule over every aspect of life, but it was assisted from the very beginning by other Israeli agencies. One of these was the general trade union, the Histadrut. This pre-state outfit had already been very effective in ousting Palestinians from the Mandatory labour market, and yet it was accepted in the Western world – including by the British trade union movement – as a paragon of socialist organization devoted to the welfare and wellbeing of the workers. It was incorporated into the mechanism of the occupation from the second week of June 1967. The government granted it monopoly over trade and industry – and it acted there not as a trade union but, rather, as a mammoth industrial complex.[19]

But it provided employment and thus the recollection of that decade, even among Palestinians, is of years that were not all doom and gloom. More importantly, perhaps, the early years might have held the promise and potential for a very different reality to develop, but this was not the intention of the policymakers. Any kind of improvement in their living conditions depended on total Palestinian consent to living in the secluded areas in the Occupied Territories, whose space would constantly be reduced by Judaization and land grabbing.

Interaction with Israelis who were not part of the bureaucracy was less traumatic. A few days after the end of the war, Moshe Dayan visited Uzi Narkiss, the Governor General of the West Bank, and noticed a long queue growing outside his office. 'What is this?' he inquired. 'These are Israelis who want to enter the West Bank and need licences from the military governor.' 'No need,' said Dayan. 'Open the gates.' Thousands of Israelis, including myself as a young boy of twelve, swarmed into the West Bank, as if travelling abroad was possible now without boarding a ship or a plane.[20]

The Israelis were attracted by the concept of visiting a foreign land with new goods to buy and the archaeological richness of the West Bank to explore. Or at least the richness that was still to be excavated – not out of intellectual curiosity, but, rather, as part of the attempt to prove that this was the heart of the ancient and biblical Jewish kingdom. By 22 June the Israeli archaeological authority had already taken over all the sites in the West Bank and the Gaza Strip. Intentionally or otherwise, they would map out for future settlers the early sites they should colonize.[21]

In July 1967 I went on just such a trip to see the archaeological sites. Like others, I did not notice the roads churned up and destroyed by tanks, the burned-out cars beside the roads, the convoys of refugees – most of them expelled – heading hungry and thirsty towards the shelled bridges crossing the River Jordan. We went in the early days, when one could, if one wanted, still see the human corpses that had not yet been evacuated or buried. In 1997 a journalist in the daily *Maariv* recalled that the local military governor reported that thousands of livestock – donkeys, cows, sheep and goats – were roaming the cities after losing their owners or fields. Many of them were taken by the Israelis; others died and the governors were worried that the cadavers would spread diseases that could not be controlled.[22]

But Moshe Dayan in his autobiography, *Aveni Derech* ('Milestones'), described the initial encounter as a happy one. Some Palestinians added to this picture with similarly positive recollections, as did the first mayor of Bethlehem, Elias Freij.[23] The better-off Palestinians, such as mayors, rich traders and lawyers, may well have experienced some measure of relief at not having been expelled, as had happened in 1948, and they were also allowed to trade and conduct business with the Israelis, and consequently they reaped material dividends. But these were the exceptions, and their numbers diminished as the years went by. Most of the people had to choose between the open-prison model or risk the maximum security one.

These early years of relative calm were the prelude to the first Intifada. And, just as the late, devoted Palestinian historian Samih Farsoun described the Mandatory period in Palestine as 'the Road to the Nakbah' (the 1948 catastrophe), so one can also describe these first ten years as 'the road to the Intifada'.[24] The model collapsed first of all because of the Labour government's inability to sell the open prison as a peaceful process of reconciliation. The government instead opted to collaborate with the new messianic movement of settlers, Gush Emunim, and the twofold pressure ignited once more with a Palestinian resistance that would increase once the Likud took office in 1977. Let us examine these factors more closely.

FROM LABOUR TO LIKUD

Two decades passed between the occupation and the outbreak of the first Intifada. Each decade was influenced by whoever was in power in the Israeli government. The first decade was a Labour period and the second a Likud one. Dan Bavli, who served as a senior officer in the early days of the occupation, published a book summarizing his years as part of that Labour bureaucracy. He provided the principal explanation why the Labour years were as crucial in explaining the first uprising in December 1987 as were the harsher policies by the Likud in the next decade.

Bavli stated in his retrospective view:

> In all the years of Mapai's [Labour] reign in power, with all its dovish and hawkish wings, and up to the 1977 upheaval, peace or the desire for peace was not a prominent political goal on Israel's agenda. Military might was the only option offered vis-a-vis the Palestinians. And the increasing employment of military power, accentuated even more Israel's intransigency.[25]

Bavli belonged to a group of officials who were attempting to search for Palestinian collaborators in the Labour project of building a mini-autonomy instead of the occupation – an effort described at the end of the previous chapter – and he assumed that, had it been adopted, history would have developed in a better way for both sides. To me this seems doubtful, but, of course, we know what happened, not what *could* have happened. In any case, his assessment is very valuable.

His overview of the Mapai (or Labour) impact and responsibility for the uprising is valid and convincing, as I tried to show in the previous chapter. The Israeli agenda in the Occupied Territories during Labour's ten years in power was totally disconnected, as it would be up to the present day, from the international agenda. The former was a blueprint for how to maintain the biggest prison on earth for as long as possible; the latter wished to end the conflict between the Israelis and the Palestinians on the basis of a two-state solution.

As Labour was considered the left, or the peace, party of Israel it was not exposed to much international pressure. For a while there was some impact from the outside. The 1973 war produced some new interest, if not in the fate of the territories, then at least in the so-called peace process. The principal initiative was a peace conference that was convened in Geneva by the USA and the USSR at the very end of the year; Israel, Jordan and Egypt were invited to what was described as a historical event – one which like so many before and after had no bearing on the lives of the people under occupation. As if to mock history, while (and this may have been genuine) Western diplomats, including President Jimmy Carter, talked about comprehensive peace, the Israeli official reaction was to deepen the occupation even further.

The discourse of Geneva was totally alien as far as official Israel was concerned. On the ground, if anything, the irreversibility of the unilateral Israeli colonization and demarcation became even more evident with two major developments. One was a more systematic planning of colonization from above, and the other a more lenient and supportive attitude towards the new movement of Jewish settlers, who began by settling in Gush Etzion, south of Jerusalem, with the blessing of the government, and in Hebron, without its blessing, in the first year of the occupation.

It was alien since the Ministry of the Interior, from the first decade of the occupation, regarded the Occupied Territories as economically and administratively part of the State of Israel. The official discourse used by politicians, diplomats, pundits and bureaucrats followed the reality faithfully. At first, Israeli diplomats talked about the Occupied Territories, but soon started to follow the language of the officials in the Interior Ministry and called it Judea, Samaria and the Gaza Strip – a reference that would become obligatory under the Likud in 1977 (and imposed on radio and television broadcasts as well).[26]

Every passing day made the disentanglement of Israel from the West Bank impossible, and while Israeli diplomats in yet another peace conference convened by President Carter in 1977 would talk about 'territorial compromise' with Jordan, facts on the ground rendered anything like this both insignificant and irrelevant. This was seven years too late. What mattered was a master plan prepared in 1970 by the Ministry of the Interior entitled 'A Blueprint for Physical and Regional Planning' for the Occupied Territories, a plan that considered the next stages in the colonization of the Palestinian territories. The geographer Elisha Porath was asked by the ministry to work on the plan and he eventually published it as a scholarly work.[27]

The blueprint explained how areas such as the Dead Sea and the Jordan Valley would be incorporated into Israel without their *de jure* annexation. It also suggested a new means of expanding the land robbery – 'agricultural expansion' that would include not only land pillage but also taking over water resources (the option of connecting new Jewish colonies to the water system in Israel was specifically ruled out). Not everything it proposed was eventually implemented; such was the fate of the recommendation to evict the refugee camps and push the refugees into larger villages and by that 'developing the periphery of Judea and Samaria so that they could be integrated into the rest of the country'.[28]

In order to make sure that unexpected agencies or bodies would not interrupt this land pillage, a crucial step was taken in 1971 when a special decree on the law of urban, rural and building planning (Judea and Samaria), No. 418, was passed. This decree transferred almost all the authority to plan to a new supreme council for planning. The vast majority of its members were representatives of the Israeli military rule.[29]

Thus from above the new project was a wish to strengthen the Jewish presence in the West Bank, and to a lesser extent in the Gaza Strip. The reality, however, was also shaped by the new licence given to the settler movement that emerged in 1968 and was intensively seeking new locations for building colonies in the midst of the Palestinian areas. However, their impact was not felt until the Likud came to power in 1977.

Chapter Nine

On the Road to the Intifada, 1977–1987

On 26 September 1975 Menachem Begin, the leader of what would become the Likud, then in opposition, promised that, if elected, he would never return territories Israel had occupied in the June 1967 war.[1] Either by design or by unexpected development, it transpired that he was only referring to the West Bank and the Gaza Strip (and in a way to the Golan Heights as well). When, soon after Begin's election, Egypt's President Anwar Sadat made a historic visit to Jerusalem, he did give up territories, but only the Sinai Peninsula. The Camp David Accord that followed was presented as a peace effort that included Palestine's future, but this reference to Palestine was lip service by an Egyptian president who opted to take Egypt out of the conflict with Israel, even if the price was leaving the occupation intact.

The Likud took office in May 1977 with the promise of annexing the West Bank and the Gaza Strip to Israel. Its electorate, mainly from the Mizrahi Jewish community, voted for the party in the hope of improving their socio-economic conditions. This is probably why most of them did not much care when it transpired that, all in all, the Likud continued the same policies, of control without annexation, of the previous government.

THE REIGN OF THE SETTLERS, 1977–1987

If there were a difference, it was in the Likud's close ties with the settler movement, Gush Emunim. However, there is a clear continuity with the colonization of Palestine before 1967 and after. The impulse for taking over the West Bank and the Gaza Strip is the same that led the Zionist leadership to ethnically cleanse much of Palestine in 1948 and to other policies of oppression and dispossession implemented against the Palestinians wherever they were. This is why the veteran ideologues of the Zionist Labour movement played such a crucial role in the lobby for allowing Jews to settle in the Occupied Territories after 1967.

The settler movement itself was located conveniently, from the perspective of Israel's external image, on the right of the Israeli political system, and thus could easily be distinguished from the secular, social democratic Zionist forces that had conceived and exercised the policy of dispossession since 1882. In essence, however, this colonization drive was born in 1882 and not in 1967.

The two motivating forces of the Likud, to cater for the socio-economic problems of marginalized Jewish groups, the Mizrahi and the ultra-Orthodox Jews, and a commitment to a Greater Israel, were fused into the particular impact the new government had on the nature of the Judaization of the West Bank.

Mizrahi Jews from poor neighbourhoods were offered a new life in the West Bank settlements (and to an extent also in the Gaza Strip settlements). They would later be referred to as economic settlers, namely those who, so the Israeli left hoped (in vain), might be returned to Israel with financial compensation. Their younger generation would be indoctrinated by the settler movement (one such graduate was Yigal Amir who assassinated Yitzhak Rabin in November 1995).

The ultra-Orthodox who had been crammed into inhabitable slums in Jerusalem and Bnei-Brak near Tel Aviv moved to new exclusive ultra-Orthodox towns in the West Bank. Apart from serving the demographic strategy of the Likud government, they were also allowed to create for themselves autonomous theocratic enclaves, immune from Israel's legal practices or cultural norms.

Thus, ultra-Orthodox non-Zionist Jews created their devout entities that were not tolerated in the more secular Jewish State and could impose the rule of exclusion and inclusion – which was impossible within the pre-1967 borders. If you want to know what the ultimate theocratic Jewish State looks like, you should visit one of these enclaves.

The isolated colony of Kedumim, one of the veteran post-1967 settlements, still exists today as an Orthodox enclave where women wearing trousers are not welcome and men dress like early American settlers in the Wild West, down to their beards and guns in their holsters, like Al-Qaeda fighters. In such colonies the synagogue is the centre of the community and the rabbis' sermons are a mixture of anti-Arab racism and Jewish messianism.

The colonies also developed as the equivalent of offshore tax havens. Cheap Palestinian labour was employed, taxes were cut, as the Likud government regarded these colonies as deserving preferential treatment since they were located in 'security risk' areas, which granted them special tax concessions and allowed for subsidy in every aspect of life.[2]

A kind of dualism developed. On the one hand, the colonization became the main tool for downsizing the Palestinian presence in the occupied areas and the settlers became an integral part of Israeli rule in the Occupied Territories. On the other hand, some sections of this community created a state within a state, which was both challenging and affecting the more secular nature of the Jewish State inside the pre-1967 borders.

However, the main change from the previous decade was the licence to act freely given by the Likud government to the more ideological religious national settlers. The integration of the more violent settler activity within the overall structure of control was not a feature everyone in the bureaucracy of the occupation welcomed. But the hooligans and vigilantes among the settlers who frequently carried out their own punitive actions, such as uprooting trees, burning fields or in general harassing Palestinians, were tolerated, as their activity added to the accentuation of Israel's control and presence, especially on the liminal boundaries between the 'pure' Palestinian enclaves and the newly defined 'no-go areas' for anyone who was not a Jew.

In 1982 Yitzhak Mordechai, the central region commander, decided that a reserve company of settlers would be employed in the Hebron area as a 'regional defence unit'. This model was taken up elsewhere, with settlers serving as soldiers near their colonies, quite often empowering them to intimidate and abuse the local population even more.[3]

THE SHARONIZATION OF THE MEGA-PRISON: THE FIRST PHASE, 1977–1987

As noted at the end of the previous chapter, there were clear signs that the Palestinians would not surrender totally to an Israeli dictate. Nonetheless, the Begin government (1977–1981) continued to act as if the formula of an open prison would be attractive to most Palestinians. Begin, notwithstanding his inflammatory rhetoric as opposition leader, was willing as a prime minister to trust the policy-makers of the past, and in particular Moshe Dayan.

Dayan, as the newly appointed Foreign Minister, stepped up the marketing of the open prison as a peace plan and found allies in the Arab world who accepted it as a permanent solution for the Occupied Territories. This was the 'autonomy plan' Dayan brought to the Israeli–Egyptian peace talks in 1979, which included twenty-six points. All of them in one way or another assumed that the territory's sovereignty, control and resources were to remain for ever in the hands of Israel, while the Palestinians, apart from those living in areas designated for Jewish colonization, would enjoy 'autonomy'.[4]

The PLO did not remain idle in the face of these developments and intensified its struggle outside Israel, announcing its rejection of this Egyptian–Jordanian–Israeli engineering of the Palestinian issue. In March 1978 the PLO was trying to make its mark on the conflict by hijacking a bus on the way from the north to Tel Aviv and executed an operation that went badly wrong, ending with the death of thirty-five Israeli citizens. This botched operation gave the Israeli army the ostensible reason to occupy southern Lebanon and meddle in the Lebanese civil war (which had broken out three years earlier) by creating its own militia there, the Southern Lebanese Army (SLA), after completing the occupation of southern Lebanon up to the Litani River.[5] Two thousand Palestinians and Lebanese lost their lives in this operation (twenty Israeli soldiers also died), and yet another quarter of a million Palestinians and some Lebanese were expelled and had to move north of the river.[6] A new UN body was created, UNIFIL, which observed a shaky truce after the operation and involved the international body in the murky waters of Israel's northern front with more complications yet to unfold in the future. As a precursor of things to come, shortly after the first UNIFIL soldiers appeared their barracks were shelled by the SLA, killing eight members of the UN peace force.[7]

The Litani operation, as it was called, was a prelude to a new piece in the overall strategic Israeli puzzle in Palestine. Its aim was to persuade domestic and international public opinion that there was no credible alternative, or force, to Israel's unilateral management of the occupation and that only the Jewish State could determine the future of the West Bank and the Gaza Strip.

The new piece in the puzzle was translated into an active war against the PLO with the aim of eliminating this alternative voice. The architect of this part of the strategy was Ariel Sharon.

The 1973 war hero had, by 1977, become a shrewd politician. The muscle man had turned into an obese, bulky leader whose uncontrollable appetite for good food matched his craving for more land and settlements all over historical Palestine.

His first appointment was Minister of Agriculture, which came about when Ezer Weizman resigned as Minister of Defence. As long as Weizman was in office, the Begin government pursued more dovish policies towards the Occupied Territories based on the autonomy plan agreed with Egypt. In 1980 Weizman felt that he did not receive genuine backing for this policy from Begin and left office bitterly.

Sharon hoped to replace him, but Begin, wisely at that time of his life, resisted the temptation and refused to appoint him to this powerful position. Yet, a different Begin would emerge after the elections of 1981: a weaker and more disoriented man, easily manipulated by those around him. The door was now open for Sharon's appointment to the coveted Ministry of Defence. Begin claimed in retrospect that he appointed Sharon as he needed him to dismantle the Jewish settlements in the south and north of the Sinai Peninsula in order to fulfil Israel's obligation under the peace treaty with Egypt, which required Israel to withdraw fully from the peninsula.[8] This might also have paved the way for Sharon to reach the top. It should be said that Sharon delivered the goods, and the eviction of the settlers there was completed in April 1982.

Sharon now had licence to kill the PLO in whichever way he deemed necessary. His first aim was to disconnect as much as possible the Palestinian territories from their national leadership and movement. Together with his generals in the army he escalated the tensions on Israel's northern border – preparing for a full invasion of Lebanon in order to eliminate the PLO presence there.[9]

His strategy in Lebanon was compounded by a similarly harsh policy in the West Bank and the Gaza Strip. One of Sharon's earlier moves was to disband the national bodies that emerged after the 1976 municipal elections, and the first one he dismantled was Lajnat al-Tawjih, an organization that attempted to coordinate activities during the first Intifada.[10]

Since 1977, Sharon had been trying to deepen the level of collaboration and lower the resistance by founding what he believed would be his kind of leadership (an old Zionist, and generally colonial, tactic of finding the leaders of your own choice). It is not clear whether the personalities to whom he gave his blessing saw themselves as his agents or acted in ways that satisfied him – in any case it was a short-lived episode. The outfits he was encouraging were the brainchild of his orientalist advisor, a professor from the Hebrew University, Menachem Milson.

Milson was brought into the picture as part of another piece in Sharon's overall strategy of trying to establish the open prison as a permanent solution. Sharon abolished military rule in an act that should have enraged the international community since it signalled the end of the Israeli charade of temporality of the occupation. If there was no military rule, it meant that there was no military occupation and hence the areas Israel had taken in 1967 were now part of Israel to all intents and purposes. But the world, in particular the USA, maintained the attitude of 'don't ask, don't tell'.

The military rule was replaced by a Civil Administration for Judea, Samaria and the Gaza Strip and Milson was appointed its first head.[11] Part of this body's authority was transferred to the Palestinian Authority in 1995. So if one day there is a sovereign state in Palestine (namely, in the West Bank and the Gaza Strip), perhaps this step will be regarded as a positive landmark on the way to Palestinian statehood. I have serious doubts about this as an appropriate narrative: the narrative of an incremental politicide of the Palestinians, which is how the late Baruch Kimmerling described Sharon's strategy, seems a more appropriate way of looking at things at this moment in time.[12]

Milson's main interlocutor on the ground was the former Jordanian Minister of Agriculture, Mustafa Dudin. Together they founded the Village Leagues, ostensibly an attempt to improve local life in the rural areas, but in essence a ploy to create an alternative leadership to that of the PLO. The Leagues were hated by most, but enlisted tens of thousands of members. The head of the League in Ramallah, Yusuf al-Khatib, was assassinated. The alleged personal corruption of the major personalities involved in the Leagues did even less to endear them to the occupied people. The height of their activity was a meeting in 1982 in which they created a movement for democracy calling for peace with, and according to the terms of,

Israel (among other issues they declared giving up the Right of Return for the 1948 refugees). When Milson was replaced as the head of the Civil Administration, his successors, in particular Fuad Ben-Eliezer, later on an Israeli Minister of Defence from the Labour party, disbanded them and banned their activity altogether. He described the League members as 'quislings'.[13]

Sharon's strategy was not only based on destroying the PLO inside and outside or building alternative leadership; intensifying colonization was also an important part of the puzzle. With Sharon's encouragement, the settlers adopted more aggressive colonization tactics. One of the most notorious groups, the settlers of Beit Hadassah in the heart of the old city of Khalil, Hebron, was already making its mark as one of the more fanatic and aggressive bunch of settlers.

At the very beginning of May 1980, the harassed Palestinians had had enough and in reprisal killed six settlers. The punishment was quick in coming and was a typically stark violation of international law and human rights. The mayor of Khalil, its Qadi (judge in a Shari'a court) and the mayor of the nearby town Halhul were expelled at the end of that month. Typical of this method of official punishment, it was accompanied by vigilante retaliation by the settlers themselves who planted bombs in the cars of Bassam Shaq'a, the mayor of Nablus, and Karim Khalaf, the mayor of Ramallah, both of whom were badly injured. This turned out to be a step too far for the government, who feared this could become a 'Jewish Underground', which is indeed what happened. It transpired that a group of vigilantes was operating under the name 'The Jewish Underground'. They were caught while preparing a terrorist attack on Haram al-Sharif, the Temple Mount, with the intention of blowing up the mosques there,[14] and were eventually outlawed by the secret service and the army.

While the right-wing government was unhappy about having such vigilante terrorist activity carried out in its name, it looked for other and no less brutal ways to unilaterally solidify the new reality that Israel had created in the West Bank and the Gaza Strip in the aftermath of the 1967 war. Apart from the action against the local

leadership and the PLO in Lebanon, the Begin government acceler-
ated the annexation of Jerusalem by passing a new law on 30 July
1980 that defied all the UN resolutions on the city and granted Israel
exclusive sovereignty over it. When powerful voices of condemnation
from the Vatican, the Muslim world and European powers had no
impact on the reality on the ground, it showed once more the immunity from criticism that Israel enjoyed.

Sharon's principal activity, however, was in dramatically expanding the Judaized areas in the Occupied Territories, and in particular
in the West Bank. The image of his bulky figure, hopping from one
hill to another, usually with the aid of a helicopter and a huge bundle
of rolled-up maps under one arm, were engraved on the Israeli public
consciousness, a testimony to his determination and commitment to
the colonization project.

More specifically, Sharon was looking for ways of overcoming the
hurdle put in his way by the Israeli Supreme Court, which ruled that
only public land could be confiscated. Under his guidance, and with
the help of the legal experts of the military rule in the Occupied
Territories, the Civil Administration, land ownership there was rede-
fined in a way that allowed Israel to claim that much of the land was,
or would become, state (public) land. One of the leading bureaucrats
in the military administration came up with the idea in a meeting
Sharon had with all of the relevant officials following another clear
decision by the Supreme Court not to allow confiscation of private
land. This individual was what one might call an 'orientalist' – an
expert on such subjects as Ottoman law – and he suggested that
certain land in the West Bank could be defined as *mawat*, or 'dead'
land, in accordance with the Ottoman land law of the nineteenth
century. According to that law, land that was not cultivated for three
years could pass into the hands of the Ottoman Empire or state. The
next day, Sharon flew off in his helicopter, and in an apparently endless
exercise pointed out to his subordinates from the air land that looked
deserted, before flying back to instruct his staff toiling away at the
drawing board to include it as *mawat* land on the map. It goes without

saying that the Ottoman experience was entirely irrelevant to the colonization of the West Bank and the Gaza Strip, but it was part of the tacit agreement between the Supreme Court and the existing bureaucracy as to how to kosherize, within a respectable legal infrastructure, the colonization of more and more areas within the West Bank.[15]

So the judicial system legalized the land robbery *a priori* and retrospectively. Such a powerful tool enabled the bureaucrats to grab any land it wanted from either the West Bank or the Gaza Strip for Jewish settlement, military bases or anything else that was needed to swallow the territories, and without the people.

By 1979 the area that was first confiscated for urgent military requirements had been transformed into colonies, such as Matityahu, Neve Zuf, Rimonim, Beit El, Kochav Hashahar, Alon Shevut, Elazar, Efrat, Har Gilo, Migdal Oz, Gitit, Yitav, Qiryat Arba and others. Some of them had grown into little towns and others remained small communities. This new urban sprawl served not only the purpose of territorial expansion of the Jewish State, but also provided major observation and monitoring centres in the midst of the mega-prison the Israelis had built.

The Likud government did, in fact, obey one injunction by the Supreme Court that had pronounced the transformation of military bases into colonies illegal. But this first ever ruling of the court in accordance with international law did not protect the Palestinians from further pillage – it only caused a change in the method, not in the purpose, of the Israeli policies.

By 1985 Israel had taken over 2,150,000 dunams, 39 per cent of the West Bank.[16] Almost all of it was public land as previously defined by the Jordanian authorities. The next step was the takeover of private land to complete total spatial control of the West Bank. The expropriation of private land was something never attempted by the Jordanian authorities, nor before that by the British Mandate. Moreover, even the seizure of public land by the Jordanians was limited to the establishment of a few military bases. The appropriation of private land was carried out through Ariel Sharon's trickery, devised by the legal apparatus of the military rule of turning private land into *mawat*, in an absurd interpretation of the mid-nineteenth-century Ottoman law.

Contrary to popular belief, the later Oslo Accord was not a game changer in this respect. The accord, even during its more optimistic phase, introduced only minor changes to this Israeli spatial control. A new wave of energetic decrees followed the 'peace process', continuing the settlement expansion. What was new was the addition of dozens of bypasses and roads for Jewish use only – for which private land was expropriated, as all the public land had already been taken.

A more complex, but equally effective, spatial takeover occurred in East Jerusalem, which was officially annexed to Israel early on and therefore the same legal practices that were employed in Israel itself from 1948 until 1967 were intact here. So while Ottoman and Jordanian laws were used to justify the takeover of land in the West Bank and the Gaza Strip, in East Jerusalem, as they had been since 1970, the Israeli government activated Mandatory laws for expropriation of land (as it did in the Galilee and the Negev). There was very little state or public land there as most of the land stolen in Jerusalem was private.

In both Greater Jerusalem and the rest of the Occupied Territories, limiting Palestinian space was achieved not only through expropriation of land and Jewish colonization. Other means included decrees and regulations that prevented extensions of building and licence fees for new ones that were beyond the ability of the average Palestinian to pay.

All these initial efforts of de-Arabizing and Judaizing the occupied space were fused into a more systematic policy with the appointment of Ariel Sharon as the Minister of Housing in the wake of his removal from the Ministry of Defence, in circumstances that will be discussed presently, following the public inquiry into his role in the Sabra and Shatila massacre in 1982. He would remain in this and similar ministerial posts (such as the Minister for the National Infrastructure), which gave him ample resources and licence to expand the Jewish colonization of the Occupied Territories. It was only when he became Prime Minister in 2001 that he and his deputy and successor, Ehud Olmert, in their newly founded party Kadima, would slightly change Israeli policy. They would remove the Jewish settlers from the Gaza Strip and expand even more the Jewish presence in the West Bank.

Sharon's principal contribution to the solidification of the mega-prison was a systematic approach that removed any ambiguity in the implementation of the 1967 strategy. He brought colonization to every corner of the West Bank.

One significant change was the exclusion of Palestinians from planning bodies and committees. Finding, for instance, that there were token Palestinians in the Planning Council, Sharon replaced it with a new one called the Chamber of Planning, which had hardly any Palestinian members. The Chamber of Planning was an incredible exercise in cynicism and deception. Officially, its remit was to help with the future development of the 400 Palestinian villages in the West Bank in the next decade (the 1980s). When the Chamber announced it would look into planning issues concerning such a large number of villages in the West Bank, what it meant in essence was that it would search for further ways of confining and containing these villages in order to limit their natural expansion and growth. Such decisions eventually became a mirror image of those taken with regard to the Jewish colonies; those taken with regard to Palestinians were intended to curb the natural growth of the population while the Jewish ones were meant to encourage such growth and development. To the outside world this newspeak bought Israel immunity from criticism – after all, what was wrong with catering to the needs of the occupied rural areas?[17]

As noted before in reference to Glenn Bowman's term 'encystation', forbidding the rural or urban development of Palestinians in the Occupied Territories was plan B for the ethnic cleansing of Palestine. Expulsion was the preferred alternative, encystation the second best.

THE COLLAPSE OF THE OPEN-PRISON MODEL

On 3 June 1982 an attempt was made on the life of the Israeli ambassador in London, Shlomo Argov, while he was leaving a dinner party at the Dorchester Hotel. Hussein Ghassan Said, the would-be assassin, was a member of Abu Nidal – an organization for all seasons. No one ever knew who was employing whom at any point in the story of this group. We know that at one point the group's founder, Abu Nidal, also worked for the CIA and among his victims were many PLO members after he left the organization in 1973.[18]

But, of course, the identity of the killer was of no interest to Ariel Sharon, who had been preparing an overall assault on Lebanon ever since his appointment as Minister of Defence. The next day, he ordered a massive aerial bombardment of PLO bases in Lebanon and used the PLO response to activate a plan he had already prepared in 1981. Most accounts say he presented the government with a minimal plan for invasion while enacting a wider one that included, ultimately, the occupation of Beirut and beyond.[19] Israeli atrocities in that war were recorded in Seán MacBride's report to the UN in 1983. This Irish statesman, then chair of the UN General Assembly, documented, with his other committee members, the war crimes in great detail. The report was shelved and was completely ignored by the international community. The only global outrage the invasion triggered was the Israeli collaboration with the Maronite Christian militias in the Sabra and Shatila massacre in September 1982. So great was the outcry that it forced Begin to remove Sharon from the Ministry of Defence.[20]

Tragically, these horrific events in Lebanon – and this is always true about the correlation between regional developments and Palestine – did not affect Sharon's strategy in the Occupied Territories.

Out of that particular ministry and in command of other ministries, Sharon intensified the strangulation policies in the Occupied Territories well into the mid-1980s. The facts he established on the ground drove home the message of what life would be like in years to come. If the occupied people looked for guidance to their principal representative body, the PLO, they would have found very little response. Since the destruction of its headquarters in the 1982 Israeli invasion of Lebanon, it was too far away in Tunis and too disempowered to assist. In the immediate years preceding the first Intifada, it was busy looking for a rapprochement with Jordan, but to no avail, as the Hashemite dynasty was distancing itself from any involvement in the West Bank, as were most of the member states of the Arab League.[21]

Inspiration came from elsewhere – from the resistance in Lebanon, by both Palestinian and Shi'ite fighters. At the beginning of 1985 policymakers in Israel were deeply involved in the Lebanese quagmire. Although the Occupied Territories were relatively calm, the constant interchange of Israeli troops on duty from occupied southern Lebanon, where there was active fighting, to the West Bank and Gaza Strip, where they just had to police the areas, has blurred the boundaries of the two arenas. The time was ripe in both occupied areas to try a more active resistance: the armed one in Lebanon was more successful, the non-violent one in Palestine was less effective.

From 1985 to 1987 the Israeli army treated the two occupied areas in the same way. Even before the first Intifada, the Israeli army employed what it called an 'iron fist' policy towards any sign of resistance. The open-prison model was slowly collapsing. The iron fist policy was executed not by the Likud alone: in 1984 the Likud and Labour formed a unity government that would hold power until 1989. The callous, punitive policy of that government preceded the uprising. Gad Yaacobi, who was the Minister of Finance in that government, said years later that the policy was not really a retaliation against Palestinian activity, since there was very little activity. The unity government, he asserted, wanted to accelerate what he called the 'creeping de-facto annexation' policy. In hindsight he regretted that policy, writing that it 'contributed to a growing militancy of the Palestinian society'.[22] Thus the Israelis themselves could not stick for too long to the open-prison model.

The only feature of the open prison that remained in place until the first Intifada was the right to work in Israel. Already by 1977, half of the occupied areas' hired workers were employed in Israel (it grew from 5000 in 1969 to about 100,000 in the 1980s) and the Palestinian areas became, after the US, the second preferred destination of Israeli exports.[23]

This 'privilege' was actually the right to participate in a modern-day slave market – working with no social rights or health insurance, no unions or labour rights. The privilege, so to speak, was still granted until the outbreak of the second Intifada. The first Intifada produced some fifty instances of frustrated Palestinian employees venting their fury on their employers, or random people in the street, more often than not using a knife. This wave of violence reached a peak in 1989 and it was the pretext for the beginning of a new policy of barring and limiting Palestinian workers in Israel. The labour market preferred young males, but the security system now barred more and more young men in Israeli building companies, agricultural markets and in other non-skilled occupations in which a labour force was needed.

Israeli experts, who were surprised by the outbreak of the first Intifada, put some of the explanation down to the socio-economic conditions in the Occupied Territories, which they deemed to have dramatically improved under Israeli rule.[24] Their Palestinian counterparts disagreed vehemently. They claimed that the Occupied Territories' economy was run very much like that of a colony during the colonial period. Such policies created a total dependency of the colony on the colonist, and in the case of the Palestinian areas led to the ruination of both agriculture and industry. Even if wage earners briefly had a 15 per cent rise in their monthly earnings, compared to the pre-occupation period, with no infrastructure for investment or savings and the rise of the cost of living, this did not mean much at the end of the day. To this can be added the lack of access to traditional Arab export markets and unrestricted competition from cheap Israeli products. Israeli restrictions on Palestinian economic activity and the Israeli claims for land and water resources during the expansion of settlements rendered the additional income insignificant in the long run for most Palestinians.[25]

And yet, this was still a more complex reality, as long as the open-prison model persisted. The most troubling aspect of it was that any rights to work in Israel, or even to earn a reasonable wage in the Occupied Territories, were not rights at all – they were rewards. 'Rewards' for good behaviour only exist in the world of the prison and detention centres. But within this context it is important to note that the open-prison model enabled daily commuters such as merchants, students and workers to move freely on the main roads.

But it was still a prison, and as much a part of this everyday reality was the Israelis' constant and systematic punitive policy against the Palestinian people. From 1967 to 1982 Israel's military government demolished 1338 Palestinian homes on the West Bank. Also over this period, more than 300,000 Palestinians were detained by Israeli security forces without trial for various lengths of time.[26]

It is indicative of the official Israeli mindset that the oppressive side of the open-prison model never seemed to register in the Jewish State's overall strategy. In the analysis of the first Intifada by both mainstream politicians and academics, the collapse of the open-prison model was almost exclusively attributed to what were deemed to be faulty prisoner exchanges back in 1985. This was a deal struck with Ahmed Jibril's PFLP organization in the wake of the successful Palestinian abduction of Israeli soldiers in Lebanon. The theory, put forward in the most widely read book in Israel about the first Intifada, by Ze'ev Schiff, the late *Haaretz* chief military correspondent, and Ehud Ya'ari, Israeli television's leading orientalist, was that those released in the deal incited the population and instigated violence.[27] One reason for the Israeli retrospective attempt to explain the uprising on the Jibril deal, was a genuine inability to grasp the level of Palestinian suffering and the evil nature of the Israeli oppression, as the main causes for the uprising. This is why the Minister of Defence at the time, Yitzhak Rabin, did not bother to interrupt his visit to the USA and return home when the Intifada broke out. He assumed it was a routine disruption that would soon be over.

Finally, in this period it is possible to provide a fine distinction between the West Bank and the Gaza Strip. Human rights organizations took their time in providing a better idea of the living standards and conditions under the occupation. The first reports suggested that overall conditions in the Strip were incomparably better and this is confirmed by a kind of oral history of the Strip that one can intuitively refer to; there were, in the words of one report, 'lesser levels of distress'. This could be attributed to stronger traditional structures of society and a greater sense of cohesiveness and solidarity.[28]

In August 1987 the Israeli military in the West Bank and the Gaza Strip published a booklet proudly announcing how successful its rule in the last twenty years had been. Colour photographs of happy Palestinians were juxtaposed with black and white pictures of gloomy Palestinians from the pre-June 1967 period. The main reason for such pride was the increased standard of living in comparison to the 1950s. Who is to say it would not have grown under Jordanian rule as well, but that was hardly the point. When, four months later, the first Intifada erupted it was clear that the improved standard of living, if indeed this is what it had been, was part of the open-prison concept against which the Palestinians rose. The booklet was withdrawn hastily from bookshops at the beginning of the Intifada.[29]

But anyone with an eye for the future – and there were a few, men such as the former deputy mayor of Jerusalem turned independent researcher and observer, Meron Benvenisti – understood that the 'facts on the ground' policy dramatically changed the West Bank and the Gaza Strip to such an extent that one uprising could not turn the clock back – as it turned out, two uprisings could not do it either.[30] What changed most was the physical landscape of the Occupied Territories in a way that fundamentally limited the living space of their inhabitants. It wasn't just the geography that was altered beyond recognition; the demography was transformed as well. Intensive Jewish colonization was accompanied by the stealthy transfer of

Palestinians who left and were not allowed to return. The number of people deported for political activity – quite often without any official charge – was, in 1987 alone, around 1500.[31] Ostensibly, the reason for issuing a deportation order was to pre-empt any terrorist activity from the individual being deported. In practice, however, deportation more than once served as a punitive action.

Deportation of residents from their homes in occupied territory, whether to another place in the occupied territory or to somewhere outside the territory, is prohibited by international humanitarian law. However, international humanitarian law provides small exceptions by which the occupying state may evacuate residents from their homes, for 'imperative military reasons' or for the greater security of the local population. In such cases, the evacuation must be temporary and, during that time, the occupying power must ensure the basic needs of the evacuees. Israel's previous deportation policy failed to meet either of these criteria and therefore was flagrantly in breach of international humanitarian law (not that anyone who drafted that law could seriously have believed occupation could continue for more than four decades!). On top of that, quite often deportees had no idea why they were being treated in such a way.[32]

With the coming to power of the Likud, the Labour party would become more vociferous about such violations. A new reality developed on the Israeli political map: a voice (which had a party or two representing it in the parliament) that wanted to see nothing less than an unconditional end to the occupation, and which was aroused when blatant violations of human rights were reported, succeeded in enlisting the support of about 100,000 Jews on a good day, and half of that for the rest of the year. This was the anti-occupation Zionist left, as ineffective then as it is today. It never associated the occupation with the ills of Zionism itself and therefore could not provide an alternative policy to the centre and right of the map – the one that faithfully implemented the strategic decisions described in the opening pages of this book.

A few of them did make the connection. The most Zionist among them was Boaz Evron, who left his comfort zone of power and influence for the sake of fighting the occupation; his was one of the lone voices crying in the Zionist wilderness. I make no mention of the others here because I feel they are already well known, but for some reason Evron does not appear among those who deserve to be recorded as part of a more genuine, and less Zionist, dissident movement.[33]

Evron was a senior journalist who wrote for a number of newspapers, including *Haaretz*, and a well-known publicist. What made him cross the line should have alerted many others, but alas it did not. He was moved by the monologue of a soldier who wrote in his kibbutz journal (every kibbutz in Israel has a kind of 'village voice') of what he had seen and done in the occupied West Bank. The soldier told how he and his comrades entered a Palestinian school, locked about twenty eight-year-old boys in a classroom, threw in some gas grenades and kept the children in there for quite a while, causing such panic that at least half of them jumped out of the windows, breaking their legs in the fall. This was a punishment for stone throwing by students from a nearby college, who were not caught. What drew Evron's attention was not so much the horrific story itself, but the fact that the soldier who published the story in a kibbutz publication seemed to believe that telling the story absolved him and his friends from his actions. The same applied to a group of soldiers in a famous publication, soon after the June 1967 war, entitled *Conversations Between Soldiers*. The uneasiness Evron felt in 1967 became a review of liberal Zionism and its role in sanitizing and disguising the horrors of Zionist colonization and occupation since 1882.[34]

And maybe at the end of the day, given the randomness of the event that eventually triggered the first Intifada, a road accident in the Gaza Strip, it was the daily abuse of basic human and civil rights that became both the hallmark of the 'enlightened occupation' and the most hated aspect of it.

Chapter Ten

The First Intifada, 1987–1993

On 8 December 1987 a truck that killed four inhabitants of the Jabaliyya refugee camp in Gaza became the event that signalled the beginning of the first uprising, or the Intifada. Later, historians would point to other discrete violent events before and around that date which signalled the 'official' beginning of the revolt. With historical hindsight we understand better today that it was not these particular incidents themselves that were so significant but, rather, the local and popular reaction to them; a reaction that for a while transformed radically the reality on the ground. The way the occupied people reacted to the December 1987 accident triggered a response unprecedented in its intensity and scope. Not since 1937 had Palestine witnessed such mass popular participation against oppression and dispossession.

A week later, six Palestinians had already been killed in the brutal Israeli retaliation to the stone throwing, demonstrations and make-shift roadblocks. The number of dead Palestinians rose dramatically in the first few months of the Intifada, most of them killed in non-violent demonstrations. This was followed by mass arrests and a puni-tive policy aimed at paralysing life in the Occupied Territories: schools were forced to shut down, shops and businesses were closed and people stayed at home.[1]

The international community responded as never before to the occupation. The Palestinians were virtually and visually depicted as brave 'Davids' confronting ruthless 'Goliaths' and the images of young boys slinging a stone at a tank became a hallmark of this uprising. Condemnation was heard everywhere and the UN Security Council was obliged to intervene when the repertoire of punitive Israeli actions started to include mass expulsions as well as other means of coercion. Resolutions 607 and 608 of the Security Council ordered Israel to stop these actions, to no avail.[2]

It is hard to define chronologically the Intifada, but it lasted more or less for six years. One thousand Palestinians were killed by the Israelis and more than 120,000 were arrested, many of them under the age of sixteen.[3]

As mentioned in the previous chapter, the open-prison model gradually collapsed. Several causes contributed to this. The scholarly and popular literature summarized well the reasons for the initiation of what was overall a campaign of civil disobedience and demonstrations. The uprising was attributed first and foremost to the abuse described so far in this book. Other factors were the economic oppression, the suppression of national rights, the frontal attack on the PLO inside the territories and outside in 1982, the indifference of the Arab world and a peace process that insisted on finding a way of partitioning the West Bank and the Gaza Strip between the Hashemite Kingdom of Jordan and Israel.[4]

The uprising was initiated by activists on the ground. A new body, the Unified National Leadership, directed the uprising; so impressed were they with its effectiveness in coordinating the non-violent resistance (namely, an alternative to the PLO) that two Israeli scholars defined this as the 'alternative leadership'.[5] This leadership worked mainly through the dissemination of leaflets – the same way, twenty years later, that activists would use Facebook and Twitter for similar purposes. The new body included representatives of the four main PLO factions of the time: Fatah, the PFLP, the Democratic Front for the Liberation of Palestine and the Palestinian People's Party. This body formulated the strategy in the early days of the Intifada, in tandem with local ad hoc organizations and a certain level of coordination with the PLO headquarters in Tunis. This synergy propelled a campaign that wanted to compel the world to notice the occupation and one that hoped to induce the international community to act against the continued oppression and occupation.

The uprising began in the Jabaliyya refugee camp in Gaza in December 1987. At least, this is the accepted historiographical version: it actually seems that it erupted in different places at the same time. It was a composition of civil action and resistance: general strikes, boycott of Israeli goods, refusal to pay Israeli taxes, the famous stone throwing at the occupation forces and here and there Molotov cocktails. It also included, alas, account settling with collaborators, a painful reminder of the venom that occupation injects into the bodies and minds of the occupied.[6]

Israel reacted to this basically non-violent uprising with great violence. From the very start the Israeli political and military elite was directed by one basic impulse – anger – and hence most of the Israeli actions in the first year of the Intifada were punitive in nature. The metaphor of prison wardens acting against rebellious inmates seems particularly relevant for our case study. This was graphically instructed by Yitzhak Rabin, the Defence Minister, when he toured the Jalazone refugee camp near Ramallah. He stated: 'The first priority of the security forces is to prevent violent demonstrations with force, power and blows . . . We will make it clear who is running the territories.'[7] These blows and the force were translated in many cases into a killing spree that left a large number of demonstrators dead.[8]

The outside world watched in bewilderment, as if for the first time ever it was the Israelis rather than the Palestinians who were using force. Those who could still bring themselves to challenge Israel's impunity added a new euphemism to the lexicon of double talk and newspeak with which the Western world discussed Israel: Israeli policies became 'manual management' of the occupation and therefore, as shocking as their actions may have been deemed, what they did was merely to employ 'excessive use' – which could be condemned.

'Excessive use' would indeed be employed repeatedly to describe massacres, massive killings and carpet bombing from the air.[9]

At first the international community, even those among it that were usually pro-Israeli, did not buy into the new euphemism. In fact, the first condemnation of the 'excessive use of force' came from the US State Department. American officials reported to their government that from the very beginning of the uprising Israeli troops over-reacted when faced with unarmed demonstrations that followed the accident in the Jabaliyya camp. The Palestinians, so the Americans said, saw it as deliberate murder:

> Soldiers frequently used gunfire in situations that did not present mortal danger to troops, causing many avoidable deaths and inju-ries . . . IDF troops used clubs to break limbs and beat Palestinians who were not directly involved in disturbances or resisting arrest . . . At least 13 Palestinians have been reported to have died from beatings.[10]

This 'overreaction', reported the Americans, escalated as the uprising went on. On 22 December the UN Security Council followed suit and used even stronger language in condemning Israel in Resolution 605 for violating the Geneva Convention, moved mainly by the high number of fatalities in what was basically an unarmed uprising. There was a certain chilling logic about the escalation.[11] The ineffectiveness of the international rebuke provided the immunity the occupation was seeking for quelling the uprising.

Some of the Israelis' punitive actions reminded one of pre-modern age incarceration and imprisonment methods – long outlawed in the civilized world. They included corporal punishment before and during arrests, a method particularly used with children and youths as part of the penalization operation. As the uprising continued the international community became more aware of the victimization of children that was taking place. The Swedish branch of Save the Children estimated that between 23,600 and 29,900 children required medical treatment for injuries sustained from beatings in the first two years of the Intifada, a third of whom were under the age of ten.[12]

The international response was somewhat muted when, in the years to come, the uprising was also seen as having been initiated by a new political force on the scene: Hamas. Islamophobia and an intensified struggle between Western powers and political Islamic groups worldwide gave Israel even more immunity as long as its nemesis was a 'fundamentalist' Islamic group.

Hamas thus both complicated life for the Israelis and helped them in branding the Palestinian struggle as part of a global anti-Western Islamic force involved in a clash of civilizations. This is why quite a few of the experts who wrote about the origins of Hamas accredited Israel with an important role in its foundation and emergence.

The movement was officially founded in 1987 by some members of the Muslim Brotherhood in the Gaza Strip, led by Sheikh Ahmed Yassin. He was born in 1948 Palestine in the village of Jura near Askelan (today's Ashkelon). An accident early in life left him paralysed and wheelchair-bound for the rest of his life. Like so many of the Palestinians who were ethnically cleansed in the Nakbah, his family, too, had found its way to a refugee camp in the Gaza Strip (the coastal al-Shati camp). He was a devout scholar and reader of Islam and very early on joined the Muslim Brotherhood branch in Gaza where he was politicized and became deeply involved in the struggle for a free Palestine.[13]

Yassin and his fellows were able to create a new movement mainly because there was a desperate search for a new national outfit that could deliver salvation where the old ones had failed so abysmally. The secular organizations were considered helpless in finding a way of liberating the homeland.

They also became powerful because Israel saw their emergence as a favourable counterforce to the secular national factions, and in particular Fatah.[14] The research substantiating this allegation is still thin on the ground and will probably be delayed until a more peaceful stage in the history of Palestine – if we should ever see such a thing in our lifetime.

Hamas's brand of national ideology fused with a political Islamist agenda led it to adopt policies toward the Jewish State, and not just the occupation, that Fatah was slowly forsaking when sucked into the abortive and deceptive 'peace process'. The new stances included a total rejection of Israel and clear demands about the Palestinian Right of Return. The language employed at the time, however, was strongly anti-Jewish and anti-Israeli, and although it was clear that it was still a Palestinian liberation movement fighting against a century of dispossession, colonization and occupation, and in fact one which was far more involved than other factions in charity, social welfare and education, it provided a pretext for the West to dumb down its criticism of Israel.[15] This would become even more obvious after 9/11 and the so-called War on Terror when there were attempts to associate Hamas, and its sister organization the Islamic Jihad, with international Jihad. But Hamas's pragmatism in the twenty-first century and the continued brutality of Israel have rendered that kind of justification for Israel's action irrelevant and marginal.[16]

When the shootings, the beatings and the wholescale arrests began to subside at the end of 1988, Israeli retribution was extended to include the population at large, not just those who had participated in the uprising. Once more these familiar punitive actions were read as the normal repertoire of rough treatment and severe penalties commonly exercised in the world of the modern-day prison.

It is important, even at this late stage in the book, to remind readers once more, if it is not obvious by now, that international law, and indeed civil and criminal law all around the world, state very clearly that any form of collective punishment is illegal. Clause 50 of the 1907 Hague Convention stated unequivocally the international community's rejection of such policies, and this was reiterated by the Fourth Geneva Convention in Clause 33 of 1949.[17] Needless to say, the fact that the Hague Convention was incorporated into Israeli law by legislation (although the Geneva Convention was not) had no impact whatsoever on Israel's punitive policies.

Nor did it matter that in 1981 Israel had established the Civil Administration as a body that allegedly replaced the internationally condemned military rule. Officially, this body was meant to manage the life of the people in the West Bank and the Gaza Strip in all matters that were not security oriented. However, every action of this Civil Administration had to be approved by a general in the army who was appointed as 'Active Coordinator in the Territories'. So, in essence, this was just another arm of the Israeli military continuing to inflict the same abusive and punitive actions against the local population. The army was quite inventive when it came to collective punishment against the local population; the Civil Administration had turned this repertoire of evil into a daily routine.

CIVIL ADMINISTRATION

Thus it was the Civil Administration, and not just the army, that provided, on a daily basis, the human face for what it meant to be subjected to a collective and sustained punitive action against the population as a whole. The worst was probably the restriction on the freedom of movement. The most conservative reports in the archives of memory of what that meant for an average person are the reports of the Israeli human rights organization B'Tselem; the worst come from the memories of Palestinians, still fresh in the mind twenty years or so later. Even in its most guarded way the strategy of making movement almost impossible is hard for most people living in the free world to comprehend. In that particular period, 1987 to 1993, every trip took twice as long as it should have and had to be undertaken on new, more dangerous and less reliable roads. In the open-prison days, Jerusalem was accessible to most Palestinians; it ceased to be so under the punitive code. Access to it and through it was denied for Palestinians, which meant that their financial, social, commercial and political hub was inaccessible. With time, even in more relaxed periods, the Israeli authorities retained this kind of blockade – and it would only be towards the end of 2012 that the Western world would recognize that such restriction of movement was not in response to Palestinian aggression but, rather, part of a more systematic plan for the Greater Jerusalem area. When these restrictions were accompanied by massive Jewish colonization in that area, they pre-empted any chance of implementing a two state, or any other similar political, solution. It was too late for those in the EU who believed they could contribute towards the implementation of such a solution. It was also, as always the case with the EU, a matter of stating the obvious but doing nothing to change it on the ground. The EU declared it understood that what had begun as punitive action rendered any aspiration for Palestinian independence in the West Bank impossible and unrealistic.[18] Needless to say, even in 2012 there were no repercussions from this recognition.

Movement was now governed by permits. A particular nuisance was the need to be physically present when these permits were requested. The Civil Administration had several headquarters. One of them was located on the northern border between the new Jewish colonies of Greater Jerusalem (Pisgat Ze'ev and Neve Yaakov); this was the main headquarters of the Civil Administration. All major decisions about people's lives were taken there between 1981 and 1993. The Civil Administration not only regulated the freedom of movement; it also had the power to rob anyone it wished of the right to work, to study, to build and to trade. Any such elementary activity required a permit that would be withheld or denied.[19]

The very location of this headquarters was one of the main obstacles to freedom of movement for anyone living there. As time passes and our memories become blurred, I should emphasize that I am describing here a pre-Oslo reality. It would, of course, become worse when the Oslo cartography bisected the West Bank and the Gaza Strip into official no-go areas for the Palestinians. I am describing a siege reality, long before the Israeli authorities could justify it under the pretext of defending themselves against suicide bombs and terrorism. This was a response to the 1987 attempt by the Palestinians to shake off peacefully a twenty-year-old occupation.

In those days Palestinians were not allowed to drive in this vicinity. In fact, Palestinians were prohibited from using cars in roads close to settlements, army bases or offices of the Civil Administration. The headquarters in the north-western side of Jerusalem seemed to be the source of all evil – the magnet of brutality: the closer you lived to it, the less normal your life became, to the point of it being unbearable.

This monstrous headquarters on the hill truly reflected the cynicism and inhumanity of the administration. This was a location that had to be visited frequently but could not be reached easily. You could not get there by car. Nor could you easily walk there. There was no footpath to the Civil Administration, since there was no paved way, and the only passable route was dangerously close to the Pisgat Ze'ev and Neve Yaakov settlements. 'A Palestinian who walked in this way endangered his life, as soldiers and settlers who would notice him could have harmed him,' warned a report from B'Tselem at the time.[20]

The daily routine of permits and blockades was interrupted by more severe restrictions on human movement. The worst was the frequent closures. The pretexts for such closures varied: they might be in response to Palestinian protests, a peaceful demonstration or a terrorist attack; to Jewish holidays, public events or a religious celebration in one of the many settlements. All such events were considered equally justifiable reasons for enforcing a closure.

This was the pretext, but not the usual reason, for closures. In most cases, the purpose was to tighten the supervision and the closures were used to round up people, 'suspects' as the Israelis called them, accompanied by the confiscation of 'inciting' material and the search for arms. Such actions were usually conducted with violence, leaving a scene of havoc and destruction in the homes visited. The members of the household were beaten, abused and their furniture destroyed. These victims of brutality should be given names, and I shall do this presently.

THE CALENDAR OF THE OCCUPATION

A more reduced form of closure was the curfew imposed by the army for a few days on towns and villages and during Jewish festivals on the West Bank and the Gaza Strip as a whole. This kind of action began in 1967 in the early days of the occupation and continued daily. I have chosen one year in particular, 1993, on the very eve of the Oslo Accord, to illustrate what kind of a reality the accord promised – and utterly failed – to achieve. As one NGO monitoring the curfew policy noted, 'every Palestinian living in the Occupied Territories had spent an average of 10 weeks under house curfew'.[21]

The worst period in the calendar of the occupation, apart from the aftermath of a particularly daring or violent operation by one of the Palestinian factions, was the three days around Israel's day of independence (celebrated according to the Hebrew calendar, which in 1993 occurred in April).

The town of Khan Yunis in the Gaza Strip, like all the other towns and villages in the West Bank and the Strip, was placed under military curfew for three days. This short period was enough for the army to perform its routine devastation. Muhammad Ahmad al-Astal, who was then twenty-four years old, recalled how the soldiers burst into the house where his friends usually gathered, about ten Palestinian men in all. The soldiers took four of them to another room. He remained with three other members of the family. Two of them were taken by the soldiers to a corner of the room and beaten with rifle stocks; they were also punched, slapped and kicked. He and another family member were ordered to empty the cupboard of its contents, clothing and other household items.

In his own words: 'The soldiers called me over, slapped me on the face and told me, 'You are Hamas'. I returned to empty the cupboard but I was called over again. This time they told me, 'You are Islamic Jihad', and slapped me again.' There was a third round of abuse in which he was told, 'You are PLO'. Another man in the room was treated in a similar way. Then they were both summoned: 'one soldier held me by the neck and banged our heads together'.

It turned out that in the next room the same abuse was taking place and then they were united with two men from the other room and ordered to stand facing the wall with their hands up in the air: 'the soldiers gave us back our ID cards to hold up in the air and told us to remain like this'. After half an hour the older members of the family told them the soldiers had left.[22]

Hassan Abd al-Sayidi Abu Labada, twenty-nine years old and married with two children, also a resident of Khan Yunis, was woken up by soldiers at two in the morning with a blow in the face from a soldier's rifle, followed by more blows. His brother Mannar, twenty-three years old, was taken out of his bed and thrown onto the family car, parked in the yard. The soldiers asked about the whereabouts of Jamal Abu Samhadana,[23] a man he did not know. He was punched in the face and then forced into the routine emptying of cupboards. The soldiers cut up the sofa with a knife. And in his own words:

> They found a kitchen knife in the kitchen. 'What is it?' 'It is a bread knife,' I answered. The soldiers punched me on the nose with the knife. I was wounded and bled. The soldier took a sack of rice and demanded that I empty it on the floor. I said it was only rice, so he emptied it himself and then took an oil can and poured it on the cloths and the rice. They left. Nobody was arrested and nothing was taken.[24]

Fatmah Hassan Tabashe Sufian, sixty-one years old, married and a mother of four, was woken up on 6 April 1993 at three o'clock in the morning. Soldiers broke into her house, pushed her up against the wall and asked her where her children were; they are asleep, she replied. They woke up her son Saad, thirty years old, kicking him and beating him with their hands and rifle stocks, until he was spitting blood all over the place. Her other son, Ibrahim, was badly beaten, and the B'Tselem researcher who took Fatmah's evidence testified that long after the incident he could still see signs of ecchymosis – subcutaneous bleeding – on his back. Both sons were taken out to the yard and put against a wall. The soldiers found two toy guns and began slashing the two men with them until the toys broke. Then they gathered everyone in the complex, twenty-seven people, into one room and threw in a shock grenade. Saad and Ibrahim were ordered to empty the cupboard while they were continuously beaten by the soldiers shouting at them, 'You are Hamas and we are Golani [the name of the military brigade to which they belonged].' Nor did they spare Fatmah's old, blind brother who was a hundred years old. He too was abused by the soldiers, who threw mattresses and blankets at him.[25]

Thus, every April from 1987 until 1993 this was the routine of the collective punishment. But it was not only these three days that mattered. Collective punishment in March–May 1993 robbed 116,000 Palestinian workers of their source of living, bisected the Occupied Territories into four disconnected areas and barred any access to Jerusalem.[26] Seen from that perspective, when the Oslo Accord was implemented as a territorial and security arrangement, it was just official confirmation of a policy already in place since 1987.

CONSOLIDATING METHODS OF OPPRESSION

The years 1987 to 1993 were indeed a formative period during which some of the realities of today in the West Bank, and in the Gaza Strip until 2005, were formulated. It was a time during which the bureaucracy of occupation showed its absolute power by transforming ad hoc policies, including punitive ones, into routine policies. This is how the checkpoint system was introduced to the world. It was put into systematic effect in 1993. Just before Israel publicly signed a peace agreement with the PLO, the Israeli government of the time experimented with the first set of checkpoints in Jerusalem (although these were used extensively in the Palestinian areas inside Israel during the period of the military rule there, from 1948 to 1967).[27]

Installing checkpoints started out as a policy aimed at excluding Jerusalem from the West Bank and a more determined wish to de-Palestinize it. This system was in a way the inevitable continuation of the wedge policies described in Chapter Four. The planning of the wedges and the installation of the checkpoints would later be followed by the actual and final physical construction of the wedges. So it was around 1987 that a chain of checkpoints and physical barriers appeared around the city entrances, hindering access to places of worship, employment, education, institutions and families. When the Oslo proposal was put on the table by Israel, its leaders already knew they had established irreversible facts on the ground in Jerusalem that would defeat the very notion of peace. Israel's calculated strategy of extricating Jerusalem from the rest of the West Bank rendered any suggestion of making Jerusalem the capital of a future Palestinian state both hollow and impossible. This entire manoeuvre would be completed with a hurried settlement of Jews in the area that would tip the city's demographic and geographic balance in favour of Jewish residents.

A similar praxis that became a fact of life was the dramatic change in the function and purpose of the IDF's elite units. These became death squads and agents provocateurs during Palestinian demonstrations, dressed in civilian clothing or wearing full military gear when attacking 'the enemy' – more often than not a poor dwelling in a refugee camp. No wonder these units had strong parallels with, and developed similar weaponry and other lethal means of warfare to, the death squads that operated in the favelas of Brazil.[28] People whom Israel was obliged by international law to bring in front of a court of law were executed before it was established whether they were guilty or not.

The units spearheaded the operations of mass arrests and the systematic abuse and torture of those arrested. It is very disappointing that the world continued to remain silent at that point, because that particular activity was investigated by a few American congressmen, a rarity in the history of the occupation. Paul Findley reported in 1991 that human rights groups had published 'detailed credible reports of torture, abuse and mistreatment of Palestinian detainees in prisons and detention centres'.[29] Although this was totally ignored by Western governments, it did generate for the first time a far wider response from what one might call Western civil societies. A more genuine and widespread movement of solidarity emerged – to this day still unable to impact the policies of the governments and hence the reality on the ground.

Needless to say, this kind of treatment reported by Findley was not unique to 1991. The people arrested during the punitive years were added to the thousands who had already been in jail since June 1967.

Maybe what was different was the growing media transparency and exposure of information which allowed people around the world to see for themselves, without relying on Israeli narrative and propaganda, the daily reality (a process that would be reinforced with the arrival of the first young volunteers of the International Solidarity Movement in the Occupied Territories). The first shocking aspect for a world that could now see with its own eyes what it meant be on the receiving end of Israeli cruelty was the high number of children and women among this never-ending community of suffering.

Quite a few aspects of the punitive action were still hidden from the public eye in the early 1990s. They would become an integral part of the reality in the years to come. To those already mentioned can be added the prevention of work inside Israel. In 1992 a third of the Palestinian workforce was employed in Israel, mostly in low-skilled, manual labour jobs in construction, agriculture and government services. This contributed 25 per cent of the territories' GNP. The denial of the right to work became part of the punitive action. The fact that even in the days of the open prison, up until 1987, Palestinian exports to Israel constituted only 1 per cent of the aggregate Israeli market, and the workers formed only 7 per cent of the Israeli labour market, this showed that economically you could impose a mega-prison without integrating the two economies. The Israeli 'success' in this respect transpired clearly only in the 1980s (and thus the fears of Pinchas Sapir, the former Finance Minister of the 1967 government, described in Chapter Three, proved to be unfounded). When the punishment became, like so many of the other punitive actions, a part of the reality of the mid-1990s, Israel replaced Palestinian labour, primarily in construction and agriculture, with low-paid workers from foreign countries. It was the nature of such economic dependency that while the Israeli economy was not affected by the end of Palestinian labour at its very heart, this new development had a devastating effect on the Occupied Territories. Unemployment increased, driving down family income and living standards.[30] This was not about economy but about incarceration, penalization and oppression.

Alas, the list of state-sponsored brutality did not end there. The Palestinians faced demolition of their houses (unlike before, this time without prior warning); the destruction of their rural infrastructure – the uprooting of olive trees and the ruination of crops; and probably the most sinister of all in this list of evils, the redirection of water away from their towns and villages, in many cases to the benefit of Jewish settlements (which, after the Intifada, sold that water for a higher price back to the Palestinians from whom the water had been stolen in the first place).[31]

The head of the Israeli military intelligence, Shlomo Gazit (whom we met as the first coordinator of the military rule after 1967), explained that this destruction of the infrastructure was intentional. Israel wanted the Palestinians to 'face unemployment and a shortage of land and water and thus we can create the necessary conditions for the departure of the Palestinians from the West Bank and Gaza'.[32]

On top of all of these measures during the period when the official mentality in Israel was that the occupied people had to be punished, there was yet more licence for the settlers' violence and intimidation. In periods like this, the courts were particularly lenient in their attitude to the killing of Palestinians by settlers. Of the forty-eight cases concerning the killing of Palestinians between 1988 and

1992 by settlers only one culprit was charged with murder. Settlers also abused life in other ways. In those years of 'peace' they were allowed to act as organized gangs terrorizing the Palestinians around them. It began in the early 1980s and has not stopped. It appeared first as the famous 'Jewish Underground' that in 1981 targeted the political elite of the West Bank, seriously wounding several leading politicians, and then became a more systematic form of aggression that escalated during the days of the maximum prison model of 1987 to 1993 and from 2000 until today.[33]

And, indeed, once the first Intifada broke out in 1987, settler provocation against the people of the West Bank and the Gaza Strip increased and became more brutal by the day. At the time, the settlers were mercilessly using their own children to provoke aggression, as happened in the village of Beita, a few miles south-east of Nablus. There, in January 1988, a battalion commander rounded up a large number of youths from Beita and the nearby village of Hawara, tied their hands behind their backs and ordered his soldiers to ruthlessly beat them with sticks and rocks. This was caught on camera and the officer was subsequently tried and discharged from the army (and became quite a sought-after TV pundit afterwards).[34]

But this did not end the trials and tribulations of this village. Three months later, in April 1988, sixteen Israeli boys and girls from the neighbouring settlement of Alon Moreh set out on a journey of provocation into the village of Beita. Their armed escort opened fire on Palestinian youths who threw stones at them, and in the raging whirlwind of the confrontation that developed, two Palestinian youths, one settler girl and an armed escort were killed. The village was severely punished as a result.[35]

The final act in this punitive period of imposing the maximum security model on the people was the massive expulsion of activists at the very end of 1992. This was the year Labour returned to power after a long period of Likud rule. Yitzhak Rabin was elected as the new Prime Minister that summer, his second and last term in office before his assassination by a Jewish terrorist in 1995.

The expulsion ended a long phase of harsh confrontation between Hamas and the Israeli army that had begun in the late 1980s. The charismatic but crippled Ahmed Yassin, who became a moral yardstick for the Hamas movement, was behind several daring operations against Israeli soldiers and settlers. Each such operation, however, offered further opportunities for the Israelis to impose harsher versions of the various punitive actions.

The brutalization of the actions was not only the result of the new methods of resistance offered by the various Palestinian factions, the worst of which were suicide bombs inside Israel. It was also caused by the almost total obedience of the legal system to the whims and requests of the government and the army. This enabled the politicians and generals to go beyond the red lines the Israelis had created for themselves. Around the mid-1990s, the Israeli judicial system became unconditionally and organically integrated into the running of the mega-prison, even in its most vicious and ultra-high security version.

THE LEGAL CHARADE

The bureaucrats who run the legal side of the mega-prison are some of Israel's finest. Since 1967 Israeli law faculties have produced annually, among other graduates, one particular group of proud licentiates: the jurists who would grace the Israeli judicial system with their wisdom and expertise. This system was, and still is, very active as a governmental tool against the Palestinian population in the Occupied Territories, both as part of the web of military courts in the territories themselves and as a system of civil courts inside Israel proper.

It is in these law schools that the future members of Israel's legal system – the ultimate manifestation of Israel's claim for being a liberal democracy – acquired the qualifications needed to operate the massive machinery of arrests and detention in action ever since 1967. Thousands of Palestinians passed along the legal Via Dolorosa paved for them by the State of Israel. The stations on that road are familiar by now – arrest, interrogation, detention for many days without telephone contact or access to a lawyer, appearance in court several times for the extension of the detention, and then a long period in jail without trial as part of 'administrative detention'. The numbers were already staggering in the early 1990s. Until the outbreak of the second Intifada it already looked like a huge campaign of arrest that systematically violated the Fourth Geneva Convention on human rights adopted in 1949. Up until 1992 some 14,000 people had been subjected to this process.[36]

Israel's immunity from prosecution is best demonstrated by judges' blind application of this inhuman method to any Palestinian action – be it a violent attack or a Gandhi-like non-violent protest movement. In 1989 local committees in the village of Beit Sahour initiated a non-violent movement that called upon the people of the West Bank and the Gaza Strip to join a tax rebellion, their slogan being 'No Taxation Without Representation'.[37] The response came quickly, and typically, from the then Minister of Defence in the Labour–Likud unity government, Yitzhak Rabin: 'We will teach them there is a price for refusing the laws of Israel.'[38] When incarceration in prison failed to stop the activists, Israel crushed the boycott by imposing heavy fines, and seizing and disposing of equipment, furnishings and goods from local stores, factories and homes. But you could be subjected to the same treatment for less; a common, non-violent Palestinian form of protest in those days was the use of graffiti to express resistance. This often led to the arrest and collective punishment of the entire family of the perpetrator.

The intensification of the Palestinian struggle spearheaded by the political Islamic and left groups numbed the Israeli legal system even further. The judges were particularly blind to the way coerced collaboration sustained the judicial system. It was no different from a Stasi state, where it was possible to arrest and punish without a reason, but it sat better if an informer provided the evidence.

The construction of such an elaborate system reached new levels in the early 1990s.

The judges provided the collaborators and the secret service furnished the evidence from these collaborators. The judicial system of arrest without trial gave the secret service an opportunity to coerce people into collaborating in return for a reduced sentence (such collaborators were not released immediately so as not to raise suspicion, which did not help them since everyone already inside knew what was going on). In this way, the secret service recruited hundreds of Palestinians and actually succeeded in planting informants inside Hamas and its sister organization, the Islamic Jihad. Unfortunately, it also triggered a ruthless counter-campaign of punishing collaborators. Between 1987 and 1992, several hundred (there are conflicting accounts) Palestinians were killed for being such collaborators.[39]

The Israelis were not genuinely worried about the internal Palestinian engagement with the issue of collaboration. As many of those who were deeply involved in such collaboration would find out, whether they were from Lebanon, the West Bank or the Gaza Strip, Israel always deserted them at some point. Although others were offered sanctuary inside Israel, they were pushed to the criminal margins of society and created a hub of disquiet and intimidation among the Palestinian communities already inside Israel, which were forced to accept their presence in their midst.[40]

The Israeli fake concern for the fate of the collaborators was manifested when the spiritual leader of Hamas, Sheikh Ahmed Yassin, was arrested, allegedly for this incitement against collaborators. His arrest was the opening shot of the first of many Israeli attempts to wipe out Hamas. Yassin was blamed by the Israeli army for being behind the abduction of two soldiers who were later killed, and therefore he was arrested and sentenced to life imprisonment in 1991.[41]

When the body of the second soldier was found, as well as arresting Yassin the army rounded up more than a thousand Hamas activists and expelled 415 of them to southern Lebanon. This was such a stark violation of any international convention that even the American administration – these were the days of Bill Clinton's first term – was furious and threatened to join a condemnation of Israel in the UN Security Council. And thus most of those who were expelled were allowed to return after a relatively short period.[42]

I once gave a lecture to a typical Israeli Jewish audience on that particular period in history leading up to the Oslo Accord, and ended it with condemnation of this expulsion. The usual response from the audience was that this was a perfectly reasonable reaction, like all the other punitive actions Israel carried out, which the listeners admitted were quite ruthless and inhuman with regard to the Palestinian suicide bombs. All my efforts to explain that suicide bombs began after the expulsion and were not the cause of the expulsion were in vain. The first suicide bomb attack was launched on 16 April 1993 – directed at soldiers at one of the checkpoints. So this form of action, which was first practised against soldiers and only later against civilians, was the consequence of the punitive action, not the reason for it. This does not mean that Israeli civilians were not targeted or killed during the first Intifada; in fact, sixteen of them were, as well as eleven soldiers. The number of wounded was much higher: more than 1400 Israeli civilians and 1700 Israeli soldiers were injured.[43]

Not surprisingly, the official Israeli narrative of the first Intifada for domestic and external consumption was that the Israeli army was fighting terrorist organizations. The international community, including the US administration for the first time since 1967, refused to accept this narrative. The Intifada, and the positive international reception to it, led a group of young Israeli politicians and academics to offer a new version of the open-prison model. They suggested de-terrorizing the PLO and allowing it to run the prison instead of Israel. (To my great shame I was one of this group, albeit playing a very marginal role at the beginning of the process.) In September 1993 this formula became the famous Oslo Accord.

It was an important move because there was a genuine opportunity for the world to react to what were now clearly the real intentions of Israel on the ground; and then came the Oslo Accord, which mesmerized – almost anesthetized – Western consciences.

It was also a moment of opportunity, to my mind the last one, to free the Occupied Territories and experiment seriously with the idea of a two-state solution (although I do not believe this would have been the right solution, it nonetheless could have been more seriously tested). During the first Intifada, the Palestinians began to build from their meagre means and resources an independent structure for their society. They made do with Israeli goods, established their own mobile medical clinics and provided independent social services (such as distributing food and clothing for those in need). The restrictions Israel imposed on universities and high schools led to underground teaching with high-quality learning, and other aspects of independence began to mature.[44]

Even the issue of security was addressed in an unprecedented manner. There was no sense of lawlessness as the body coordinating the uprising, named by the locals as the Unified Command, organized local watches over villages and refugee camps at night against army and settler raids. Security was not used to serve as the extended arm of the Israeli forces, but was employed for self-defence.

It was also a moment when collective national pride was directed towards constructing a new reality, not just destroying an old one. Or, as the Australian social activist Sonja Karkar put it when summarizing the first Intifada: it was a moment of national empowerment.[45] In particular it was true for women, who established committees in their struggle to shake off not only the occupation but also the more oppressive side of tradition. (This was another missed opportunity to build an alternative reality; if only the West had been willing to deem the Intifada as a legitimate liberation struggle or the precursor of the Arab Spring.) The Palestinian flag and its colours, rather than weapons or the blood dripping from a map of the homeland, became the symbol of the day, whether it was waved over rooftops or sewn into clothing and embroidery.

In the end, the first uprising produced another version of the open-prison model and when this collapsed another far more severe uprising broke out. The Israelis quelled the second uprising with a severe model of an ultra-security prison in 2000, which lasted for a few years and was transformed by a mixed model of both around 2005.

Chapter Eleven

The Oslo Charade and
the Second Intifada

On 13 September 1993 Israel and the PLO signed a Declaration of Principles, known as the Oslo Accord, on the White House lawn under the auspices of President Bill Clinton. Yasser Arafat, the leader of the PLO, Israel's Prime Minister Yitzhak Rabin and Foreign Minister Shimon Peres would later receive a Nobel Peace Prize for this agreement.

It ended a long period of negotiations between the PLO and Israel that began in 1992. Until that year, Israel refused to negotiate directly with the PLO over the fate of the West Bank and the Gaza Strip, or about the Palestinian question in general. Successive Israeli governments preferred negotiating with Jordan, but since the mid-1980s had allowed PLO representatives to join the Jordanian delegations.

There were several reasons for the change in the Israeli position that enabled direct negotiations with the PLO. The first was the victory of the Labour party in the 1992 elections (for the first time since 1977) and the formation of a government that was more interested in a political solution than the previous Likud-led ones. This government understood that its attempt to negotiate directly with the local Palestinian leadership about autonomy was stalled because every Palestinian decision was referred back to the PLO headquarters in Tunis; thus, a direct line was more useful.

The second reason was the Israeli apprehensions from the Madrid peace initiative, an American enterprise to bring Israel, the Palestinians and the rest of the Arab world to agree on a solution after the first Gulf War. President George Bush Sr and his Secretary of State, James Baker, fathered this initiative in 1991. Both politicians asserted that Israel was the obstacle for peace and pressured Israel to agree to a halt of settlement building so as to give a two-state solution a chance. Israeli–American relations at this time were at an unprecedented low. This administration also initiated direct contact with the PLO. The Madrid Conference of 1991 and the peace efforts conducted under its aegis were probably the first genuine US effort to offer a solution for the West Bank and the Gaza Strip based on Israeli withdrawal. The Israeli political elite wanted to thwart the move and nip it in the bud. They preferred to initiate their own peace proposal and convince the Palestinians to accept it. Incidentally, Yasser Arafat also was unhappy with the Madrid framework since the local Palestinian leadership in the Occupied Territories, headed by the Gazan leader Haidar Abdel-Shafi and Faisal al-Husseini from Jerusalem, in his eyes threatened his leadership and popularity by taking the lead in these negotiations.

Thus the PLO in Tunis and the Israeli Foreign Office in Jerusalem began back-track negotiations while the Madrid peace effort continued. They found a willing mediator in Fafo, a Norwegian research foundation based in Oslo, for these early negotiations. The two teams eventually met in the open in August 1993 and, with American involvement, finalized the Declaration of Principles. This was hailed as the end of the conflict when it was signed with a lot of histrionics on the White House lawn in September 1993.

There are two myths associated with the Oslo process. The first is that it was a genuine peace process at all and the second is that Yasser Arafat wrecked it intentionally by instigating the second Intifada as a terrorist operation against Israel.

The first myth was born out of the wish by both sides at the beginning of the process in 1992 to reach a solution. However, when this failed, it quickly became a game of who to blame. The hardliners pointed the finger at the Palestinian leadership. A more nuanced, and a liberal Zionist, version of this assumption laid the blame on Yasser Arafat until his death and on the Israeli right, in particular Benjamin Netanyahu, for the impasse after the PLO leader's death. In either scenario, the peace process was a real one albeit a failure.

However, the truth is more complex. The terms of the negotiation were impossible to fulfil. The claim that Arafat refused to respect the Palestinian pledges made in the 1993 accord does not bear scrutiny. He could not enforce pledges that were impossible to keep. For example, the Palestinian authorities were called upon to act as Israel's security sub-contractor inside the Occupied Territories and assure there would be no resistance activity. More implicitly, Arafat was expected to accept the Israeli interpretation of the final settlement emerging from this accord without debate. The Israelis presented this fait accompli to the PLO leader in the summer of 2000 at the Camp David Summit, where the Palestinian leader was negotiating the final agreement with the Israeli Prime Minister, Ehud Barak, and President Clinton.

Barak demanded a demilitarized Palestinian state, with a capital in a village near Jerusalem, Abu Dis, and without parts of the West Bank such as the Jordan Valley, the big Jewish settlement blocks and areas in Greater Jerusalem. The future state would not have an independent economic and foreign policy and would be autonomous only in certain domestic aspects (such as running the education system, tax collection, municipalities, policing and infrastructure maintenance). The formalization of this arrangement signified the end of the conflict and terminated any future Palestinian demands (such as the right of the 1948 Palestinian refugees to return).

PARTITION

The peace process was a busted flush from the outset. In order to understand better the failure of Oslo, one has to widen the analysis and relate the events in particular to two principles that remained unanswered throughout the process. The first was the primacy of geographical or territorial partition as the exclusive foundation of peace; and the second, the denial of the Palestinian refugees' Right of Return and its exclusion from the negotiating table.

The proposition that the physical partition of the land was the best solution for the conflict appeared for the first time in 1937 as part of the British Royal Commission's Peel Report. At that time the Zionist movement offered that Jordan – Transjordan in those days – would annex the 'Arab parts of Palestine', but the idea was rejected by the Palestinians.[1]

It was later re-adopted as the best way forward in November 1947 in the UN partition resolution. The UN Special Commission on Palestine (UNSCOP) was established to try to find a solution. The members of the Commission came from countries that had very little interest in and knowledge of Palestine. The Palestinian representative body, the Arab Higher Committee, and the Arab League boycotted UNSCOP and refused to cooperate with it. This left a vacuum filled by the Zionist diplomats and leadership, who fed UNSCOP with ideas for a solution. The Zionist leadership suggested the creation of a Jewish State over 80 per cent of Palestine; the Commission reduced it to 56 per cent.[2] Egypt and Jordan were willing to legitimize the Israeli takeover of Palestinian land that it occupied in 1948 in return for bilateral agreements with Israel (which were eventually signed in 1979 with Egypt and in 1994 with Jordan).

This then resurfaced as a formula for peace in the efforts led by the Americans after 1967, when the concept of partition reappeared in different names and references. It was hidden as a discourse with the emergence of two new concepts. The first was 'territories for peace', which every peace negotiator treated as a sanctified formula for peace – the more territory Israel withdrew from the more peace it would get. Now the territory in Palestine that Israel could withdraw from was within the 22 per cent it had not taken over in 1948. Therefore, in essence the idea was to build peace on the basis of partitioning the remaining 22 per cent of Palestine between Israel and whoever it would legitimize as a partner for peace (which at first were the Jordanians until the late 1980s and then the Palestinians ever since).

Unsurprisingly, therefore, it became the cornerstone of the logic that informed the opening discussion in Oslo. However, it was easily forgotten that every time in history when partition was offered, it was followed by more bloodshed and did not produce the desired peace.

Yet at no point did the Palestinian leaders ever demand partition. It was always a Zionist and, later, an Israeli idea. In addition, the proportional share of territory demanded by the Israelis at each instance grew as their power increased. Thus as partition gained growing global support it increasingly appeared to the Palestinians like an offensive strategy by other means. It was only due to a lack of alternatives that the Palestinian parties accepted this set of circumstances as the lesser evil within the terms of negotiation. In the early 1970s Fatah acknowledged partition as a necessary means on the way to full liberation, but not as a final settlement by itself.[3]

So, in truth, without the application of extreme pressure, there is no reason in the world why a native population would ever volunteer to partition its homeland with a settler movement. And therefore we should see that the Oslo process was actually not a fair and equal pursuit of peace, but a compromise made by a defeated, colonized people. As a result the Palestinians were forced to seek solutions that went against their interests and endangered their very existence.

This same argument can be made about the debates concerning the two state solution that was offered in Oslo. However, this offer should be seen for what it is: partition through different wording. Even in this scenario, although the terms of the debate appear different, Israel would not only decide how much territory it concedes but also what would happen in the territory it leaves behind. While the promise of statehood initially proved persuasive to the world and to some of the Palestinians, it soon came to sound hollow.

Nonetheless, these two intertwined notions of territorial withdrawal and statehood were successfully incorporated as parts of a peace deal in Oslo in 1993.

Yet, within weeks of the joint signature of the Declaration of Principles on the White House lawn, the writing was on the wall. By the end of September, the vague principles had already been translated into a new geopolitical reality under the terms of what was called the Oslo II (or Taba)[4] agreement. This included not just partitioning the West Bank or the Gaza Strip between 'Jewish' and 'Palestinian' zones, but partitioning further all the Palestinian areas into small cantons or Bantustans. The peace cartography, or map, of 1995 was a bisected Palestinian series of zones that resembled, in the words of quite a few commentators, a Swiss cheese.[5]

After this programme became clear, the decline of the negotiations was swift. Before the final summit meeting in the summer of 2000, Palestinian activists, academics and politicians had realized that the process they supported did not incur an actual Israeli military withdrawal from the Occupied Territories, nor did it promise the creation of a real state. The charade was unmasked and progress ground to a halt. The ensuing sense of despair contributed to the outburst of the second Palestinian uprising in the autumn of 2000.

The Oslo peace process did not fail only due to its adherence to the principle of partition. In the original accord there was an Israeli promise that the three issues that trouble the Palestinians most – the fate of Jerusalem, the refugees and the Jewish colonies – would be negotiated when the successful interim period of five years came to an end. Within this interim period, the Palestinians had to prove they could serve effectively as Israel's security sub-contractors, preventing any guerrilla or terror attacks against the Jewish State, its army, settlers and citizens.

Contrary to the promise made in the Oslo Declaration of Principles, when the five years of the first stage was over, the second stage, in which the more substantial issues for the Palestinians were meant to be discussed, did not commence. The Netanyahu government claimed that it was unable to begin the more substantial phase in the negotiations because of the Palestinian 'misbehaviour' (which included 'incitement in schools' and weak condemnations of terror attacks against soldiers, settlers and citizens). In truth, however, the process stalled mainly because of the assassination of the Israeli Prime Minister, Yitzhak Rabin, in November 1995. His murder was followed by the victory of the Likud party, headed by Benjamin Netanyahu, in the 1996 national elections. The new Prime Minister's overt objection to the accord put the brakes on the process. And when the Americans forced him to reignite it, it moved very slowly until the return to power of the Labour party under Ehud Barak in 1999. Barak was determined to end the process in a final peace agreement, an impulse fully supported by the Clinton administration.

Israel's final offer, delivered during discussions at Camp David in the summer of 2000, proposed a small Palestinian state, with a capital in Abu Dis, without significant dismantling of any settlements and no hope for return of the refugees. After the Palestinians rejected the deal, there was an informal attempt by the deputy Israeli Foreign Minister, Yossi Beilin, to offer a more reasonable deal. On the issue of refugees he now agreed to their return to a future Palestinian state and symbolic repatriation to Israel. Yet these informal terms were never ratified by the state. Thanks to the leaking of key documents, known as the Palestine papers, we have a better insight into the nature of the negotiations, and readers who wish to examine other aspects of the Israeli–Palestinian negotiations between 2001 and 2007 are advised to have a look at this accessible source.[6]

And yet, as negotiations collapsed, it was the Palestinian leadership, rather than the Israeli politicians, who were accused of being intransigent, leading to the collapse of Oslo. This does a disservice to those involved and how seriously the prospects of partition were taken.

RIGHT OF RETURN

The exclusion of the Palestinian Right of Return from the peace agenda is the second reason that made Oslo irrelevant as a peace process. While the partition principle reduced 'Palestine' to the West Bank and the Gaza Strip, under the Oslo Accord, the exclusion of the refugee issue, and that of the Palestinian minority inside Israel, shrunk the 'Palestinian people' demographically to less than half of the Palestinian nation.

The lack of attention to the refugee question during the peace negotiation was not new. Ever since the beginning of the peace efforts in post-Mandatory Palestine refugees have been exposed to a campaign of repression and negligence. Ever since the first peace conference on post-1948 Palestine, the Lausanne meeting of April 1949, the refugee problem was excluded from the peace agenda and disassociated from the concept of 'The Palestine Conflict'. Israel participated in this conference only because it was a precondition for its acceptance as a full member in the UN,[7] which also demanded that Israel sign the May Protocol, in which it had to commit itself to the UN General Assembly Resolution 194. This included an unconditional call for the Palestinian refugees to be allowed to return to their homes, or to be given appropriate compensation. A day after the protocol was signed in May 1949, Israel was admitted to the UN and immediately retracted from its commitment to the protocol.

In the wake of the June 1967 war, the world at large accepted the Israeli claim that the conflict in Palestine emerged from the territories that had to be occupied by the army. Several Arab regimes also cooperated with this notion, abandoning the refugee problem as an issue in their peace negotiations. However, the refugee camps soon became the site of intensive political, social and cultural activity. It was there, for example, that the Palestinian liberation movement was reborn.

It was only the United Nations that mentioned in several of its resolutions the obligation of the international community to ensure the full and unconditional repatriation of the Palestinian refugees. This was a commitment first made in Resolution 194, dated 11 December 1948. Still today the UN includes a body named the Committee on the Exercise of the Inalienable Rights of the Palestinian People, though this has had little effect on the peace process.

The Oslo Accord is no different. In this document, the refugee issue has been shuffled into a sub-clause, made almost invisible in the mass of words. The Palestinian partners to the accord contributed to this obfuscation, probably out of negligence not bad intention, but the result is the same. The refugee problem, the heart of the Palestine conflict, a reality acknowledged by all the Palestinians wherever they are and by anyone sympathizing with the Palestinian cause, was marginalized in the Oslo documents. Instead, the issue was handled by a short-lived multilateral group who were asked to focus on the 1967 refugees, namely the Palestinians who were expelled or left after the June war.

The Oslo Accord in fact substituted an embryo attempt, born out of the 1991 Madrid peace process, to form a multilateral group that would discuss the refugee issue on the basis of UN General Assembly Resolution 194. The multilateral group, led by the Canadians (who regarded the Right of Return as a myth), met throughout 1994 but then it petered out. Without any official announcement, this body finally stopped meeting and even the fate of the 1967 refugees (more than 300,000) was abandoned.[8]

After 1993, the implementation of the accord only made things worse. The rules of the agreement defined the abandonment by the Palestinian leadership of the Right of Return. Thus only five years after the cantonization of 'the Palestinian entity' and its transformation into a Bantustan, the Palestinian leadership was given the permission to express its wish to deal with the refugee problem as part of the negotiations over the permanent settlement of the Palestine question. Nevertheless, the Israeli state was able to define the terms of discussion and so chose to distinguish between the introduction of the 'refugee problem' as a legitimate Palestinian grievance, on the one hand, and, on the other, the demand for the Right of Return, which it was able to describe as a Palestinian provocation.

The final stage of the peace process took place at Camp David in 2000. Here, the refugee issue did not fare any better in this last ditch attempt to save the agreement. In January 2000 the Barak government presented a paper, endorsed by the American negotiators, which defined the parameters of the negotiations. This was an Israeli diktat and, until the summit was convened in the summer, the Palestinians failed to produce a counter-proposal. In the summer, the final 'negotiations' were in essence a combined Israeli and American effort to get the Palestinians to accept the paper. The paper included, among other things, an absolute and categorical rejection of the Palestinian Right of Return. It left open for discussion the number of Palestinian refugees that might be allowed to return to the territories controlled by the Palestinian Authority; all the sides concerned understood that these crammed areas were unable to absorb more people, while there is plenty of space for repatriating Palestinian refugees in the rest of Israel and Palestine. This part of the discussion was a meaningless gesture, introduced to silence criticism without offering any real solution.

The peace process of the 1990s was no such thing. The insistence on partition and the exclusion of the refugee issue from the peace agenda rendered the Oslo process at best a military redeployment and rearrangement of Israeli control in the West Bank and the Gaza Strip. At worst, it became a new arrangement of control that made life for the Palestinians in the West Bank and the Gaza Strip far worse than it was before.

After 1995, the impact of the Oslo Accord as a factor that ruined Palestinian society, rather than bringing peace, became painfully clear. After Yitzhak Rabin's assassination and the election of Benjamin Netanyahu in 1996, the Oslo Accord became a discourse of peace that had no relevance to the reality on the ground. During the period of the talks – between 1996 and 1999 – more settlements were built, more collective punishments were inflicted on the Palestinians. Even if you believed in the two-state solution in 1999, a tour of either the West Bank or the Gaza Strip would convince you, in the words of the Israeli scholar Meron Benvenisti, that Israel killed the two-state solution.[9]

So the Oslo process was not a peace process, and the Palestinian participation in it and their reluctance to continue it was not a sign of their intransigence and alleged violent political culture, but a natural response to a diplomacy that solidified and deepened Israeli control over the Occupied Territories.

THE ARAFAT MYTH

This then leads on to the second myth concerning the Oslo process: that Arafat's intransigence caused the Camp David Summit to fail in 2000. Two questions have to be answered here. The first: what happened in the summer of 2000 in Camp David – who was responsible for the failure of that summit? Secondly, who was responsible for the violence of the second Intifada? The two questions will help us engage directly with the common assumption that Arafat was a warmonger who came to Camp David to destroy the peace process and returned with a determination to start a new Intifada.

Before we answer these questions, we should remember the reality in the Occupied Territories on the day Arafat left for Camp David. My main argument here is that Arafat came to Camp David to change that reality while the Israelis and the Americans arrived there determined to maintain it. The Oslo process transformed the Occupied Territories into a geography of disaster, which meant that the Palestinians' quality of life was far worse after the accord than it was before.

Already in 1994, Rabin's government had forced Arafat to accept its interpretation of how the Oslo Accord would be implemented on the ground. The West Bank was divided into the infamous areas A, B and C. The Palestinian Authority controlled area A and jointly with Israel, Area B. Area C was the one directly controlled by Israel and constituted half of the West Bank. Movement between, and inside, the areas became nearly impossible and the West Bank was cut off from the Gaza Strip. Israel also divided the Gaza Strip. The settlers were a given small part of it and took over most of the water resources and lived in gated communities. The Palestinians were cordoned within barbed wire. Thus, here too, the end result meant that the peace process deteriorated the quality of Palestinian life.

This was Arafat's choice in the summer of 2000 as he arrived at Camp David. He was being asked to sign off as a final settlement the irreversible facts on the ground that turned the idea of a two-state solution into an arrangement that at best would allow the Palestinians to have two small Bantustans and at worst would allow Israel to annex more territory. This agreement would also force him to give up any future Palestinian demands or propose a way of alleviating some of the daily hardships most Palestinians suffered.

We have a very authentic and reliable report of what happened in Camp David by the US State Department's Hussein Agha and Robert Malley. Their detailed report appeared in the *New York Review of Books*[10] and begins by dismissing the Israeli claim that Arafat wrecked the summit. The article makes the point that Arafat's main problem when coming to the summit was that, in the years since Oslo, life for the Palestinians in the Occupied Territories had only got worse. Quite reasonably, according to these two American officials, Arafat suggested that instead of rushing within two weeks 'to end the conflict for once and for all', Israel should agree to some measures that might restore the Palestinians' faith in the usefulness and benefits of the peace process. The period of two weeks, by the way, was not so much an Israeli demand, but rather a foolish timeframe insisted upon by President Clinton, who was considering his own legacy.

There were two major issues that Arafat signalled as potential areas of discussion and which might improve the reality on the ground. The first was de-escalating the intensive colonization of the West Bank that had increased after Oslo. The second was putting an end to the daily brutalization of normal Palestinian life, manifested in severe restrictions of movement, frequent collective punishment, arrest without trial and constant humiliation at the checkpoints. All these practices appeared in the most callous way within every area where there was contact between the Israeli army, or the Civil Administration (the body running the territories), and the local population.

According to the testimony of the US officials, Barak refused to change Israel's policy towards the Jewish colonies or the daily abuse of the Palestinians. He took a tough position, which left Arafat with no choice. Whatever Barak depicted as a final settlement did not mean much if he could not promise immediate change in the reality on the ground.

Arafat was, as expected, blamed by Israel and its allies of being a warmonger who, immediately after returning from Camp David, contemplated the second Intifada. The myth here is that the second Intifada was a terrorist attack sponsored and perhaps even planned by Yasser Arafat. The truth is, it was a mass demonstration of dissatisfaction with the betrayal of Oslo, compounded by the provocative action of Ariel Sharon. In September 2000 Sharon, as the leader of the opposition, toured Haram al-Sharif, the Temple Mount, with massive security and media presence, igniting an explosion of protests.

The initial Palestinian anger was translated into non-violent protest that was crushed by brutal force by Israel. The callous repression of these demonstrations led to a more desperate response – the suicide bombs that appeared as the last resort in the face of the strongest military power in the region. There is telling evidence by Israeli newspaper correspondents that their reports on the early stages of the Intifada – as a non-violent movement that was crushed violently by the Israeli army – were shelved by their editors so as to fit the narrative of the government. One of them was a deputy editor of *Yeidot Achronot*, the main daily, who wrote a book about the misinformation produced by the Israeli media on the early days of the second Intifada.[11] At the same time, official Israeli propagandists claimed this behaviour reaffirmed the famous saying of the veteran Israeli superdiplomat, Abba Eban, that the Palestinians do not miss an opportunity to miss an opportunity for peace.

We have a better understanding today of what triggered such a furious Israeli reaction. In their book *Boomerang*, two senior Israeli journalists, Ofer Shelah and Raviv Drucker, interviewed the General Chief of Staff and strategists in the Ministry of Defence and offered inside knowledge on the way these officials and generals were thinking about the issue.[12] Their conclusion was that in the summer of 2000 the IDF was a frustrated outfit following its humiliating defeat by Hezbollah in Lebanon, who had forced the army to withdraw totally from Lebanon. There was a fear that this retreat made the army look weak. And so a show of strength was much needed.

The reassertion of dominance within the occupied Palestinian territories was just the kind of display of sheer power the 'invincible' Israeli army needed. The army was ordered to respond with all its might, and so it did. When Israel retaliated against a terror attack on a hotel in the sea resort city of Netanya in April 2002 (where thirty people were killed) it was the first time the IDF used aeroplanes to bomb the dense Palestinian towns and refugee camps in the West Bank. Instead of hunting down the individuals who carried out these attacks, the most lethal and heavy weapons were brought to bear on innocent civilians.

Another common reference that accompanied the blame game Israel and the US played after the failure of the Camp David Summit was reminding public opinion that there was a chronic problem with Palestinian leaders, who, at the moment of truth, exposed their warmongering ways. 'There is no one to talk to on the Palestinian side' reappeared in that period as a common analysis by local pundits and commentators in Israel, Europe and the USA.

These allegations are particularly cynical. The Israeli government and army had tried by force to impose their own version of Oslo – one that was meant to perpetuate the occupation for ever but with Palestinian consent – and even an enfeebled Arafat could not accept it. He and so many other leaders, who could have led their people to reconciliation, were targeted by the Israelis; and most of them, probably Arafat himself included, were assassinated.

Target killing of Palestinian leaders, including moderate ones, was not a new phenomenon in the conflict. Israel began this policy with the assassination of Ghassan Kanafani in 1972, a poet and writer, who could have led his people to reconciliation. The fact that he was targeted, a secular and leftist activist, is symbolic of the role Israel played in killing those Palestinians it 'regretted' later for not being there as partners for peace.

In May 2001 President George Bush Jr appointed Senator George J. Mitchell as a special envoy to the Middle East conflict. Mitchell produced a report about the causes for the second Intifada. He concluded: 'We have no basis on which to conclude that there was a deliberate plan by the PA to initiate a campaign of violence at the first opportunity; or to conclude that there was a deliberate plan by the [Government of Israel] to respond with lethal force.'[13] On the other hand, he blamed Ariel Sharon for provoking unrest by visiting and violating the sacredness of the al-Aqsa mosque and the holy places of Islam.

In short, even the disempowered Arafat realized that the Israeli interpretation of Oslo in 2000 meant the end of any hope for normal Palestinian life and doomed the Palestinians to more suffering in the future. This scenario was not only morally wrong in his eyes, but also would have strengthened, as he knew too well, those who regarded the armed struggle against Israel as the exclusive way to liberate Palestine. At any given moment, Israel could have stopped the second Intifada, but the army needed a 'success'. Only when this was achieved through the barbaric Operation Defensive Shield in 2002 and the building of the infamous 'apartheid wall' did the Israelis succeed temporarily in quelling the second Intifada.

THE WEST BANK, 2005–2017

By 2007, 40 per cent of the West Bank was already under direct rule by Israel; or, in other words, annexed, for all intents and purposes, to Israel. Within this 40 per cent Israel solidified its presence with barriers, military bases and closed military areas (cynically, Israel declared them nature reserves).[14] This policy focused on Area C of the West

Bank and its main purpose was to downsize the Palestinian population there (there were also calls from senior Israeli politicians to annex the area). In 1967 around 300,000 Palestinians lived in Area C; today there are a mere 50,000. The Jewish population has increased from about a thousand in 1967 to more than 400,000 today.[15]

Very much as in 1967, there has been constant fine-tuning of the mega-prison. The West Bank is not as much under siege as the Gaza Strip, but movement in and out is very restricted. People of the West Bank are banned from using Ben-Gurion airport in Tel Aviv. There are two major crossings for them into Jordan, one being the Allenby/King Hussein Bridge. This crossing is controlled by Israel. The other crossing, the Damia Bridge, has been officially annexed to Israel; it is for commercial use and allows only the export of goods to Jordan, banning imports of any kind.

Movement within the West Bank is also severely restricted. All major roads (in all about 700 kilometres) are apartheid roads; in other words, Palestinians are banned from using them. Control of the roads has tightened since 2007. Movement has become even more of a challenge since the Israeli authorities recently finished building a new highway (divided by a wall segregating the road into Jewish and Palestinian lanes), which bisects the West Bank in two from north to south.

All over the West Bank, by December 2016, about 400,000 Israelis inhabited 121 settlements officially recognized by the Israeli government, while about 375,000 Israelis live in settlements in East Jerusalem. There are approximately a hundred further settlement outposts that are not officially recognized by the government and are illegal under Israeli law, but have been provided with infrastructure, water, sewage and other services by the authorities.[16]

Whether Palestinians lived among the 40 per cent or elsewhere in the West Bank, as the Independent Commission for Human Rights reported in 2010, they were exposed to a systematic campaign of human rights abuses by the Israelis, and quite often, and regrettably, also by the Palestinian Authority. Since 2005 the security forces of the

PA have also been responsible for quite a few cases of torture, arrest and arbitrary detention.[17] This aspect of life still falls within the paradigm of the open prison, where prisoners themselves are observing the peace for the prison authorities.

Gradually the international community has become aware that not only are human and civil rights being endangered by the continued oppression, but the very economic existence of the West Bank is also threatened. According to a 2007 World Bank report, the Israeli occupation of the West Bank has destroyed the Palestinian economy.[18] The only thing that has kept the economy alive to a certain extent is international aid. If this should cease, the economic reality would become even more precarious. As things currently stand it is unlikely it will increase to the point where it can substantially alleviate the economic hardship faced by the people of the West Bank. The number of Palestinians who succeed in finding work in Israel (and for that matter in the settlements) is unclear as many of them are there illegally. Recent estimates have put that number at around 100,000. This is also unlikely to help sustain the crumbling economy.

The peace charade continued after 2005. It was injected with some hope when Barack Obama entered the White House, but all was in vain. The discourse of peace in Obama's time was about the Palestinian state. In May 2011 Obama officially announced US support for a future Palestinian state based on borders prior to the 1967 war, allowing for land swaps where they were mutually agreeable between the two sides. Obama was the first US president to formally support this idea. The fact that such a statement had no bearing whatsoever on the reality on the ground proved that the decision taken by Israel in June 1967 to offer the charade of peace as a substitute for international intervention in a genuine peace process was highly successful.

This is a point further accentuated by the zero impact of similar initiatives effected by other countries. By September 2013, 134 (69.4 per cent) of the 193 member states of the United Nations had recognized the State of Palestine within the Palestinian territories and a few more probably followed suit, to no avail.

The international community's unwillingness to act is demon-strated even when there are, on the face of it, concrete promises to act against Israeli policy. In January 2012 the European Union approved the 'Area C and Palestinian State Building' report. The report said that Palestinian presence in Area C has been continuously undermined by Israel and that state-building efforts in Area C of the PA and the EU were of the 'utmost importance in order to support the creation of a contiguous and viable Palestinian state'. The EU will back various projects to 'support the Palestinian people and help maintain their presence'.[19] In 2017 the incremental annexation of the West Bank continues and the Palestinian state is more of a distant reality than ever.

The last Palestinian campaign triggered a process in the UN for ending Israeli occupation. In September 2014 the PA appealed to the UN Security Council demanding that a timetable for such a process should be put into effect. Failing that, the PA threatened that it would appeal to the International Criminal Court in The Hague.

Since 2005 more Israelis have joined movements that harshly condemn Israeli policies, but even if they are numerous they will only be effective if external pressure on Israel, as suggested and practised by the Boycott, Divestment and Sanctions movement, is applied.

The situation in the West Bank was not influenced by the ongoing condemnation by international jurists of this reality as a severe viola-tion of the Hague and Geneva conventions. For a moment in December 2007, as so often in the past, an Israeli leader juggled impressively with words in an effort to deflect international outcry. Prime Minister Ehud Olmert decreed that all settler activities, includ-ing planning, in the West Bank, required the approval of both the Israeli Prime Minister and the Minister of Defence.

Deposed and imprisoned for corruption, Olmert had no oppor-tunity to follow through this measure. The next government of Benjamin Netanyahu approved almost all the settlers' requests.

In their turn, since 2005 the settlers have become even more brutal and barbarous in their treatment of the people of the West

Bank, culminating in the burning alive of a teenager and an entire family.

The Palestinians' steadfastness in the West Bank continues. Popular resistance is a daily occurrence but with limited resources it is easily quashed by the Israeli occupation. However, in its tenacity it suggests that the final chapter to what began in 1967 has yet to be written.

Today there are nearly three million Palestinians in the West Bank and almost 400,000 settlers. Zionism as a settler colonial movement was able to colonize Palestine almost in its entirety regardless of its demographic minority. These settlers, however, are much more powerful than the early Zionists and it is unlikely that anyone will prevent them from taking over the rest of the West Bank, by one way or another.

During that same period, Israel subjected the Gaza Strip to even harsher oppression and the most callous version of the maximum security prison to date.

Chapter Twelve

The Ultimate Maximum Security Prison Model: the Gaza Strip

In 2004 the Israeli army began building a dummy Arab city in the Negev Desert. It was the size of a real city, with streets (all of them given names), mosques, public buildings and cars. Built at a cost of $45 million, this phantom city became a fake Gaza in the winter of 2006, after Hezbollah fought Israel to a standstill in the north, so that the Israeli army could prepare to fight a 'better war' against Hamas in the south.[1]

When the Israeli Chief of General Staff, Dan Halutz, visited the site after the Lebanon war, he told the press that soldiers 'were preparing for the scenario that will unfold in the dense neighbourhood of Gaza City'.[2] A week into the bombardment of Gaza, Ehud Barak attended a rehearsal for the ground war. Foreign television crews filmed him as he watched ground troops conquer the mock city, storming the empty houses and no doubt killing the 'terrorists' hiding in them.[3]

In 2009 the Israeli NGO Breaking the Silence published a report of its members', reserve soldiers' and other soldiers' preparation for Operation Cast Lead, when the attack on the dummy city was replaced by an assault on the real Gaza. The gist of the testimonies was that the soldiers had orders to attack Gaza as if they were attacking a massive enemy stronghold: this became clear from the firepower employed, the absence of any orders or procedures about acting properly within a civilian environment, and the synchronized effort from land, sea and air. Among the worst practices they rehearsed were the senseless demolition of houses, the spraying of civilians with phosphorus shells, the killing of innocent civilians by light weaponry and obeying orders from their commanders generally to act with no moral compass. 'You feel like an infantile child with a magnifying glass that torments ants, you burn them,' one soldier testified.[4] In short, they practised the total destruction of the real city as they trained in the mock city.

This was the new version of the maximum security prison that awaited the Palestinians in the Gaza Strip, as the Israeli government and its security policymakers realized that the open-prison model, which was meant to enclose the people of the Strip under a collaborative rule of the PA, had been foiled by the people themselves. The retaliation that came in the form of besieging and blockading the Strip into surrendering to the preferred Israeli model had not worked either. The Palestinian political groups in the Strip, led by Hamas, decided to retaliate by launching occasional barrages of primitive missiles so that the world, and Israel, would not forget them and their life within a hermetically closed prison.

This is how the Israeli fiasco unfolded in 2005, which turned into what I have referred to elsewhere as the incremental genocide of Palestine. The Israelis referred to their first operation against Gaza as 'First Rain'; it was more a rain of fire from the sky than of blessed water from above.

2005: THE FIRST RAIN

The militarization of the Israeli policy towards the Gaza strip began in 2005. That year Gaza became an official military target from the Israeli point of view, as if it were a huge enemy base rather than a place of civilian habitation. Gaza is a city like any other in the world, and yet for the Israelis it became a dummy city for soldiers to experiment with the most recent and advanced weapons.

This policy was enabled by the Israeli government's decision to evict the Jewish settlers who had colonized the Gaza Strip since 1967. The settlers were allegedly moved as part of what the government described as a unilateral policy of disengagement, the argument being that since there was no progress in the peace talks with the Palestinians, it was up to Israel to determine how its borders with the Palestinian areas would ultimately look. In essence, Prime Minister Sharon was willing to turn the Strip into a West Bank Area A and in turn strengthen Israel's grip on the West Bank (and in evicting the Gazan settlers against their will, it would create an alleged trauma that would absolve Israel from ever repeating it again).

But things did not turn out as expected. The eviction of the settlers was followed by a Hamas takeover, first in democratic elections, then in a pre-emptive coup staged to avert an American-backed seizure by Fatah. The immediate Israeli response was to impose an economic blockade on the Gaza Strip, to which Hamas retaliated by firing missiles at the nearest town to the Strip, Sderot. This gave Israel the pretext to use its air force, artillery and gunships. Israel claimed it was firing at the launching areas of the missiles, but in practice this meant anywhere and everywhere in the Strip.

Creating the prison and throwing the key into the sea, as UN Special Rapporteur John Dugard has put it,[5] was an action against which the Palestinians in Gaza reacted with force in September 2005. They were determined to show that at the very least they were still part of the West Bank and Palestine. That same month they launched the first significant barrage (in number only, not quality) of missiles into the western Negev – as so often, these resulted in damage to some properties but very rarely in human casualties. The events of that month deserve to be mentioned in detail, because the early Hamas response before September had been the sporadic trickle of missiles. The launching in September 2005 was in response to an

Israeli campaign of mass arrests of Hamas and Islamic Jihad activists in the Tul Karem area; one could not escape the impression at the time that the army was looking to trigger a Hamas response. Indeed, when it came, it was a harsh policy of massive killings, the first of its kind, code-named 'First Rain'.

It is worth dwelling for a moment on the nature of that operation. The discourse that accompanied it was one of punishment and it resembled the punitive measures inflicted in the more distant past by colonial powers, and more recently by dictatorships, against rebellious imprisoned or banished communities. A frightening show of aggression by the oppressor ended with large numbers of dead and wounded among the victims. In Operation First Rain, supersonic flights took place over Gaza to terrorize the entire population, followed by the heavy bombardment of vast areas from the sea, sky and land. The logic, the Israeli army explained, was to create pressure in order to weaken the Gaza community's support for the rocket launchers.[6] As everyone expected, the Israelis included, the operation only increased support for the rocket launchers and gave impetus to their next attempts.

In hindsight, and especially given the Israeli military commanders' explanation that the army had long been preparing the 2008–2009 Operation Cast Lead,[7] it is possible that the real purpose of that particular operation was experimental. And if the Israeli generals wanted to know how such operations would be received at home, in the region and in the wider world, it seems that the quick answer was 'very well'; namely, no governments showed any interest in the scores of dead and hundreds of wounded Palestinians left behind after First Rain subsided.[8]

Subsequent operations were along similar lines. The difference was in their escalation: more firepower, more casualties and more collateral damage and, as to be expected, a tighter siege and blockade. The Palestinians reacted with more Qassam missiles.

THE LEBANON HUMILIATION AND
THE GAZA 'COMPENSATION'

Tank shelling, bombing from the air and the sea and brutal incursions were frequent occurrences throughout 2006. But when Israel was defeated on another front, this time in southern Lebanon in the summer of 2006, the army intensified its punitive policy even more against one and a half million people living in the most densely populated 40 square kilometres on the planet. Such was the brutality of the Israeli policy that it met the UN Article 2's definition of genocide, which stressed that it can be applied to actions against part of an ethnic or national population (and not necessarily against all of it). The kinds of weapon used by Israel – 1000-kilo bombs, tanks, missiles from the air and shelling from the sea against civilian areas – were not intended to deter, wound or warn. They were intended to kill.

Not surprisingly, Hamas's reaction became more desperate. Quite a few observers inside and outside Israel attributed the escalation to a determination to show that the Israeli army had swiftly recovered from the humiliation meted out to it by Hezbollah in Lebanon.[9] The army needed to show its superiority and deterrence capability, which it considered to be the primary safeguard of the Jewish State's survival in a 'hostile' world. The Islamic nature of both Hamas and Hezbollah, and an alleged, and totally false, association of both with Al-Qaeda, enabled the army to imagine an Israel spearheading a global war against Jihadism in Gaza. While George W. Bush was in office, the killing of women and babies in Gaza could be accepted even by the American administration as part of that holy war against Islam.

The worst month in 2006 for the Gazans was September, when this new pattern in the Israeli policy became all too obvious. Almost daily, civilians were killed by the IDF: 2 September 2006 was one such day. Three citizens were killed and an entire family injured in Beit Hanoun. This was just the morning's harvest; before the end of the day many more were killed. In September an average of eight

Palestinians died every day in Israeli attacks on the Strip, many of them children. Hundreds were maimed, wounded and paralysed.[10]

More than anything else the systematic killing had the appearance of an inertia killing due to the absence of a clear policy. The Israeli leadership in September 2006 seemed to be at a loss as to what to do with the Gaza Strip. Reading its statements at the time you get the impression that the government was quite confident about its policy towards the West Bank, but not towards the Strip. It perceived the West Bank, unlike the Strip, as an open space, at least on its eastern side. Hence Israel – under a strategy the Prime Minister of the day, Ehud Olmert, defined as 'ingathering' – was entitled to take unilateral action in the West Bank, since there was no progress in the peace process.[11] In practice, it meant that the 2006 government wished to annex the parts it coveted – more or less half of the West Bank – and to try to push out, or at least enclose within it, the native population, while allowing the other half of the West Bank to develop in a way that would not endanger Israeli interests (either by being ruled by a submissive Palestinian Authority or by associating directly with Jordan). This was a fallacy, but it nonetheless won the enthusiastic backing of most of the Jews in the country when Olmert turned it into a key policy of his election campaign.

However, this strategy could not be applied to the Gaza Strip. As early as 1967, Egypt, unlike Jordan, had succeeded in persuading the Israelis that the Gaza Strip was a liability for it and would never form part of Egypt. So one and a half million Palestinians remained an 'Israeli' problem and responsibility – although geographically the Strip is located on the margins of the State of Israel, psychologically it still lay very much in its midst in 2006.

The inhuman conditions in the Strip made it impossible for the people living there to reconcile themselves to the imprisonment Israel had imposed on them since 1967. There were relatively better periods when movement to the West Bank and into Israel for work was permitted, but such better times had gone by 2006. Harsher realities had been in place since 1987. Some access to the outside world was allowed as long as there were Jewish settlers in the Strip, but once they were removed the Strip was hermetically sealed. Ironically, most Israelis, according to the 2006 polls, regarded Gaza as an independent Palestinian state that Israel had graciously allowed to emerge.[12] The leadership, and particularly the army, saw it as a prison with the most dangerous community of inmates, which had to be managed ruthlessly one way or another.

The conventional Israeli policy of ethnic cleansing employed successfully in 1948 against half of Palestine's population, and against hundreds of thousands of Palestinians in the West Bank in 1967, was of no use here.[13] You could slowly transfer Palestinians out of the West Bank, and in particular out of the Greater Jerusalem area, but you could not do it in the Gaza Strip – once you had sealed it as a maximum security prison camp.

The result, as I have argued elsewhere, was the onset of a policy of incremental genocide by Israel against the Gaza Strip. I have also explained how the various legal and moral definitions of genocide have been relevant to the Israeli policy in the Gaza Strip since 2006, so I will not repeat them here. Let me just say that every year I ponder afresh this problematic definition and nothing on the ground suggests that I am wrong. This is not necessarily an intentional policy of annihilation, but it is one that has brought about the slow destruction of the ability of people in the Strip to survive (as was recognized by a UN report in 2016 that predicted that in 2020 life in the Strip would be unsustainable).

As with the ethnic cleansing operations, the unfolding genocidal policy that began in 2006 was not formulated in a vacuum. Since 1948, the Israeli army and government needed a pretext to commence such policies.[14] The takeover of Palestine in 1948 produced the inevitable local resistance that in turn allowed the implementation of an ethnic cleansing policy, pre-planned in the 1930s. Twenty years of Israeli occupation of the West Bank eventually led to some sort of Palestinian resistance. This belated anti-occupation struggle unleashed a new cleansing policy that was still intact in the West

Bank in 2006 and an aggressive policy of massive killing in the Gaza Strip. The daily business of slaying Palestinians only reached the back pages of the local press.

The Lebanon war provided the screen for a while, covering the sheer scale of destruction being wreaked on the Gaza Strip. However, the policies raged on even after the conclusion of the ceasefire up in the north. It seems that the frustrated and defeated Israeli army was even more determined to enlarge the killing fields in the Gaza Strip. The political elite seemed unable, or unwilling, to stop the generals. The daily killing of up to ten civilians throughout 2006 left a large number dead by the end of the year.[15] Such numbers are, of course, different from the destruction of a million people in a single campaign, an act more commonly defined by the international community as genocide. Indeed, one felt, at least until the 2009 massacre in Gaza, that, if only out of deference to Holocaust memory, official Israel would baulk at the prospect of committing genocide.

On 28 December 2006 the Israeli human rights organization B'Tselem published its annual report about Israeli atrocities in the Occupied Territories. That year Israeli forces killed 660 citizens.[16] The number of Palestinians killed by Israel in 2006 tripled in comparison to the previous year (around 200). According to B'Tselem, the Israelis killed 141 children in 2006. Most of the dead were from the Gaza Strip, where Israeli forces demolished almost 300 houses and slew entire families. This means that since 2000, Israeli forces have killed almost 4000 Palestinians, many of them children; more than 20,000 were wounded.

B'Tselem is a conservative organization, and the numbers it quotes may be higher. It did not describe the killings as part of a policy of genocide. In a series of articles written that year and after, I chose to differ. The point I made was that the question of definition was not just numeric; it related to the trend and the strategy. As 2007 began, Israeli policymakers faced two very different realities in the West Bank and the Gaza Strip. In the former, they were closer than ever to completing the delineation of their eastern border. Their internal ideological debate about the fate of the West Bank was nearly over and their master plan for annexing half of the West Bank was being implemented at an ever-growing speed by the last months of 2006. The last phase was delayed because of the promises made by Israel, under the road map for peace, not to build new settlements. Israel found two ways of circumventing this alleged prohibition. First, it defined a third of the West Bank as Greater Jerusalem, which allowed it to build towns and community centres within this new annexed area. Secondly, it expanded old settlements to such an extent that there was no need to build new ones. This trend was given additional impetus in 2006 when hundreds of caravans were installed to delineate the boundaries of the Jewish 'sphere' within the Palestinian territories. The planning schemes for the new towns and neighbourhoods were finalized and the apartheid bypass roads and highway system was completed. In all, the settlements, the army bases, the roads and the wall would allow Israel to complete the annexation in the following years.

Within these territories there are still a considerable number of Palestinians against whom the Israeli authorities pursue slow and creeping transfer policies – too boring a subject for the Western media to bother with and too elusive for human rights organizations to make a general point about. There was no hurry as far as the Israelis were concerned; they felt at the beginning of 2007 that they had the upper hand there: the daily abusive and dehumanizing mechanisms of army and bureaucracy were as effective as ever in contributing their own share to the process of dispossession.

This strategy was first conceived by Ariel Sharon in 2001 and became a political consensus. It won the day and was deemed the preferred strategy for the future in 2006 and much preferable to the one offered by the blunt 'transferrists' or ethnic cleansers such as Avigdor Lieberman (he would repeat his advocacy for transfer once more at the end of 2016 as Defence Minister). It was endorsed as the way forward in 2006 and was accepted by everyone in the 2006 government, from Labour to Kadima (the new centre party that Ariel

Sharon founded with Shimon Peres and which lasted for a few years after Sharon's departure from political life in 2006). The *petit* crimes of state terrorism were also effective as they enabled critical, but loyal, support of the state around the world to softly condemn Israel and yet categorize any genuine criticism of Israel's criminal policies as anti-Semitism.

This clarity on the policy towards the West Bank highlighted the confusion about Gaza. There was no clear Israeli strategy for the Gaza Strip at the beginning of 2007; but the difference between 2006 and 2007 was that the daily activity by the army in the Strip transformed into the strategy itself. Gaza, in the eyes of the Israelis, was a very different geopolitical entity from that of the West Bank. Hamas had already been controlling the Gaza Strip for almost a year, while the leader of Fatah, Abu Mazen (aka Mahmoud Abbas), was running the fragmented West Bank with Israeli and American blessing. Israel did not covet any chunk of land in the Strip, as it did in the West Bank; nor did the Strip have a hinterland, like Jordan, to which the Palestinians of Gaza could have been expelled. As mentioned before, ethnic cleansing was an ineffective option here.

Up to 2007, the salient strategy in Gaza had been ghettoizing the Palestinians there, but this was no longer working. The ghettoized community continued to express its zest for life by firing primitive missiles into Israel. Ghettoizing or quarantining unwanted communities, even if they were regarded as sub-human or dangerous, had historically never been a solution. The Jews knew it best from their own history.

Hamas's counter-operation culminated in the capture of the Israeli soldier Gilad Shalit on Gaza's soil in June 2006. This incident was irrelevant in the general scheme of things, but nonetheless provided an opportunity for the Israelis to escalate even more the components of the tactical and allegedly punitive missions. After all, there was still no strategy that followed the tactical decision of Ariel Sharon to remove 8000 settlers whose presence complicated punitive missions and whose eviction almost made him a candidate for the

Nobel Peace Prize. Thereafter, the 'punitive' actions continued and themselves became a strategy.

The Israeli army loves drama and therefore also escalated its discourse. Operation First Rain was replaced by Summer Rains, a general name given to the 'punitive' operations since June 2006 (in a country where there is no rain in the summer, the only precipitation that one can expect are showers of F-16 bombs and artillery shells landing on the people of Gaza).

Summer Rains introduced a novel component: the land invasion into parts of the Gaza Strip. This enabled the army to kill citizens even more effectively and to present it as a result of heavy fighting within densely populated areas, an inevitable result of the circumstances and not of Israeli policies. With the end of summer came Operation Autumn Clouds, which was even more efficient: on 1 November 2006, in less than forty-eight hours, the Israelis killed seventy civilians; by the end of that month, with additional mini-operations accompanying it, almost 200 were killed, half of them children and women.[17]

From First Rain to Autumn Clouds one could see escalation in every parameter. The first was the removal of the distinction between civilian and non-civilian targets: the senseless killing turned the population at large into the main target for the army's operation. The second was the escalation of the means to kill: employment of every possible killing machine the Israeli army possessed. Thirdly, the escalation was conspicuous for the number of casualties: with each operation, and each future operation, a much larger number of people were killed and wounded. Finally, and most importantly, the operations became a strategy – the way Israel intended to solve the problem of the Gaza Strip.

A creeping transfer in the West Bank and a measured genocidal policy in the Gaza Strip were the two strategies Israel also employed in 2007. From an electoral point of view, the one in Gaza was more problematic as it did not reap any tangible results, while the West Bank under Abu Mazen was yielding to Israeli pressure and there seemed to be no significant force that could arrest the Israeli strategy of annexation and dispossession. However, Gaza continued to fire back. On the one hand, this enabled the Israeli army to initiate more massive genocidal operations; but on the other hand, there was also the great danger, as had happened in 1948, that the army would demand a more drastic and systematic 'punitive' and collateral action against the besieged people of the Gaza Strip.

2007–2008: THE POLICY BECOMES A STRATEGY

The casualties were rising in 2007. Three hundred people were killed in the Gaza Strip, dozens of them children. However, during the George W. Bush administration and definitely after, the myth of fighting the world Jihad in Gaza had started to lose credibility. So a new mythology was proposed in 2007: the Strip was a terrorist base determined to destroy Israel. The only way the Palestinians could be 'de-terrorized', so to speak, was eliciting from them a consent to live in a Strip encircled by barbed wire and walls. Supply, as well as movement, in and out of the Strip depended on the political choice made by the Gazans. Should they persist in supporting Hamas, they would be effectively strangled and starved until they changed their ideological inclination. Should they succumb to the kind of politics Israel wished them to adopt, they would suffer the same fate as those on the West Bank: life without basic civil and human rights. They could either be inmates in the open prison of the West Bank or incarcerated in the maximum security one of the Gaza Strip. If they resisted they were likely to be imprisoned without trial, or killed. This was Israel's message in 2007 and the people of the Gaza Strip were given a year, 2008, to make up their minds.

A bilateral ceasefire was officially declared in the summer of 2008, brokered by Egypt. The Israeli government did not achieve its goals. It needed to prepare more seriously for the next step and used that year for such preparations. Its strategy not only depended on silencing Hamas in the Gaza Strip, but also consisted of desperate attempts to prove to the international body appointed to deal with the Israel/

Palestine conflict, the Quartet (consisting of representatives from the EU, Russia, the USA and the UN), and the Palestine Authority, that the situation in the Strip was sufficiently under its control that it could be incorporated into an Israeli peace vision of the future.

The summer of 2008 was two years after the humiliation of Lebanon. The Olmert government, which had led Israel into that war, was bitterly criticized in a damning report by an official inquiry into its failure in the north. The government did not want the Israeli public to dwell on this open wound for too long. Winds of change were also blowing from Washington where it was feared a new administration would not be as sympathetic to the Israeli strategy; and, all in all, world public opinion, at least bottom up, as it had been since 2000, seemed restless and antagonistic.

The old method of waiting for the right pretext to move ahead and escalate the struggle against the only resistance still intact was at work once more. The training in the dummy city now became operational and was turned into a proper doctrine in the Israeli policy towards the Gaza Strip. It was known as the 'Dahiya Doctrine'. In October 2008 *Haaretz* referred to this for the first time. The gist of it was the comprehensive destruction of areas in their entirety and the employment of unparalleled force in response to the launch of missiles. *Haaretz* referred to it as a possible scenario that could unfold in Lebanon, hence the Dahiya reference (a Shi'ite quarter in Beirut that was blown to smithereens in the 2006 Israeli air attack on the city). Gadi Eizenkot, the then Chief of the Northern Command, said that 'for us villages are military bases'. He talked about the total destruction of villages as a punitive action. His colleague at the top of the army, Colonel Gabi Siboni, confirmed that this would apply to the Gaza Strip as well. He added: 'this is meant to damage in such a way that it will take a long period to recover'.[18]

Thus, all was ready for reigniting the Strip. The first step was tightening the siege on the Strip. This produced a shortage of basic foodstuffs, a lack of the simplest medicines and caused massive claustrophobia for a million and a half people who were not allowed to move out. The siege also included severe restrictions of fishing rights, which is one of the Strip's main sources of income. The highly sophisticated yet idle Israeli navy has been mainly occupied in chasing small dinghies and fishing boats in recent years.

Hamas did not budge and refused to go away in return for the lifting of the blockade. Thus another pretext was sought: Israel violated the ceasefire in several attacks from the air and by incursion on the land on a daily basis during one week in June 2008. Consequently, groups that were not affiliated to Hamas retaliated with several rockets and the public opinion in Israel was now prepared for a larger operation.

To reinforce the point, in November 2008 the Israeli army attacked a tunnel, one of many dug in order to survive the blockade, and claimed that it was a pre-emptive strike against a future Hamas operation. This time Hamas fired the rockets. It lost six people in the attack and launched a barrage of more than thirty rockets. At the end of the month, Hamas declared that such Israeli actions, which had become a daily occurrence, had terminated the ceasefire.

On 18 November 2008, Hamas declared the end of the ceasefire and on the 24th intensified the barrage of missiles for a short time in response to the previous Israeli action, before ceasing after a while. As before there were hardly any casualties on the Israeli side, although houses and flats were damaged and the afflicted citizens traumatized.

The 24 November missile attack was what the Israeli army was waiting for. From the following morning until 21 January 2009, it bombarded the million and a half people of Gaza from the air, land and sea. Hamas responded with missiles that caused three casualties and another ten Israeli soldiers were killed, some by friendly fire.

The evidence collected by Israeli-based human rights organizations, by international agencies and the media (although the Israelis barred the media from entering the Strip) – some of it repeated in the Goldstone Report, which was both a very conservative and guarded summary of what occurred – reveals the true dimension of the massacre in Gaza in that period. (The South African Justice, Richard Goldstone was appointed by the UN at the head of a fact finding mission for the events in Gaza in 2009.)

The nearly 1500 killed and thousands of wounded, and tens of thousands who lost their homes, do not tell the whole story. Only the use of military force in the confines of such a space populated by civilians could produce the kind of collateral damage that was seen. It also displayed a desire on the army's part to try out new weaponry, all intended to kill civilians as part of what the former Chief of the Army General Staff, Moshe 'Bogie' Yaalon, termed the need to imprint upon the Palestinian consciousness the fearsome might of the Israeli army.[19]

A new, more cynical dimension was now added: international and Arab aid promised billions to help rebuild what Israel would probably destroy again in the future. Even the worst disaster can be profitable.

The next round of aggression occurred in 2012 with two operations: Returning Echo, which was smaller than the previous ones and escalated from a border clash; and, more significantly, Pillar of Defense in July 2012, which ended that summer's social protest movement in Israel. Hundred of thousands of middle class Israelis demonstrated for a few months, threatening to bring down the government for its economic and social policies. There is nothing like a war in the south to convince young Israelis to stop their protesting and go and defend the homeland. It worked before, and it worked this time as well.

In 2012 Hamas reached Tel Aviv for the first time, with missiles that caused little damage and no casualties. Typical of the familiar imbalance that year, 200 Palestinians were killed, including ten children.

This was not a bad year for Israel. An exhausted EU and US administration did not even condemn the 2012 attacks; in fact, they repeatedly cited 'Israel's right to defend itself'. No wonder that two years later the Israelis realized they could go even further.

Operation Protective Edge, in the summer of 2014, had been in the planning stage for two years and the abduction and killing of three settlers in the West Bank provided the pretext for a destructive operation that killed 2200 Palestinians. Israel itself was paralysed for a while as Hamas rockets even reached Ben-Gurion airport.

For the first time the Israeli army tried to take on the Palestinian guerrillas face to face in the Strip and lost sixty-six soldiers in the confrontation. This was a bit like a police force entering a maximum security prison in which the prisoners are besieged and running their own lives; you control them mainly from the outside parameters and you put yourself in danger if you try to invade it, to confront the desperation and resilience of those you are trying to starve and slowly squeeze the life out of. The Israelis knew all too well that such confrontation had to be avoided and therefore they still opted to use massive firepower, which, in the words of the army, contained the situation in the Strip rather than leading to the destruction of Hamas.

The war in Syria and the refugee crisis left little room for international action or interest. However, it seems everything is poised for yet another round of aggression against the people of Gaza. The UN predicted that, at such a rate of hostilities, by 2020 the Strip would become uninhabitable. This would be caused not only by military force but by what the UN called 'de-development' – a process whereby development is reversed.

> Three Israeli military operations in the past six years, in addition to eight years of economic blockade, have ravaged the already debilitated infrastructure of Gaza, shattered its productive base, left no time for meaningful reconstruction or economic recovery and impoverished the Palestinian population in Gaza, rendering their economic wellbeing worse than the level of two decades previous.[20]

This death sentence is even more likely since the military coup in Egypt. The new regime there has added its own closure on the only opening Gaza has, outside of Israel. Since 2010 the civil societies have sent flotillas of ships to show solidarity and break the siege. One of them, the *Mavi Marmara*, was viciously attacked by Israeli commandos, who killed nine of the passengers and arrested the rest. Other flotillas were treated better. However, the 2020 prediction still remains, and it seems that in order to avoid this happening the people of the Gaza Strip will need more than peaceful flotillas to persuade the Israelis to stop bringing about the slow death of Gaza.

The monstrous mega-prison Israel contemplated in 1963, and then built in 1967, is fifty years old as this book comes to a close. The third generation of inmates are still there waiting for the world to acknowledge their suffering and to realize that, as long as their oppression continues, it will be impossible to engage constructively with oppression elsewhere in the Middle East, and in particular in Syria. The immunity Israel has received over the last fifty years encourages others, regimes and oppositions alike, to believe that human and civil rights are irrelevant in the Middle East. The dismantling of the mega-prison in Palestine will send a different, and more hopeful, message to everyone living in this troubled part of the world.

Bibliography

Abudi, Yosi and Lachish, Zeev, 'The Moked Operation' in A. Shmuelevitz (ed.), *The Theatre of War – Decisive Battles in Eretz Israel*, Tel Aviv: Ministry of Defence Publications, 2007 (Hebrew)

Agha, Hussein and Malley, Robert, 'Camp David: The Tragedy of Errors', *New York Review of Books*, 9 August 2001

Alon, Yigal, *A Curtain of Sand*, Tel Aviv: Hakibbutz Hameuchad, 1960 (Hebrew)

Amos, John W., *Palestinian Resistance: Organization of a Nationalist Movement*, New York: Pergamon Press, 1980

Appleby, Scott, *Spokesmen for the Despised: Fundamentalist Leaders of the Middle East*, Chicago: Chicago University Press, 1996

Bar-Joseph, Uri, 'Rotem: The Forgotten Crisis on the Road to the 1967 War', *Journal of Contemporary History*, Volume 31, no. 3, July 1996

Bar-Siman-Tov, Yaacov, *Israel and the Peace Process 1977–1982: In Search of Legitimacy for Peace*, Albany: SUNY Press, 1994

Bavli, Dan, *Dreams and Missed Opportunities, 1967–1973*, Tel Aviv: Carmel, 2002 (Hebrew)

Benvenisti, Meron, *West Bank Data Project: A Survey of Israel's Policies*, New York: American Enterprise Institute for Public Policy Research, 1984

Benvenisti, Meron and Khayat, Shlomo, *The West Bank and Gaza Atlas*, Jerusalem: The West Bank Data Base Project, 1988

Benziman, Uzi, *Sharon: An Israeli Caesar*, New York: Adama, 1985

Bornstein, Avram S., *Crossing the Green Line: Between Israel and the West Bank*, Philadelphia: University of Pennsylvania Press, 2002

Bowker, Robert, *Palestinian Refugees: Mythology, Identity, and the Search for Peace*, Boulder: Lynne Rienner Publishers, 2003

Bowman, Glenn, 'Israel's wall and the logic of encystation: Sovereign exception or wild sovereignty?', *Focaal*, Volume 2007, no. 50, Winter 2007

Bowman, Glenn and Harrison, David, 'The Politics of Tour Guiding: Israeli and Palestinian Tour Guides in Israel and the Occupied Territories' in D. Harrison (ed.), *Tourism and the Less Developed Countries*, London: Belhaven Press, 1992

Budeiri, Musa, 'Democracy ... And the Experience of National Liberation: The Palestinian Case' in Ilan Pappe and Jamil Hilal (eds.), *Across the Wall: Narratives of Israeli–Palestinian History*, London and New York: I. B. Tauris, 2010

Caplan, Neil, '"*Oom-Shmoom*" Revisited: Israeli Attitudes towards the UN and the Great Powers, 1948–1960' in Abraham Ben-Zvi and Aharon Klieman (eds.), *Global Politics: Essays in Honour of David Vital*, London: Frank Cass, 2001

Chomsky, Noam, *Fateful Triangle*, Chicago: South End Press, 1983

Chomsky, Noam and Pappe, Ilan, *Gaza in Crisis: Reflections on Israel's War against the Palestinians*, London: Penguin, 2010

Cohen, Ayelet, 'The Power of Words', *Toar*, Volume 11, April 2001 (Hebrew)

Dayan, Moshe, *Aveni Derech*, Tel Aviv: Idanim, 1976 (Hebrew)

Dor, Daniel, *The Suppression of Guilt: The Israeli Media and the Reoccupation of the West Bank*, London: Pluto Press, 2005

Drucker, Raviv and Shelah, Ofer, *Boomerang*, Jerusalem: Keter, 2005 (Hebrew)

Efrat, Elisha, *Judea and Samaria: A Blueprint for Physical and Regional Planning*, Jerusalem: Ministry of the Interior Publication, 1970 (Hebrew)

European Union, Internal Report on 'Area C and Palestinian State Building', Brussels, January 2012, excerpts, *Journal of Palestine Studies*, 41/3, Spring 2012

Farsakh, Leila, *Palestinian Labour Migration to Israel: Labour, land and occupation*, London: Taylor and Francis, 2005

Farsoun, Samih K. (with Christina E. Zacharia), *Palestine and the Palestinians*, Boulder: Westview Press, 1997

Findley, Paul, *Deliberate Deceptions: Facing the Facts about the US–Israeli Relationship*, Washington: American Educational Trust, 1995

Finkelstein, Norman, *The Rise and Fall of Palestine: A Personal Account of the Intifada Years*, Minnesota: University of Minnesota Press, 1996

Fisk, Robert, *Pity the Nation: The Abduction of Lebanon*, New York: Nation Books, 2002

Freshwater, L. (pseudonym), 'Policy and Intelligence: The Arab-Israeli War', *Studies in Intelligence*, Volume 13, no. 1, Winter 1969 (declassified 2 July 1996)

Gazit, Shlomo, *The Carrot and the Stick: Israel's Policy in Judea and Samaria, 1967–68*, Tel Aviv: Kinert, Zamora-Bitan, 1985 (Hebrew)

Gluska, Ami, *Eshkol: Give an Order*, Tel Aviv: Ministry of Defence, 2004 (Hebrew)

Goldstein, Yossi, *Eshkol: Biography*, Jerusalem: Keter Publishing, 2003 (Hebrew)

Gordon, Neve, *Israel's Occupation*, Berkeley: University of California Press, 2008

Gorenberg, Gershom, *The End of Days: Fundamentalism and the Struggle for the Temple Mount*, New York: Oxford University Press, 2000

Hajjar, Lisa, Rabbani, Mouin and Beinin, Joel, 'Palestine and the Arab–Israeli Conflict for Beginners' in Zachary Lockman and Joel Beinin (eds.), *Intifada: The Palestinian Uprising Against Israeli Occupation*, Cambridge, MA: South End Press, 1989

Halabi, Usama, 'The Israeli Law in the Service of the Expropriation, Planning and Settlement Policies', *Mahbarot Adalah*, no. 2, Winter 2002 (Hebrew)

Heiberg, Marianne and Øvensen, Geir, 'Palestinian Society in Gaza, West Bank and Arab Jerusalem: A Survey of Living Conditions', Fafo Report 151, Oslo, 1993

Henriksen Waage, Hilde, 'Postscript to Oslo: The Mystery of Norway's Missing Files', *Journal of Palestine Studies*, Volume 38, no. 1, Autumn 2008

Hershberg, Marshal A., 'Ethnic Interest Groups and Foreign Policy: A case study of the activities of the organized Jewish community in regard to the 1968 decision to sell Phantom jets to Israel', unpublished PhD Dissertation, University of Pittsburgh, 1973

Huberman, Hagai, 'The Early Settlement of Gush Katif – The Five Fingers Plan' in Yehuda Zoldan (ed.), *The Bible and the Land*, Volume 7, Gush Etzion: The Biblical Institute, 2004 (Hebrew)

Hunter, F. Robert, *The Palestinian Uprising: A War by Other Means*, Berkeley: University of California Press, 1991

Inbar, Zvi, 'The Military Attorney General and the Occupied Territories', *The Law and the Army*, Volume 16, no. 1, 2002 (Hebrew)

Israeli, Rafi, *The First Decade of Israeli Rule in Judea and Samaria*, Jerusalem: The Truman Institute, 1977 (Hebrew)

Johnson, Penny, O'Brien, Lee and Hiltermann, Joost, 'The West Bank Rises Up' in Zachary Lockman and Joel Beinin (eds.), *Intifada: The Palestinian Uprising Against Israeli Occupation*, Cambridge, MA: South End Press, 1989

Kenan, Amos, *Israel: A Wasted Victory*, Tel Aviv: Amikam, 1970 (Hebrew)

Khalidi, Walid, 'Revisiting the UNGA Partition Resolution', *Journal of Palestine Studies*, Volume 27, no. 1, Autumn 1997

Kimmerling, Baruch, *Politicide: The Real Legacy of Ariel Sharon*, London and New York: Verso, 2003

Kretzmer, David, *The Occupation of Justice: The Supreme Court of Israel and the Occupied Territories*, New York: SUNY Press, 2002

Kurth Cronin, Audrey, 'How fighting ends: asymmetric wars, terrorism, and suicide bombing' in Holger Affelbach and Hew Strachan (eds.), *How Fighting Ends: A History of Surrender*, New York: Oxford University Press, 2012

Lein, Yezekhel and Weizman, Eyal, *Land Grab: Israel's Settlement Policy in the West Bank*, Special Report for B'Tselem, May 2002

Lenczowski, George, *American Presidents and the Middle East*, Durham, NC: Duke University Press, 1990

Louis, Wm. Roger, 'Britain: The Ghost of Suez and Resolution 242' in Wm. Roger Louis and Avi Shlaim (eds.), *The 1967 Arab–Israeli War: Origins and Consequences*, Cambridge: Cambridge University Press, 2012

Lustick, Ian S., *For the Land and the Lord: Jewish Fundamentalism in Israel*, New York: Council for Foreign Relations, 1988

Masalha, Nur, *Expulsion of the Palestinians: The Concept of 'Transfer' in Zionist Political Thought, 1882–1948*, Washington: Institute for Palestine Studies, 1992

Mishal, Shaul and Aharoni, Reuben, *Speaking Stones: The Words Behind the Palestinian Intifada*, Tel Aviv: Kibbutz Meuhad, 1989 (Hebrew)

Morris, Benny, *Israel's Border Wars, 1948–1956: Arab Infiltration, Israeli Retaliation, and the Countdown to the Suez War*, Oxford: Oxford University Press, 1997

Müller, Patrick, 'Occupation in Hebron: Settlements and the State of Israel', *News from Within*, Volume 20, Issue 6, September 2004

Mustafa, Issa, 'The Arab–Israeli Conflict over Water Resources', *Studies in Environmental Science*, Volume 58, 1994

Mutawi, Samir, *Jordan in the 1967 War*, Cambridge: Cambridge University Press, 2002

Nasrallah, Nami, 'The First and Second Palestinian Intifadas' in David Newman and Joel Peters (eds.), *The Routledge Handbook on the Israeli–Palestinian Conflict*, London and New York: Routledge 2013

Neff, Donald, 'The Intifada Erupts, Forcing Israel to Recognize Palestinians', *Washington Report on Middle Eastern Affairs*, December 1997

Newman, David, 'The Evolution of a Political Landscape: Geographical and Territorial Implications of Jewish Colonization in the West Bank', *Middle Eastern Studies*, Volume 21, no. 2, 1985

Oren, Michael B., *Power, Faith, and Fantasy: America in the Middle East, 1776 to the Present*, New York: W. W. Norton, 2007

— *Six Days of War: June 1967 and the Making of the Modern Middle East*, New York: Persidio Press, 2003

Oz, Amos, *My Michael*, Tel Aviv: Am Oved, 1976

Pappe, Ilan, 'Clusters of history: US involvement in the Palestine question', *Race & Class*, Volume 48/3, 2007

— 'De-Terrorising the Palestinian National Struggle: The Roadmap to Peace', *Critical Studies in Terrorism*, Volume 2, no. 2, August 2009

— *The Ethnic Cleansing of Palestine*, London and New York: Oneworld, 2006

— *The Forgotten Palestinians: A History of the Palestinians in Israel*, New Haven and New York: Yale University Press, 2011

— *A History of Modern Palestine: One Land, Two Peoples*, Cambridge: Cambridge University Press, 2006

— 'Jordan between Hashemite and Palestinian Identity' in Joseph Nevo and Ilan Pappe (eds.), *Jordan in the Middle East 1948–1988: The Making of a Pivotal State*, Ilford: Frank Cass, 1994

— 'The Junior Partner: Israel's Role in the 1948 Crisis' in Wm. Roger Louis and Roger Owen (eds.), *A Revolutionary Year: The Middle East in 1958*, London and New York: I. B Tauris, 2002

— *The Making of the Arab–Israeli Conflict, 1947–1951*, London and New York: I. B. Tauris, 1992

— 'Moshe Sharett, David Ben-Gurion and the "Palestinian Option"', *Studies in Zionism*, Volume 7, no. 1, Spring 1986

— 'Understanding the Enemy: A Comparative Analysis of Palestinian Islamist and Nationalist Leaflets, 1920s–1980s' in Ronald L. Nettler and Suha Taji-Farouki (eds.), *Muslim-Jewish Encounters: Intellectual Traditions and Modern Politics*, Amsterdam: Harwood, 1998

Pearlman, Wendy, *Violence, Nonviolence, and the Palestinian National Movement*, Cambridge: Cambridge University Press, 2011

Perlmutter, Amos, 'The Middle East: A Turning Point?: Begin's Rhetoric and Sharon's Tactics', *Foreign Affairs*, Volume 61, no. 1, Fall 1982

Playfair, Emma (ed.), *International Law and the Administration of Occupied Territories*, New York: Oxford University Press, 1992

Quigley, John, *Palestine and Israel: A Challenge to Justice*, Durham, NC: Duke University Press, 1990

Robage, David S., 'CIA Analysis of the 1967 Arab–Israeli War: Getting it Right', *Studies in Intelligence*, 49/1 in https://www.cia.gov/library/center-for-the-study-of-intelligence/csi-publications/csi-studies/studies/vol49no1/html_files/arab_israeli_war_1.html

Rokach, Livia, *Israel's Sacred Terrorism: A Study Based on Moshe Sharett's Personal Diary and Other Documents*, Belmont: AAUG Press, 3rd edition, 1986

Rosental, Rubik, 'The First One Hundred Days', *Panim – the Journal of the Teachers Union in Israel*, no. 39, 2007 (Hebrew)

Roy, Sara, *Hamas and the Civil Society in Gaza: Engaging the Islamist Social Sector*, Princeton: Princeton University Press, 2013

Said, Edward, 'Zionism from the Standpoint of Its Victims', *Social Text*, 1, Winter 1979

Sayigh, Yusif A., 'The Palestinian Economy under Occupation: Dependency and Pauperization', *Journal of Palestine Studies*, Volume 15, no. 4, Summer 1986

Schiff, Ze'ev and Ya'ari, Ehud, *Israel's Lebanon War*, New York: Simon and Schuster, 1984

— *Intifada: the Palestinian Uprising – Israel's Third Front*, New York: Simon and Schuster, 1989

Seal, Patrick, *Abu Nidal: A Gun For Hire*, London: Hutchinson, 1992

Segev, Tom, *1967: The Landscape Has Changed*, Jerusalem: Keter, 2005 (Hebrew)

Shafir, Gershon, 'The Miscarriage of Peace: Israel, Egypt, the United States, and the "Jarring Plan" in the Early 1970s', *Israel Studies Forum*, Volume 21, no. 1, Summer 2006

Shapira, Anita, *Yigal Allon, Native Son: A Biography*, Philadelphia: University of Pennsylvania Press, 2007

Shapira, Avraham, *Conversations Between Soldiers*, Tel Aviv: The Kibbutz Movement, 1967 (Hebrew)

Sharett, Moshe, *Personal Diary*, Tel Aviv: Maariv, 1978 (Hebrew)

Shehadeh, Raja, *The Third Way: A Journey of Life in the West Bank*, London: Quartet Books, 1982

Shindler, Colin, *A History of Modern Israel*, New York: Cambridge University Press, 2013

Shlaim, Avi, *Collusion Across the Jordan: King Abdullah, the Zionist Movement, and the Partition of Palestine*, New York: Columbia University Press, 1987

— 'Conflicting Approaches to Israel's Relations with the Arabs: Ben-Gurion and Moshe Sharett, 1953–1956', *The Middle East Journal*, 37/2, 1983

Smith, Charles, 'The United States and the 1967 War' in Wm. Roger Louis and Avi Shlaim (eds.), *The 1967 Arab–Israeli War: Origins and Consequences*, Cambridge: Cambridge University Press, 2012

Smith, Grant F., *Foreign Agents: The American Israel Public Affairs Committee from the 1963 Fulbright Hearings to the 2005 Espionage Scandal*, Washington: Institute for Research, 2007

Spiegel, Steven L., *The Other Arab–Israeli Conflict: Making America's Middle East Policy, from Truman to Reagan*, Chicago: Chicago University Press, 1985

Sprinzak, Ehud, *Brother Against Brother: Violence and Extremism in Israeli Politics From Altalena to the Rabin Assassination*, New York: Simon and Schuster, 1999

Stenberg, Petter, 'Creating a State of Belligerency: A Study of the Armistice Negotiations between Israel and Syria in 1949', Masters Thesis, University of Oslo, 2009

Tafakji, Khalil, 'The Impact of the Geographical and Demographic Colonization on the Jerusalem Question', paper presented to the International Symposium for Jerusalem Affairs, General Islamic Conference for Jerusalem, Amman, 2000 (Arabic)

Tamari, Salim, 'The Palestinians in the West Bank and Gaza: the Sociology of Dependency' in Khalil Nakhleh and Elia Zureik (eds.), *The Sociology of the Palestinians*, London: Croom Helm, 1980

Tessler, Mark, 'Israeli Thinking about the Palestinians: A Historical Survey' in Robert O. Freedman (ed.), *Israel's First Fifty Years*, Miami: University of Florida Press, 2000

Teveth, Shabtai, *The Cursed Blessing: The Story of Israel's Occupation of the West Bank*, Tel Aviv: Shoken, 1982 (Hebrew)

Weizman, Eyal, *Hollow Land: Israel's Architecture of Occupation*, London and New York: Verso, 2012

Wolfe, Patrick, 'Settler colonialism and the elimination of the native', *Journal of Genocide Research*, 8/4, 2006

Zertal, Idith and Eldar, Akiva, *Lords of the Land: The War Over Israel's Settlements in the Occupied Territories, 1967–2007*, New York: Nation Books, 2009

Notes

PREFACE: ONE HILL, TWO PRISONS

AND THREE AGENCIES

1. Amos Oz, *My Michael*, Tel Aviv: Am Oved, 1976, p. 186 (Hebrew).
2. This government official was appointed in 1950 to oversee the maintenance and selling of the real estate and lands of the Palestinians who were uprooted from Palestine in 1948.
3. Described by one of the participants in a scholarly article: Inbar, 'The Military Attorney General and the Occupied Territories', pp. 147–9. The article is in fact pages from Inbar's diary from those days.
4. Gazit, *The Carrot and the Stick*, 1985, p. 21.
5. Inbar, 'The Military Attorney General and the Occupied Territories'.
6. Ibid.
7. More will be said later about the censorship after the occupation. The main source for this is a report by the Israeli human rights organization B'Tselem, 'Banned Books and Authors', October 1989, http://www.btselem.org/sites/default/files2/banned_books_and_authors.pdf.
8. Gazit, *The Carrot and the Stick*, 1985, pp. 22–4.
9. Gazit, *The Carrot and the Stick*, 1985, p. 23.
10. The publisher is stated as the School for Political Science of the Hebrew University, 1963.
11. Gazit, *The Carrot and the Stick*, 1985, p. 26.
12. Pappe, *The Forgotten Palestinians*, 2011, p. 52.
13. See *Hapraklit* (*The Advocate*), February 1946, p. 58 (Hebrew).
14. In my book, *The Ethnic Cleansing of Palestine*, I have elaborated on what ethnic cleansing means in legal and academic terms. The gist of the discussion there shows that the international consensus is that this is a

policy meant to downsize a certain group on the basis of its identity. The means by which such a population is downsized varies from expulsion to intimidation, and it is a crime under international law whether this is inflicted on the population as a whole or only on part of it. The particular means used after 1967 could be best described as incremental ethnic cleansing, which entailed a set of actions and policies, discussed in chapter six, that were intended to downsize the Palestinian population.

I have elaborated in the Preface, pp. xxiv–xxv, on why the Israeli political elite decided not to enact a massive expulsion, on the scale witnessed in 1948. One can add that had they attempted it, the population would have fully resisted, and in addition, Jordan would have intervened or responded in such a way that it would have been almost impossible for the Israelis to implement it. The Egyptians might also have intervened.

INTRODUCTION: RE-READING THE NARRATIVE OF OCCUPATION

1. See Wolfe, 'Settler colonialism and the elimination of the native', pp.387–409, and Said, 'Zionism from the Standpoint of Its Victims', p. 7.

CHAPTER ONE: THE WAR OF CHOICE

1. All this was described in my book, *The Ethnic Cleansing of Palestine*, 2006.
2. Ibid.
3. The agreement with Jordan is covered in Shlaim, *Collusion Across the Jordan*, 1987.
4. He made this comment several times; the first was to the German journal *Der Spiegel*, on 5 November 1969.
5. I have discussed this in *The Making of the Arab-Israeli Conflict, 1947–1951*, 1992, pp. 180–91.
6. I have discussed this at length in 'The Junior Partner: Israel's Role in the 1948 Crisis', pp. 245–74.
7. See Shlaim, 'Conflicting Approaches to Israel's Relations with the Arabs', pp. 180–201.
8. See Khaled Diab, 'Israel's Part in Egypt's Revolution', *Haaretz* (English), 23 July 2012.

9. Caplan, '"*Oom-Shmoom*" Revisited: Israeli Attitudes Towards the UN and the Great Powers, 1948–1960', pp. 167–99.

10. Ibid.

11. I have dealt more extensively with the American perspective on this in 'Clusters of history', pp. 1–28.

12. Sharett, *Personal Diary*, 1978, entry for 26 May 1955, p. 1021.

13. Rokach, *Israel's Sacred Terrorism*, 1986.

14. See Pappe, 'The Junior Partner'.

15. Ibid.

16. Ibid.

17. See Pappe, 'Clusters of history', pp. 1–28.

18. See Stenberg, 'Creating a State of Belligerency', 2009.

19. See Pappe, 'The Junior Partner'.

20. Ibid.

21. Ibid.

22. Ibid.

23. Ibid.

24. See Segev, *1967*, 2005, p. 202.

25. See Pappe, 'The Junior Partner'.

26. Segev, *1967*, 2005, pp. 196–7.

27. Alon, *A Curtain of Sand*, 1960, pp. 344–8.

28. See details in Bar-Joseph, 'Rotem: The Forgotten Crisis on the Road to the 1967 War', pp. 547–66.

29. See Mustafa, 'The Arab–Israeli Conflict over Water Resources', pp. 123–33.

30. Abudi and Lachish, 'The Moked Operation' in Shmuelevitz (ed.), *The Theatre of War – Decisive Battles in Erez Israel*, 2007.

31. Lenczowski, *American Presidents and the Middle East*, 1990, pp. 105–15.

32. Oren, *Six Days of War*, 2003, p. 171.

33. Morris, *Israel's Border Wars, 1948–1956*, 1997.

34. *The New York Times*, 11 May 1997.

35. See *Maariv*, 2 June 1972.

36. Israel State Archives, government meetings, 8164/4-A, 21 May 1967.

37. *Le Monde*, 28 February 1968.

38. Israel State Archives, government meetings, 8164/4-A, 21 May 1967.

39. Ibid.

40. Ibid.

41. Ibid.

42. Ibid.

43. Israel State Archives, government meetings, 8164/4-A, 28–29 May 1967.

A full report on these meetings can be found in Segev, *1967*, 2005, pp. 308–09, which also features some of these quotes (it is best to read the Hebrew edition if possible).

44. Freshwater (pseudonym), 'Policy and Intelligence: The Arab-Israeli War', pp. 3, 8; Charles Smith, 'The United States and the 1967 War', p. 188; CIA Office of Current Intelligence (OCI), 'Overall Arab and Israeli Military Capabilities', 23 May 1967, Department of State, *Foreign Relations of the United States, 1964–1968, Volume XIX, The Arab-Israeli Crisis and War, 1967*, Washington, DC: Government Printing Office, 2003, Document 44.

45. Robage, 'CIA Analysis of the 1967 Arab–Israeli War'.

46. Ibid.

47. Ibid.

48. Israel State Archives, government meetings, 29 May 1967.

49. Ibid.

50. Robage, 'CIA Analysis of the 1967 Arab–Israeli War'.

51. Ibid.

52. Israel State Archives, government meetings, 29 May 1967.

53. Ibid.

54. Ibid.

55. Segev quotes this in *1967*, 2005, p. 309, as said in the meeting on 28 June, but I think that it was said on the next day according to the Israel State Archives minutes. The meeting began in the morning and ended in the early hours of the next morning.

56. Ibid.

57. Gluska, *Eshkol*, 2004, pp. 137–42.

58. Ibid.

59. See his testimony on the Gush Shalom website, 6 July 2008.

60. *Haaretz*, 18 June 1967.

61. Ben-Gurion Archives, Ben-Gurion Diary.

62. Mutawi, *Jordan in the 1967 War*, 2002, p. 181.

63. Ibid, pp. 154–6.

64. The government meeting, 5 June 1967, is also mentioned in the publication of a summary in Hebrew of this meeting by the Israeli State Archives accessible at http://www.archives.gov.il/NR/rdonlyres/F45223CB-F8FC-4878-9FE9-D399BE70DD04/0/RabinEbook18.pdf.

65. Louis, 'Britain: The Ghost of Suez and Resolution 242' in Louis and Shlaim (eds.), *The 1967 Arab–Israeli War*, 2012, p. 240.

66. Interview with Jerome McDonnell, WBEZ 91.5, 6 June 2007.

67. Israel State Archives, government meetings, 28 May 1967.

68. Israel State Archives, government meetings, 21 May 1967.

69. See Chomsky and Pappe, *Gaza in Crisis*, 2010, pp. 19–56.

70. Oren, *Power, Faith, and Fantasy*, 2007, p. 536.

71. Grant F. Smith, *Foreign Agents*, 2007.

CHAPTER TWO: DEVISING THE MEGA-PRISON

1. These numbers were quoted in different meetings of the Israeli government. See in particular the meetings of 11–12 and 18–19 June, Israel State Archives, government meetings. The meetings of the government from those days are displayed almost in full in http://www.archives.gov.il/publication. The full texts are in the archives, files in 8164/7-A (the meetings for the whole month can be found there).

2. See *Haaretz*, 23 June 1967.

3. This is the title of Shlomo Gazit's book in Hebrew.

4. See minutes from 11 and 18 June 1967, Israel State Archives, government meetings.

5. Israel State Archives, government meetings, 18 June 1967.

6. Ibid.

7. Israel State Archives, government meetings, 19 June 1967. Bavli, *Dreams and Missed Opportunities*, 2002, p. 35 also writes that this decision was taken on the 19th.

8. Israel State Archives, government meetings, 19 June 1967.

9. *The Times*, 25 June 1969.

10. Israel State Archives, government meetings, Cabinet meeting, 18 June 1967.

11. Ibid.

12. Ibid.

13. Ibid.

14. Ibid.

15. Ibid.

16. Ibid.

17. Ibid.

18. Ibid.

19. Ibid.

20. See Pappe, *A History of Modern Palestine*, 2006, p. 51.

21. Israel State Archives, government meetings, Cabinet meeting, 18 June 1967.

22. Ibid.

23. Ibid.

24. Israel State Archives, government meetings, 19 June 1967.

25. Ibid.

26. See a very good article on this by Bowman and Harrison, 'The Politics of Tour Guiding' in Harrison (ed.), *Tourism and the Less Developed Countries*, 1992, pp. 121–34.

27. Quoted in the government meeting.

28. Diplomatic Note from Secretary of State Rusk to the Israeli Ambassador. US Department of State: Office of the Historian. US Government. Retrieved 9 November 2015.

29. Lenczowski, *American Presidents and the Middle East*, 1990, p. 105.

30. LBJ, National Security File, Box 104/107, Middle East Crisis: Jerusalem to the Secretary of State, 8 June 1967; Barbour to Department, 8 June 1967; Joint Embassy Memorandum, 8 June 1967.

31. This early period is discussed in detail in Chomsky and Pappe, *Gaza in Crisis*, 2010, pp. 19–56.

32. A prediction made in the government meeting on 19 June 1967.

33. These quotes can be found in a special report on the Israeli Settlements in the Occupied Territories, A Special Publication of the Foundation for Middle East Peace, February 1994.

34. Ibid.

35. See Chomsky and Pappe, *Gaza in Crisis*, 2010, pp. 19–56.

36. Israel State Archives, government meetings, 19 June 1967.

37. Ibid.

38. *Haaretz* published long quotes from this meeting, 2 November 2003.

39. Spiegel, *The Other Arab–Israeli Conflict*, 1985, p. 160, and Hershberg, 'Ethnic Interest Groups and Foreign Policy', 1973, pp. 27–8.

40. In *Haaretz*.

41. See, for instance, *Haaretz* and *Maariv*, 21 and 26 June 1967.

42. *Haaretz*, 7 June 1967.

43. This argument is made by Zertal and Eldar, *Lords of the Land*, 2009.

44. On Fulbright and AIPAC see Pappe, 'Clusters of history', pp. 4–27.

45. See further analysis on this in Pappe, *The Forgotten Palestinians*, 2011, pp. 94–100.

46. See Pappe, 'Moshe Sharett, David Ben-Gurion and the "Palestinian Option", pp. 77–95.

47. See 'Palestinians revive idea of one-state solution', *Toronto Star*, 15 September 2008.

48. Shehadeh, *The Third Way*, 1982.

49. *Haaretz*, 8 June 1967. *Haaretz*'s general line from 27 May 1967 was that Israel should attack Egypt, and later it supported an overall war.

CHAPTER THREE: THE GREATER
JERUSALEM AS A PILOT PROJECT

1. A dunam is a unit of land used in the Ottoman Empire and still in use in many parts of the Middle East. One dunam is about 1000 square metres, roughly equivalent to a quarter of an acre or 0.1 hectare.
2. See Goldstein, *Eshkol: Biography*, 2003, p. 736, note 914.
3. The Popular Front for the Liberation of Palestine was founded in 1967. It subscribed to Marxist-Leninist ideology and was led by George Habash.
4. Writing in *The Jerusalem Report*, 28 February 2000.
5. Segev, *1967*, 2005, p. 513.
6. See Tafakji, 'The Impact of the Geographical and Demographic Colonization on the Jerusalem Question'.
7. Lein and Weizman, *Land Grab*, 2002.
8. Weizman, *Hollow Land*, 2012, pp. 35–8.
9. Tafakji, 'The Impact of the Geographical and Demographic Colonization on the Jerusalem Question'.
10. Faisal al-Husseini was a Palestinian statesman, seated in the Orient House in Jerusalem and leading the community there in the struggle against Judaization and for Palestinian independence. A member of one of Palestine's most venerated families, Faisal was the son of Abd al-Qader al-Husseini, the revered Palestinian war hero from 1948 who was killed in the battle over Jerusalem in April 1948, the grandson of Musa Kazim Pasha al-Husseini, mayor of Jerusalem, and great-nephew of Haj Amin al-Husseini, the grand mufti of Jerusalem in the Mandatory period.
11. On this struggle read Zertal and Eldar, *Lords of the Land*, 2009, pp. 165–6.
12. A very thorough description of what happened to the Mamilla area can be read in Sylvia Schwarz, 'The Destruction of the Mamilla Cemetery: Desecration of a Sacred Site', OpedNews, 9 June 2010: www.opednews. com/articles/The-Destruction-of-the-Mam-by-Sylvia-Schwarz-100906-17.html.
13. Article 8(b)(viii).

CHAPTER FOUR: THE ALON VISION

1. Anita Shapira, *Yigal Allon, Native Son*, 2007.
2. *Foreign Relations of the United States, 1964–1968, Volume XX, Arab–Israeli Dispute, 1967–1968*, Telegram from the Embassy in Jordan to the

Department of State Department, Amman, 19 December 1968, Document 353.

3. Israel State Archives, government meetings, 18 June 1967.

4. Segev, *1967*, 2005, p. 449.

5. Goldstein, *Eshkol: Biography*, 2003.

6. www.pmo.gov.il/History/PastPMM/Pages/eshkol.aspx (Hebrew).

7. Israel State Archive, government meetings, 16718/6-G, 20 August 1967.

8. The various decrees and orders in English can be found in several sources. The internet's most accessible source for the text of these early decrees, including No. 25, can be found at www.itisapartheid.org/Documents_pdf_etc/ApartheidLawsOccupied.pdf.

9. *Haaretz*, 6 October 1995.

10. He declared this while the cabinet approved the establishment of the first colonies in the Jordan Valley but decided to make public its decision. Israel State Archives, government meetings, Cabinet meeting, 28 January 1968.

11. Eshkol Archive, Israel Galili letter to Eshkol, 14 August 1968.

12. Israel State Archives, government meetings, 8164/7-A, 26 June 1967.

13. Ibid.

14. This was reported also in the Israeli press: see *Maariv*, 19 September 1971.

15. Huberman, 'The Early Settlement of Gush Katif – The Five Fingers Plan' in Zoldan (ed.), *The Bible and the Land*, 2004.

16. Benvenisti and Khayat, *The West Bank and Gaza Atlas*, 1988, p. 62.

17. Israel State Archives, government meeting, 7927/4-A, 11 June 1967.

18. Israel State Archives, government meeting, 18 June 1967.

19. Ibid.

20. Ibid.

21. See a review of this plan, ten years after it was conceived, in 'Your Own Garden and Your Own Tank', *Haaretz*, 16 October 2001.

CHAPTER FIVE: ECONOMIC REWARDS AND PUNITIVE REPRISALS

1. See the analysis of Sayigh, 'The Palestinian Economy under Occupation: Dependency and Pauperization', pp. 46–67.

2. See Tamari, 'The Palestinians in the West Bank and Gaza' in Nakhleh and Zureik (eds.), *The Sociology of the Palestinians*, 1980, pp. 84–111.

3. Israel State Archives, government meeting, 18 June 1967.

4. On the beginning of the process see Farsakh, *Palestinian Labour Migration to Israel*, 2005, pp. 82–5.

5. See Tamari, 'The Palestinians in the West Bank and Gaza' in Nakhleh and Zureik (eds.), *The Sociology of the Palestinians*, 1980, pp. 84–111.

6. *Haaretz*, 25 June 1967.

7. Israel State Archives, government meetings, 18 June 1967.

8. Israel State Archives, government meetings, 20 June 1967.

9. www.ariel-sharon-life-story.com/08-Ariel-Sharon-Biography-1971-War-against-Terrorism.shtml.

10. The recommendation to employ the same methods as the British did in 1936 to 1939 were expressed in the doctoral dissertation of a senior army officer, the head of the history department of the IDF, submitted to the University of Haifa. 'The First Intifada: The Repression of the Arab Revolt, 1936–1939', 1998 (Hebrew).

11. *Haaretz*, 5 April 1968.

12. Lyrics by Haim Hefer; it was sung by the military choir of the Central Command.

13. Shafir, 'The Miscarriage of Peace', pp. 3–26.

CHAPTER SIX: THE ETHNIC CLEANSING OF JUNE 1967

1. For a definition of ethnic cleansing, see Note 14 in the Preface.

2. See Segev, *1967*, 2005, and the discussions reported there, pp. 558–68. According to Segev, the idea of mass expulsion was intact well into mid-1968.

3. Dor, *The Suppression of Guilt*, 2005.

4. These and other protestations were reported by Abba Eban in a letter to Eshkol, see Israel State Archives, government meetings, 7921/A/-2, 12 July 1967.

5. Israel State Archives, government meetings, 26 June 1967.

6. Ibid.

7. Reported in *Haaretz*, 21 June 1967. It was also reported here that hundreds of people were moved to Egypt by the Israeli forces, according to Egyptian sources.

8. *Haaretz*, 19 June 1967.

9. Details about them can be seen in the UNRWA website, www.unrwa.org/where-we-work/jordan.

10. *Haaretz*, 21 June 1967.

11. Israel State Archives, government meetings, 18 June 1967.

12. UN Archives, 'Report of the Special Committee to Investigate Israeli Practices Affecting Human Rights of the Population of the Occupied Territories', Document A/8389, 5 October 1971.

13. Segev, *1967*, 2005, p. 426.

14. Israel State Archives, government meetings, 25 June 1967.

15. Ibid.

16. Ibid.

17. Ibid.

18. Ibid.

19. Ibid.

20. Ibid.

21. See https://www.youtube.com/watch?v=NrhaglA5c_w. See also John Dirlik, '"Canada Park" Built on Ruins of Palestinian Villages', *The Washington Report on Middle East Affairs*, October 1991, pp. 34–5.

22. The Israeli journalist Yossi el-Gazi has put the whole diary on his blog: http://www.defeatist-diary.com/.

23. Kenan, *Israel: A Wasted Victory*, 1970, p.18.

24. Ibid.

25. Israel State Archives, government meetings, 25 June 1967.

26. Ibid.

27. Ibid.

28. Bowman, 'Israel's wall and the logic of encystation', pp. 127–35.

29. Israel State Archives, government meetings, 25 June 1967.

30. Ibid.

31. Ibid.

32. Ibid.

33. Ibid.

34. Ibid.

35. Ibid.

36. Ibid.

37. Ibid.

38. Ibid.

39. Ibid.

40. Robert Bowker estimates that roughly 300,000 Palestinians became refugees in these operations. See Bowker, *Palestinian Refugees*, 2003, p. 81.

41. Segev, *1967*, 2005, p. 548.

CHAPTER SEVEN: THE LABOUR LEGACY, 1968–1977

1. See for instance Rafi Israeli, *The First Decade of Israeli Rule in Judea and Samaria*, 1977, and Teveth, *The Cursed Blessing*, 1982.

2. For a concise history of this episode in the party's history see Shindler, *A History of Modern Israel*, 2013, pp. 128–45.

3. See Zertal and Eldar, *Lords of the Land*, 2009, pp. 66–81, and for an even more concise deconstruction of the narrative that accompanied this act see Gordon, *Israel's Occupation*, 2008, pp. 123–4.

4. On the early stages see Newman, 'The Evolution of a Political Landscape', pp. 192–205.

5. Lustick, *For the Land and the Lord: Jewish Fundamentalism in Israel*, 1988, pp. 42–72.

6. For a settler's view on this formative moment see Israel Harel, 'Not *Gush Emunim* but Zionism', *Haaretz*, 2 December 2011.

7. Gordon, *Israel's Occupation*, 2008, p. 124.

8. See the ICRC, Convention (IV) relative to the Protection of Civilian Persons in Time of War, Geneva, 12 August 1949.

9. See Amos, *Palestinian Resistance*, 1980, pp. 228–313.

10. http://www.toraland.org.il is his Hebrew website.

CHAPTER EIGHT: THE BUREAUCRACY OF EVIL

1. The documents have been published selectively, but quite tellingly, in 1971 by the Israeli Archives. See *The Israeli Ministry of Defence, The Occupied Territories, 1967-1971*, Tel Aviv: Ministry of Defence (this volume is 750 pages).

2. Ibid.

3. Gazit, *The Stick and the Carrot*, 1985, pp. 94–5.

4. Gazit, *The Stick and the Carrot*, 1985, pp. 97–8.

5. Inbar, 'The Military Attorney General and the Occupied Territories', p. 158.

6. Gordon, *Israel's Occupation*, 2008, p. 26.

7. See the discussion in Gordon, *Israel's Occupation*, 2008.

8. Decree on the Administrative Arrangements of Rule and Law (Ha-shilton ve Ha-Mishpat), the West Bank, 7 June 1967.

9. Kretzmer, *The Occupation of Justice*, 2002, p. 2.

10. https://www.hrw.org/report/2010/12/19/separate-and-unequal/israels-discriminatory-treatment-palestinians-occupied.

11. B'Tselem published a Position Paper in Hebrew entitled 'Legislation Permitting Physical and Mental Pressure in the Shabak Investigation' in January 2000, which examines the violations of human rights involved in these policies. This can be accessed at www.btselem.org/download/200001_torture_position_paper_heb.doc.

12. See Pappe, *The Ethnic Cleansing of Palestine*, 2006, p. 226.

13. Adalah, the Palestinian NGO for legal rights of the Arab Minority in Israel, began challenging this application in 2013. See Adalah news bulletin: 'Israeli Supreme Court Defers Decision in Absentee Property Cases in East Jerusalem', 10 September 2013, in www.adalah.org/eng/Articles/2202/Israeli-Supreme-Court-Defers-Decision-in-Absentee, and an article by Haneen Naamnih and Suhad Bishara, 'The Law of the Promised Land 2011: Between Absentees and Foreigners', 31 May 2008, in www.adalah.org/eng/Articles/2029/The-Law-of-the-Promised-Land-2011.

14. In 1997 the army issued a list and history of these decrees in booklet form. This one appears in 'The Legal Advisor to the areas of Judea and Samaria [*sic*], Pamphlets, Decrees and Appointments, Judea and Samaria', Issue 174, pp. 2291–997 (published in Hebrew and Arabic in 1997).

15. See Hunter, *The Palestinian Uprising*, 1991, p. 48.

16. The Palestine Liberation Army was established by the Arab League in 1964 as the military wing of the PLO.

17. Israel State Archives, government meetings, 25 June 1967.

18. See Tamari, 'The Palestinians in the West Bank and Gaza' in Nakhleh and Zureik (eds.), *The Sociology of the Palestinians*, 1980, and Israeli, *The First Decade of Israeli Rule in Judea and Samaria*, 1977, for two opposing perspectives on this.

19. *Haaretz*, 25 June 1967.

20. Rosental, 'The First One Hundred Days', *Panim*.

21. *Haaretz*, 22 June 1967.

22. This is the same journalist, Rubik Rosental named above, who originally published the *Panim* article in *Maariv*, on 18 April 1997.

23. Dayan, *Aveni Derech*, 1976, pp. 450–550.

24. Farsoun (with Zacharia), *Palestine and the Palestinians*, 1997, pp. 66–123.

25. Bavli, *Dreams and Missed Opportunities*, 2002, p. 21.

26. Menachem Begin instructed the Israeli Broadcasting Authority to use the new terms. See Cohen, 'The Power of Words'.

27. Efrat, *Judea and Samaria*, 1970.

28. Ibid.

29. Halabi, 'The Israeli Law in the Service of the Expropriation, Planning and Settlement Policies', pp. 6–13.

CHAPTER NINE: ON THE ROAD TO THE INTIFADA, 1977–1987

1. See Menachem Begin's article, 'Those Who Pave the Way for a Palestinian State', *Maariv*, 10 December 1976.

2. The financial cost of this preferential attitude was calculated only in 2009: www.peacenow.org.il/preferredareas.

3. Müller, 'Occupation in Hebron', pp. 19–24.

4. Bar-Siman-Tov, *Israel and the Peace Process 1977–1982*, 1994, pp. 68–9.

5. Chomsky, *Fateful Triangle*, 1983, pp. 187–92.

6. Ibid.

7. Fisk, *Pity the Nation*, 2002, p. 138.

8. So claims Shlomo Nakdimon who was very close to Begin. Shlomo Nakdimon, 'Begin's Legacy "Yehiel, It Ends Today"', *Haaretz*, 22 February 2012.

9. For a critical assessment of Sharon see Benziman, *Sharon: An Israeli Caesar*, 1985.

10. Budeiri, 'Democracy . . . And the Experience of National Liberation' in Pappe and Hilal (eds.), *Across the Wall*, 2010, p. 336.

11. Tessler, 'Israeli Thinking about the Palestinians' in Freedman (ed.), *Israel's First Fifty Years*, 2000, p. 110.

12. Kimmerling, *Politicide*, 2003.

13. Ibid.

14. Gorenberg, *The End of Days*, 2000, pp. 128–37.

15. The official is interviewed in Ra'anan Alexadrowicz's documentary *The Law in These Parts*. Full interviews are provided on the film's website: www.thelawfilm.com/eng#!/the-film.

16. Zertal and Eldar, *Lords of the Land*, 2009, p. 102.

17. Halabi, 'The Israeli Law in the Service of the Expropriation, Planning and Settlement Policies', pp. 6–13.

18. See Seal, *Abu Nidal*, 1992.

19. This was already noted in an article in September 1982. See Perlmutter, 'The Middle East: A Turning Point?', pp. 67–83.

20. Schiff and Ya'ari, *Israel's Lebanon War*, 1984, pp. 283–4.

21. Pappe, 'Jordan between Hashemite and Palestinian Identity' in Nevo and Pappe (eds.), *Jordan in the Middle East 1948–1988*, 1994, pp. 61–94.

22. Johnson, O'Brien and Hiltermann, 'The West Bank Rises Up' in Lockman and Beinin (eds.), *Intifada*, 1989, p. 32.

23. Tamari, 'The Palestinians in the West Bank and Gaza' in Nakhleh and Zureik (eds.), *The Sociology of the Palestinians*, 1980.

24. Schiff and Ya'ari, *Intifada*, 1989.

25. Tamari, 'The Palestinians in the West Bank and Gaza' in Nakhleh and Zureik (eds.), *The Sociology of the Palestinians*, 1980.

26. Hajjar, Rabbani and Beinin, 'Palestine and the Arab–Israeli Conflict for Beginners' in Lockman and Beinin (eds.), *Intifada*, 1989, p. 102.

27. Schiff and Ya'ari, *Intifada*, 1989.
28. Heiberg and Øvensen, 'Palestinian Society in Gaza, West Bank and Arab Jerusalem', p. 124.
29. Ori Nir, 'Not Every Day is Purim', Middle East Online, 13 March 2009, www.middle-east-online.com/english/?id=30944.
30. Benvenisti, *West Bank Data Project*, 1984.
31. A breakdown of these numbers and more information can be found in the B'Tselem website: www.btselem.org/topic/deportation.
32. Ibid.
33. Boaz Evron, 'How Can One Enjoy from All the Worlds [How can one have cake and eat it]', *Yedioth Ahronoth*, 8 December 1978.
34. Avraham Shapira, *Conversations Between Soldiers*, 1967.

CHAPTER TEN: THE FIRST INTIFADA, 1987–1993

1. Neff, 'The Intifada Erupts, Forcing Israel to Recognize Palestinians', pp. 81–3.
2. United Nations, General Assembly, Resolution 43/21, 'The Uprising of the Palestinian People', 3 November 1988.
3. Neff, 'The Intifada Erupts, Forcing Israel to Recognize Palestinians', pp. 81–3.
4. Finkelstein, *The Rise and Fall of Palestine*, 1996.
5. Mishal and Aharoni, *Speaking Stones*, 1989, pp. 14–20.
6. Human Rights Watch, 'Israel, the Occupied West Bank and the Gaza Strip, and the Palestinian Authority Territories', Volume 13, no. 4, November 2001, pp. 48–9.
7. Kurth Cronin, 'How fighting ends' in Affelbach and Strachan (eds.), *How Fighting Ends*, 2012, p. 426.
8. Nasrallah, 'The First and Second Palestinian Intifadas' in Newman and Peters (eds.), *The Routledge Handbook on the Israeli–Palestinian Conflict*, 2013, p. 56.
9. A recent summary of the real meaning of excessive use by Israel was published by Amnesty International: '"Trigger-happy" Israeli army and police use reckless force in the West Bank', 27 February 2014.
10. The US State Department, Country Reports on Human Rights Practices, 1988–1991. The report for 1988 can now be digitally accessed at www.archive.org/details/countryreportson1988unit.
11. United Nations Publications, *Repertory of Practice of United Nations Organs, Supplement No. 7, Covering the period 1 January 1985 to 31 December 1988*, Volume VI, p. 71.

12. Pearlman, *Violence, Nonviolence, and the Palestinian National Movement*, 2011, p. 114.

13. Roy, *Hamas and Civil Society in Gaza*, 2013, p. 23.

14. A very good article on this can be found in Andrew Higgins, 'How Israel Helped to Spawn Hamas', *The Wall Street Journal*, 24 January 2009.

15. Pappe, 'Understanding the Enemy' in R. Nettler and S. Taji-Farouki (eds.), *Muslim-Jewish Encounters*, 1998, pp. 87–108.

16. Pappe, 'De-Terrorising the Palestinian National Struggle', pp. 127–46.

17. See a good analysis in 'Israel Must Withdraw all Settlers or Face ICC, says UN Report', *The Guardian*, 31 January 2013.

18. See 'Europe Threatens to Withdraw Support for Israel over Settlement Building Plans', *Haaretz*, 2 December 2012.

19. Most of the information here is taken from the B'Tselem 1990 annual report, pp. 23–4.

20. Ibid.

21. See B'Tselem Report for March–May 1993.

22. Ibid.

23. Jamal Abu Samhadana was the founder of the Popular Resistance Committees in the Rafah area in Gaza; he was assassinated by the Israelis in 2006 for his involvement in military actions against them.

24. B'Tselem Report for March–May 1993.

25. Ibid.

26. Ibid.

27. There is a powerful description of the early experiences at the checkpoint in Bornstein, *Crossing the Green Line*, 2002, pp. 2–3.

28. This connection is exposed in *The Lab*, a film by Yotam Feldman (2013). More details on the film's website: www.gumfilms.com/lab.

29. Findley, *Deliberate Deceptions*, 1995, p. 88.

30. Very thorough research can be found in Farsakh, *Palestinian Labour Migration to Israel*, 2005.

31. Report to the UN, 'Economic and Social Repercussions of the Israeli Occupation', in Resolution 53/230 of the UN General Assembly, 22 December 1999.

32. Quoted in *The Jerusalem Post*, 5 March 1988, p. 7.

33. On the origins of this phenomenon see Sprinzak, *Brother Against Brother*, 1999, pp. 177–9.

34. This was not the worst of the events in that time: see 'Two Palestinians Teens Killed by Israeli Gunfire', *Los Angeles Times*, 23 February 1988.

35. A vivid description is in Chomsky, *Fateful Triangle*, 1983, p. 495.
36. According to some sources, by 2012, 800,000 Palestinians had been arrested. Mohamedd Mar'i, 'Israeli Forces Arrested 800,000 Palestinians since 1967', *Saudi Gazette*, 12 December 1967.
37. Mary Curtius, 'Palestinian Villagers are Defiant after Israeli Troops End Tax Siege', *Boston Globe*, 2 November 1989.
38. Stephen J. Sosebee, 'The Passing of Yitzhak Rabin, Whose "Iron Fist" Fuelled Intifada', *The Washington Report on Middle East Affairs*, Volume 9, no. 5, 31 October 1990, p. 9.
39. Lockman and Beinin (eds.), *Intifada*, 1989, p. 1.
40. B'Tselem Report, 'Harm to Palestinians collaborating with Israel', 1 January 2011.
41. Appleby, *Spokesmen for the Despised*, 1996, pp. 5–6, 225–6, 400–01. This is the only book I know that puts Rabbi Kook and Yassin in the same research!
42. Appleby, *Spokesmen for the Despised*, 1996, p. 238.
43. For a detailed breakdown see B'Tselem, 'Fatalities in the first Intifada', www.btselem.org/statistics/first_intifada_tables.
44. There is an excellent account of all these aspects in Sonja Karkar, 'The First Intifada 20 Years Later', The Electronic Intifada, 10 December 2007.
45. Ibid.

CHAPTER ELEVEN: THE OSLO CHARADE
AND THE SECOND INTIFADA

1. Nur Masalha, *Expulsion*, 1992, p. 107.
2. Khalidi, 'Revisiting the UNGA Partition Resolution', pp. 5–21.
3. I recommend reading thoroughly the best account of the developments leading to the Oslo Accord in Henriksen Waage, 'Postscript to Oslo', pp. 54–65.
4. See http://israelipalestinian.procon.org/view.background-resource.php?resourceID=000921.
5. See Ian Black, 'How the Oslo Accord Robbed the Palestinians', *The Guardian*, 4 February 2013.
6. See http://thepalestinepapers.com/en/projects/thepalestinepapers/20121821231215230.html.
7. Pappe, *The Making of the Arab-Israeli Conflict, 1947–1954*, 1992, pp. 203–43.
8. Bowker, *Palestinian Refugees*, 2003, p. 157.
9. Benvenisti, *West Bank Data Project*, 1984.

10. Agha and Malley, 'Camp David: The Tragedy of Errors'.

11. Dor, *The Suppression of Guilt*, 2005.

12. Drucker and Shelah, *Boomerang*, 2005.

13. For the full text see: http://eeas.europa.eu/mepp/docs/mitchell_report_2001_en.pdf.

14. UN Office for the Coordination of Humanitarian Affairs – Occupied Palestinian Territory, 'The Humanitarian Impact on Palestinians of Israeli Settlements and Other Infrastructure in the West Bank', April 2009.

15. European Union, Internal Report on 'Area C and Palestinian State Building', pp. 220–23.

16. Playfair (ed.), *International Law and the Administration of Occupied Territories*, 1992, p. 396.

17. Human Rights Watch, which ironically is banned from Israel, has annually catalogued these abuses.

18. World Bank Technical Team Report, 'Movement and Access Restrictions in the West Bank', 9 May 2007.

19. European Union, Internal Report on 'Area C and Palestinian State Building', pp 220–23.

CHAPTER TWELVE: THE ULTIMATE MAXIMUM SECURITY PRISON MODEL – THE GAZA STRIP

1. On the plans to establish the dummy city see the daily *Globes* (Hebrew), 20 May 2002 (planning actually began in 2002); there was also an interesting report of a soldier who participated in the training on the blog on 7 November 2009, www.dacho.co.il/showthread.php, although this blog has now been removed for obvious reasons (it was available until 2010). IDF's own announcement on its website in an article by Ido Elazar has also been removed.

2. See Ilan Pappe, 'Responses to Gaza', *London Review of Books*, 21, no. 2, 29 January 2009, pp. 5–6.

3. Ibid.

4. Breaking the Silence, *Report on Gaza*, 15 July 2009. The NGO has a website, www.shovrimshtik.org, where this report is available and it has also published a 96-page booklet entitled *Soldiers' Testimonies from Operation Cast Lead: Gaza 2009*.

5. John Dugard, *Report of the Special Rapporteur on the Situation of Human Rights in the Palestinian Territories Occupied by Israel Since 1967*, UN Commission on Human Rights, Geneva: United Nations, 3 March 2005.

6. See *Yedioth Ahronoth* for an analysis by the Israeli journalist Roni Sofer on 27 September 2005.

7. Amos Harel and Avi Issacharoff, 'Analysis: Gaza Gains have Softened Israel Stance on Shalit Deal', 25 January 2009, www.haaretz.com/print-edition/news/analysis-gaza-gains-have-softened-on-Shalit-deal-1.268774.

8. See the report by Amir Buhbut and Uri Glickman, 'The IDF Had Attacked in Gaza', *Maariv*, 25 September 2005.

9. Several generals and ex-generals expressed this view in a collection of articles in a strategic journal published by the Israeli Institute for National Security Studies, *Strategic Assessment*, Volume 11, no. 4, February 2009.

10. Amos Harel and Avi Issacharoff, 'One humiliation too many', *Haaretz*, 13 July 2006.

11. Ilan Pappe, 'Ingathering', *London Review of Books*, 28, no. 8, 20 April 2006, p. 15.

12. Yehuda Ben Meir and Dafna Shaked, 'The Israeli Body Politic: Views on Key National Security Issues', *Strategic Assessment*, Volume 10, no. 1, June 2007, pp. 31–35.

13. See Pappe, *The Ethnic Cleansing of Palestine*, 2006.

14. Seán MacBride et al, *Israel in Lebanon: The Report of the International Commission to Enquire into Reported Violations of International Law by Israel during Its Invasion of Lebanon*, London: Ithaca Press, 1983.

15. See the UN Office for the Coordination of Humanitarian Affairs (OCHA) Special Report of August 2007.

16. B'Tselem, '683 people killed in the conflict in 2006', press release, 28 December 2006: www.btselem.org/english/Press_Releases/20061228.asp.

17. Ibid.

18. Gabi Siboni, 'The Third Threat', *Haaretz*, 30 September 2009.

19. Breaking the Silence, *Report on Cast Lead Operation*, 15 July 2009.

20. UN News Centre, 'Gaza could become uninhabitable in less than five years due to ongoing de-development', 1 September 2015.

Maps

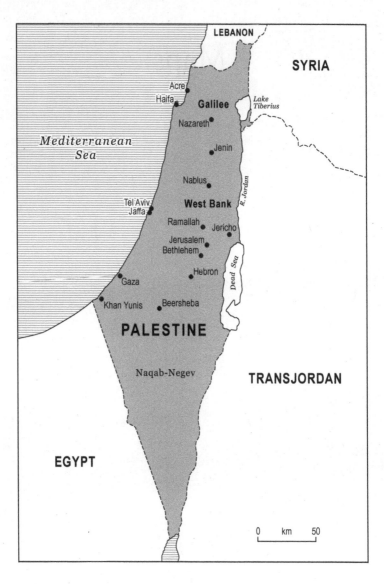

Pre-1948 Historical Palestine

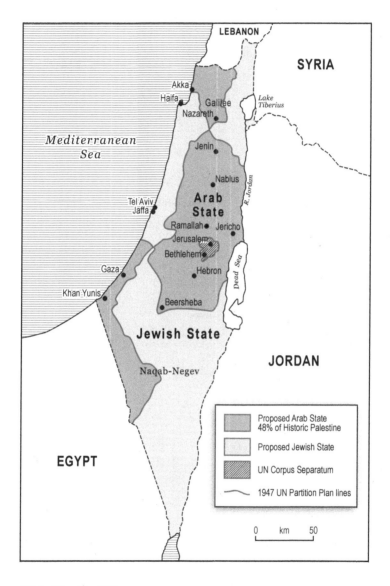

UN Partition Plan 1947

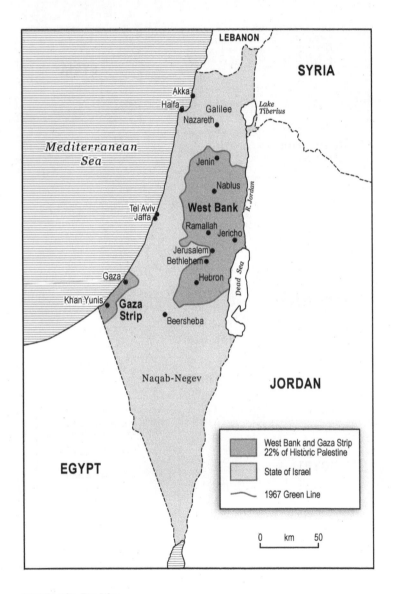

1967 Post Six-Day War

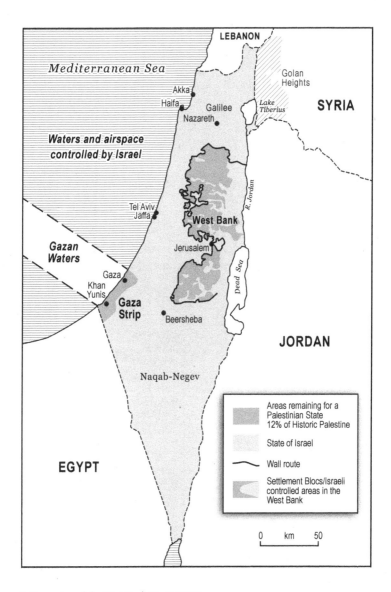

Settlements and the West Bank Barrier 2006

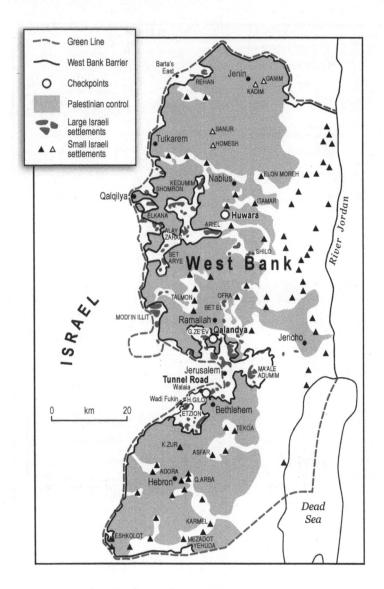

The West Bank in 2006 showing the Green Line vs. West Bank Barrier

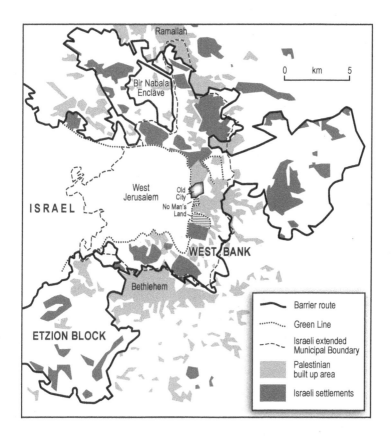

East Jerusalem 2007 showing the development of new settelements in the West Bank

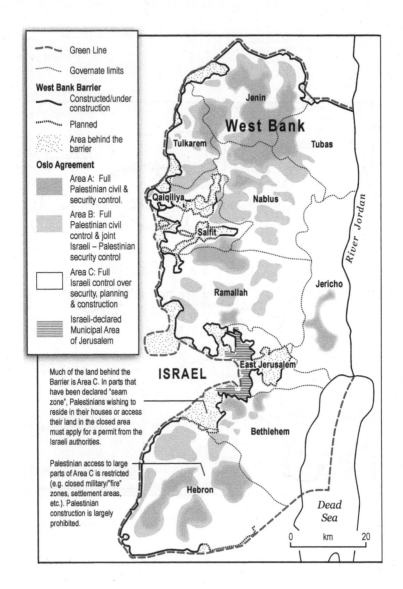

Legend

- – – – Green Line
- ·········· Governate limits

West Bank Barrier
- ——— Constructed/under construction
- ·········· Planned
- Area behind the barrier

Oslo Agreement
- Area A: Full Palestinian civil & security control.
- Area B: Full Palestinian civil control & joint Israeli – Palestinian security control
- Area C: Full Israeli control over security, planning & construction
- Israeli-declared Municipal Area of Jerusalem

Much of the land behind the Barrier is Area C. In parts that have been declared "seam zone", Palestinians wishing to reside in their houses or access their land in the closed area must apply for a permit from the Israeli authorities.

Palestinian access to large parts of Area C is restricted (e.g. closed military/"fire" zones, settlement areas, etc.). Palestinian construction is largely prohibited.

Areas A, B and C in the West Bank 2010

Index

References to notes are indicated by n.

Also by Ilan Pappe

THE ETHNIC CLEANSING OF PALESTINE

Ilan Pappe's groundbreaking book revisits the formation of the State of Israel. Between 1947 and 1949, over 400 Palestinian villages were deliberately destroyed, civilians were massacred and around a million men, women and children were expelled from their homes at gunpoint.

Denied for almost six decades, had it happened today it could only have been called 'ethnic cleansing'. Decisively debunking the myth that the Palestinian population left of their own accord in the course of this war, Ilan Pappe offers archival evidence to demonstrate that, from its very inception, a central plank in Israel's founding ideology was the forcible removal of the indigenous population.

'Pappe has opened up an important new line of inquiry into the vast and fateful subject of the Palestinian refugees'

Times Literary Supplement

'A major intervention in an argument that will, and must, continue'

Independent

ONEWORLD

ONEWORLD, MANY VOICES
WINNER OF THE 2016 MAN BOOKER PRIZE
WINNER OF THE 2015 MAN BOOKER PRIZE